2001

JANUARY

M	T	W	T	F	S	S
1	2	3	4	5	6	7
8	9	10	11	12	13	14
15	16	17	18	19	20	21
22	23	24	25	26	27	28
29	30	31				

FEBRUARY

M	T	W	T	F	S	S
			1	2	3	4
5	6	7	8	9	10	11
12	13	14	15	16	17	18
19	20	21	22	23	24	25
26	27	28				

MARCH

M	T	W	T	F	S	S
			1	2	3	4
5	6	7	8	9	10	11
12	13	14	15	16	17	18
19	20	21	22	23	24	25
26	27	28	29	30	31	

APRIL

M	T	W	T	F	S	S
						1
2	3	4	5	6	7	8
9	10	11	12	13	14	15
16	17	18	19	20	21	22
23	24	25	26	27	28	29
30						

MAY

M	T	W	T	F	S	S
	1	2	3	4	5	6
7	8	9	10	11	12	13
14	15	16	17	18	19	20
21	22	23	24	25	26	27
28	29	30	31			

JUNE

M	T	W	T	F	S	S
				1	2	3
4	5	6	7	8	9	10
11	12	13	14	15	16	17
18	19	20	21	22	23	24
25	26	27	28	29	30	

JULY

M	T	W	T	F	S	S
						1
2	3	4	5	6	7	8
9	10	11	12	13	14	15
16	17	18	19	20	21	22
23	24	25	26	27	28	29
30	31					

AUGUST

M	T	W	T	F	S	S
		1	2	3	4	5
6	7	8	9	10	11	12
13	14	15	16	17	18	19
20	21	22	23	24	25	26
27	28	29	30	31		

SEPTEMBER

M	T	W	T	F	S	S
					1	2
3	4	5	6	7	8	9
10	11	12	13	14	15	16
17	18	19	20	21	22	23
24	25	26	27	28	29	30

OCTOBER

M	T	W	T	F	S	S
1	2	3	4	5	6	7
8	9	10	11	12	13	14
15	16	17	18	19	20	21
22	23	24	25	26	27	28
29	30	31				

NOVEMBER

M	T	W	T	F	S	S
			1	2	3	4
5	6	7	8	9	10	11
12	13	14	15	16	17	18
19	20	21	22	23	24	25
26	27	28	29	30		

DECEMBER

M	T	W	T	F	S	S
					1	2
3	4	5	6	7	8	9
10	11	12	13	14	15	16
17	18	19	20	21	22	23
24	25	26	27	28	29	30
31						

= NEW MOON, PST

◻ *May Trillium 2000*

= FULL MOON, PST

WE'MOON '01

GAIA RHYTHMS FOR WOMYN

MAGIC

published by
Mother Tongue Ink

WE DEDICATE WE'MOON '01 TO GREENHAM WOMEN'S PEACE CAMP
WOMEN WHOSE POWERFUL MAGIC SUCCEEDED IN TRANSFORMING
A MILITARY BASE INTO FREE LAND ONCE AGAIN (1981–2000)
(SEE "DEDICATION" P. 187)

Dewi V
¤ *Gyps Curmi 1998*

WE'MOON '01: GAIA RHYTHMS FOR WOMYN AND WE'MOON '01 UNBOUND
© Mother Tongue Ink 2000

P.O. Box 1395-A
Estacada, Oregon 97023 USA
Phone: 503-630-7848 or for orders call
toll free: 877-O WEMOON (877-693-6666)
E-mail: wemoon@teleport.com
URL: http://www.teleport.com/~wemoon/

Crone Editor/Consultant: Musawa
Matrix Team: Beth Freewomon, Amy Schutzer and Tarie the Fairie
Creatrix/Editing Team: Beth, Bethroot, Musawa, Tarie and Amy

Front cover art *Priestess 9* © Ulla Anobile 1996; back cover art *Corn Spirit* © Diane Rigoli 1998; See "Cover Notes" on page 188.

Distributed directly by Mother Tongue Ink and by our other fine wholesale distributors: **USA:** Baker & Taylor, Bookpeople, Ingram, Koen, Lady Slipper, New Leaf, Northern Sun, Small Changes, and Vision Works. **Canada:** Dempsey (Vancouver). **International:** Airlift (London), Bookpeople (Oakland, CA). A German edition of **We'Moon '01** is distributed by Neue Erde and Labyrinth Verlag (Braunschweig). To order directly from Mother Tongue Ink, see page 186.

Astro-data and ephemerides reprinted with permission from Astro Communications Services, Inc., P.O. Box 34487, San Diego, CA 92163-4487.

We'Moon '01 is printed with soy ink on acid-free, 85% recycled paper (min. 30% post-consumer) that is ECF (elementally chlorine-free). Using this paper instead of non-recycled paper saves about 166 trees, 72,600 gallons of water, 618 pounds of air pollution effluents, 48,000 kwh of electricity and 86 cubic feet of landfill space.

As a moon calendar, this book is recyclable; every nineteen years the moon completes a metatonic cycle, returning to the same phase, sign and degree of the zodiac. If you still have **We'Moon '83** you can use it again this year (**We'Moon '01** will be reusable in 2020)!

ISBN: 1-890931-05-5 **We'Moon '01** (with lay flat binding)
ISBN: 1-890931-07-1 **We'Moon '01** (with spiral binding)
ISBN: 1-890931-06-3 **We'Moon '01 Unbound** (w/ no binding)

Printed and bound in Canada.

ᴄᴀʙʟᴇ ᴏꜰ ᴄᴏɴᴛᴇɴᴛꜱ

▽

1. ɪɴᴛʀᴏᴅᴜᴄᴛɪᴏɴ

11. ᴍᴏᴏɴ ᴄᴀʟᴇɴᴅᴀʀ*

*Feature writers for the calendar pages of **We'Moon '01**: Astrological predictions by **Gretchen Lawlor**, holy day writing with an herbal focus by **Colette Gardiner**. **Disclaimer:** any herbal or astrological information herein should be used with caution, common sense, and the approval of your health care practitioner, astrologer and/or other sources you trust.

111. ᴀᴘᴘᴇɴᴅɪx

What Is *We'Moon*? A Handbook in Natural Cycles

We'Moon: Gaia Rhythms for Womyn is more than an appointment book, it's a way of life! **We'Moon** is a lunar calendar, a handbook in natural rhythm and comes out of international womyn's culture. Art and writing by we'moon from many lands give a glimpse of the great diversity and uniqueness of a world we create in our own image. **We'Moon** is about *womyn's spirituality* (spirit'reality). We share how we live our truth, what inspires us, how we envision our reality in connection with the whole earth and all our relations.

We'moon means "women." Instead of defining ourselves in relation to men (as in *wo*man or *fe*male), we use the word *we'moon* to define ourselves by our primary relation to the natural sources of cosmic flow. Other terms we'moon use are *womyn, wimmin, womon, womb-one*. **We'Moon** is a moon calendar for we'moon. As we'moon, we seek to be whole in ourselves, rather than dividing ourselves in half and hoping that some "other half" will complete the picture. We see the whole range of life's potential embodied and ex-

Celtic Amazon Labrys
◻ *Tracy Litterick 1998*

pressed by we'moon, and do not divide the universe into sex-role stereotypes according to a heterosexual model. **We'Moon** is sacred space in which to explore and celebrate the diversity of she-ness on earth. The calendar is we'moon's space.

We'moon means "we of the moon." The moon, whose cycles run in our blood, is the original womyn's calendar. Like the moon, we'moon circle the earth. We are drawn to one another. We come in different shapes, colors and sizes. We are continually transforming. With all our different hues and points of view, we are one.

We'moon culture exists in the diversity and the oneness of our experience as we'moon. *We honor both.* We come from many different ways of life. At the same time, as we'moon, we share a common mother root. We are glad when we'moon from varied backgrounds contribute art and writing. When material is borrowed from cultures other than our own, we ask that it be acknowledged and something given in return. Being conscious of our sources keeps us from engaging in the divisiveness of either *cultural appropriation* (taking what belongs to others) or *cultural fascism* (controlling creative expression). We invite every we'moon to share how the "Mother Tongue" speaks to her, with respect for both cultural integrity and individual freedom.

Gaia Rhythms: We show the natural cycles of the moon, sun, planets and stars as they relate to earth. By recording our own activities side by side with those of other heavenly bodies, we may notice what connection, if any, there is for us. The earth revolves around her axis in one day; the moon orbits around the earth in one month (29$^1/_2$ days); the earth orbits around the sun in one year. We experience each of these cycles in the alternating rhythms of day and night, waxing and waning, summer and winter. The earth/moon/sun are our inner circle of kin in the universe. We know where we are in relation to them at all times by the dance of light and shadow as they circle around one another.

The Eyes of Heaven: As seen from earth, the moon and the sun are equal in size: "the left and right eye of heaven," according to Hindu (Eastern) astrology. Unlike the solar-dominated calendars of Christian (Western) patriarchy, the **We'Moon** looks at our experience through both eyes at once. The **lunar eye** of heaven is seen each day in the phases of the moon as she is both reflector and shadow, traveling her 29$^1/_2$-day path through the zodiac. The **solar eye** of heaven is apparent at the turning points in the sun's cycle. The year begins with Winter Solstice (in the Northern Hemisphere), the dark renewal time, and journeys through many seasons and balance points (solstices, equinoxes and the cross-quarter days in-between). The **third eye** of heaven may be seen in the stars. Astrology measures the cycles by relating the sun, moon and all other planets in our universe through the star signs (the zodiac), helping us to tell time in the larger cycles of the universe.   7

© *Germaine Knight 1999*

Measuring Time and Space: Imagine a clock with many hands. The earth is the center from which we view our universe. The sun, moon and planets are like the hands of the clock. Each one has its own rate of movement through the cycle. The ecliptic, a band of sky around the earth within which all planets have their orbits, is the outer band of the clock where the numbers are. Stars along the ecliptic are grouped into constellations forming the signs of the zodiac—the twelve star signs are like the twelve numbers of the clock. They mark the movements of the planets through the 360° circle of the sky, the clock of time and space.

Whole Earth Perspective: It is important to note that all natural cycles have a mirror image from a whole earth perspective—seasons occur at opposite times in the Northern and Southern Hemispheres and day and night occur at opposite times on opposite sides of the earth as well. Even the moon plays this game—a waxing crescent moon in Australia faces right (e.g., ☾), while in North America it faces left (e.g., ☽). **We'Moon** has a Northern Hemisphere perspective regarding times, holy days, seasons and lunar phases.

Whole Sky Perspective: It is also important to note that all over the earth, in varied cultures and times, the dome of the sky has been interacted with in countless ways. *The* zodiac we speak of is just one of many ways that hu-moons have pictured and related to the stars. In this calendar, we use the tropical zodiac.   ▫ *Musawa 1999*

How to Use This Book

Useful Information about the We'Moon

Time Zones: All aspects are in Pacific Standard/Daylight Time, with the adjustment for GMT and EDT given at the bottom of each page. To calculate for other areas, see "World Time Zones" (p. 220).

Signs and Symbols at a Glance is an easily accessible handy one-page guide that gives brief definitions for commonly used astrological symbols (p. 221).

Pages are numbered throughout the calendar to facilitate cross referencing. See Table of Contents (p. 5) and Contributor Bylines and Index (pp. 189–198). The names of the days of the week and months are in English with additional foreign language translations included (Esperanto, Swahili, German and Hawaiian).

Moon Pages mark the beginning of each moon cycle with an art-filled two-page spread near the new moon. Each Moon page is numbered with Roman numerals (ie., **Moon III**) and contains the dates of that Moon's new and full moon and solar ingress.

Month and Year at a Glance Calendars can be found on pp. 208–219 and p. 2. Month at a Glance pages include daily lunar phases.

Annual Predictions: For your annual astrological portrait, turn to Gretchen Lawlor's prediction for your sun sign. See "Astrological Predictions and Flower Essences for each Sign" (pp. 13–14).

Holydays and Herb Feature: There is an art-filled two-page holy day spread for all equinoxes, solstices and cross quarter days. These include descriptions of each holy day with an herbal focus written by Colette Gardiner (see pp. 49, 67, 85, 103, 121, 143, 157 and 177).

Planetary Ephemeris: Exact planetary positions for every day are given on pp. 202–207. These ephemerides show where each planet is in a zodiac sign at noon GMT, measured by degree in longitude.

Asteroid Ephemeris: Exact positions of asteroids for every ten days are given for sixteen asteroids in the zodiac at midnight GMT on p. 201. See "Asteroids" (p. 199) for more information.

Astrology Basics

Planets: Planets are like chakras in our solar system, allowing for different frequencies or types of energies to be expressed.

Signs: The twelve signs of the zodiac are a mandala in the sky, marking off 30° segments in the 360° circle around the earth. Signs show major shifts in planetary energy through the cycles.

Glyphs: Glyphs are the symbols used to represent planets and signs.

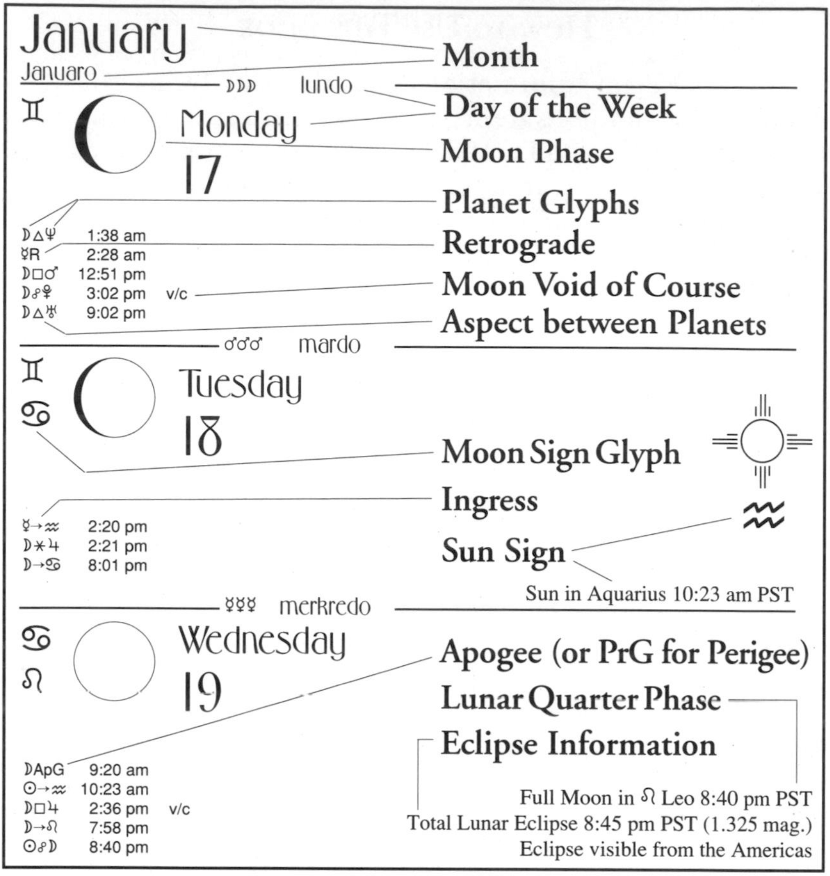
January
Januaro
☽☽☽ lundo
♊
Monday
17
☽△♆ 1:38 am
☿R 2:28 am
☽□♂ 12:51 pm
☽☍♀ 3:02 pm v/c
☽△♅ 9:02 pm
Month
Day of the Week
Moon Phase
Planet Glyphs
Retrograde
Moon Void of Course
Aspect between Planets
♂♂♂ mardo
♊
♋
Tuesday
18
☿→♒ 2:20 pm
☽✶♃ 2:21 pm
☽→♋ 8:01 pm
Moon Sign Glyph
Ingress
Sun Sign
♒
Sun in Aquarius 10:23 am PST
☿☿☿ merkredo
♋
♌
Wednesday
19
☽ApG 9:20 am
☉→♒ 10:23 am
☽□♃ 2:36 pm v/c
☽→♌ 7:58 pm
☉☍☽ 8:40 pm
Apogee (or PrG for Perigee)
Lunar Quarter Phase
Eclipse Information
Full Moon in ♌ Leo 8:40 pm PST
Total Lunar Eclipse 8:45 pm PST (1.325 mag.)
Eclipse visible from the Americas

Sun Sign: The sun enters a new sign once a month (around the 20th or so), completing the whole cycle of the zodiac in one year. The sun sign reflects qualities of your outward shining self. For a description of sign qualities see "Sun Signs" (pp. 15–17).

Moon Sign: The moon changes signs approximately every 2½ days, going through all twelve signs of the zodiac every 29½ days (the sidereal month). The moon sign reflects qualities of your core inner self. For descriptions see "Moon Signs and Transits" (pp. 18–20).

Moon Phase: Each calendar day is marked with a graphic representation of the phase that the moon is in. Although the moon is not usually visible in the sky during the new or dark moon, we represent her using miniscule crescent moon graphics for the days immediately before and after the *actual* new moon or conjunction. For more information about the moon see related articles on pp. 21–23.

Lunar Quarter Phase: At the four quarter points of the lunar cycle (new, waxing half, full and waning half) we indicate the phase, sign and exact time for each. These points mark off the "lunar week."

Day of the Week: Each day is associated with a planet whose symbol appears in the line above it (e.g., DDD is for Moon: Moonday, Monday, Luna Day, lundi, lunes). The names of the days of the week are displayed prominently in English with translations appearing in the line above them. Four languages (Esperanto, Swahili, German, Hawaiian) rotate weekly in this order throughout the calendar.

Eclipse: The time of greatest eclipse is given, which is not the exact time of the conjunction or opposition. Locations from where eclipses are visible are also given. For lunar and partial solar eclipses, magnitude is given in decimal form (e.g., 0.881 mag.), denoting the fraction of the moon's diameter obscured by the shadow of Earth. For total and annular solar eclipses, the duration of the eclipse in minutes and seconds is given. For more information see "Eclipses" (p. 24).

Aspects (□ △ ♂ ♂ ✶ ⊼): These show the angle of relation between different planets. An aspect is like an astrological weather forecast for the day, indicating which energies are working together easily and which combinations are more challenging. See "Signs and Symbols at a Glance" (p. 221) for a brief explanation of each kind.

Ingresses (→): Indicate planets moving into new signs.

Moon Void of Course (D v/c): The moon is said to be void of course from the last significant lunar aspect in each sign until the moon enters a new sign. This is a good time to ground and center yourself.

Apogee (ApG): This is the point in the orbit of a planet or the Moon that is farthest from Earth. At this time the effects of transits (when planets pass across the path of another planet) may be less noticeable immediately but may appear later on.

Perigee (PrG): This is the point in the orbit of a planet or the Moon that is nearest to Earth. Transits with the Moon or other planets when they are at perigee will be more intense.

Direct or Retrograde (D or R): These are times when a planet moves forward (D) or backward (R) through the signs of the zodiac (an optical illusion, as when a moving train passes a slower train which appears to be going backward). When a planet is in direct motion, planetary energies are more straightforward; in retrograde, planetary energies turn back in on themselves and are more involuted.

☼ *Musawa and Beth Freewomon 2000*

PLANETARY DANCE 2001

The planetary configurations of 2001 indicate we will be in for a passionate explosion of inventive thinking as people reject stifling, existing paradigms and perceptions of reality. With this will come increased global networking and community building, as well as great problems and delays with all media forms.

Uranus, Neptune, Pluto continue to transit the futuristic signs of Sagittarius (Pluto) and Aquarius (Uranus and Neptune). They ask each of us to participate in creating a more egalitarian future through courage to be authentic, true to our deepest instincts and willing to experiment until we get the future right. There is a restless seeking, questing feeling to the year.

Chiron has been travelling through Sagittarius since 1999 and shifts into Capricorn on December 11, 2001 (until 2005). Chiron shows us how we choose to deal with what fate hands to us and encourages us to change what does not serve our true essence. In Sagittarius there is a collective call to let old philosophical or political systems pass away. In the devastating loss of external principles of ethical behavior with which to guide our efforts, instinctive truth and right action emerges from our core spiritual selves.

Jupiter in Gemini, until June, encourages us to imagine all possibilities. Saturn enters Gemini on April 20 emphasizing the limitations of our reality constructs. Saturn in Gemini can block the full use of the imagination for which Jupiter longs, but also brings methodical and structured thinking (Saturn) to what might other-wise remain pure fantasy (Jupiter).

March–June, Jupiter aspects all the outer/transpersonal planets catalyzing inspiration and hope with a strong spiritual bent and a tendency towards obsessiveness. Between the end of June and December, Saturn will also aspect all the transpersonal planets, bringing idealism into practice in our everyday lives. Saturn opposing Pluto in June–August and November–December may evoke intense opposition to your efforts and will be the most explosive months of the year. This will require conciliatory efforts on your part—work hard and be willing to cut your losses in areas where you are not making any headway. By July, Jupiter will enter Cancer bringing some settling to the restless questing of Gemini. If you've been looking for a new home, Jupiter in Cancer will help you anchor.

12   © Gretchen Lawlor 2000

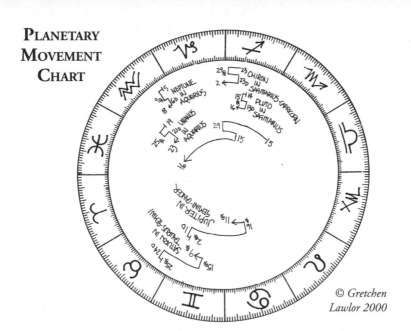

© Gretchen
Lawlor 2000

ASTROLOGICAL PREDICTIONS
AND FLOWER ESSENCES FOR EACH SIGN

Predictions for each sun sign can be found on the calendar page where the sun enters that sign. If you know your rising sign more specific information may be gathered by reading predictions for both signs watching for repeated themes as well as any jangling dissonance. The predictions can provide an excellent navigational map for your own journey through the year.

Flower essences[1] provide support for the changes indicated by the planetary dance of 2001, particularly if taken before May. Essences nudge you to closure on issues that have been dominant in your life in the last three years readying you to move swiftly forward as the year progresses. For each sign see below for areas of challenge and essences to facilitate your healing.

Aries: To clarify and consolidate your gifts and assets. *Buttercup* for knowing your true worth, independent of cultural standards. *Hound's Tongue* for recognizing emotional and spiritual gifts.

[1]I have chosen to focus upon FES Essences and Bach formulas. These flower essences can be acquired through Centergees Flower Essence Pharmacy 1-800-343-8693 or www.floweressences.com

13

Taurus: To establish a new cycle of internal growth. *Aspen* to face an unknown future with courage and enthusiasm. *Black-eyed Susan* to work with previously avoided powerful emotions.

Gemini: For closure of an old life cycle. *Sage* for insight into the deeper meaning of such huge changes. *Sagebrush* to facilitate the breakdown and clear out what does not serve your future.

Cancer: For clarification of personal goals for the future. *Wild Oat* for clarity regarding life purpose. *Indian Pink* for steadiness and commitment to your dreams despite judgements from others.

Leo: To express your true individuality to the world. *Larkspur* for balanced leadership. *Fairy Lantern* for inner strength to face the world as a healthy adult with a good relationship to the inner child.

Virgo: To assimilate years of experience that can be shared with others. *Cerato* to define your inner convictions. *Mountain Pride* to speak out for your ideals and activate their expression in your world.

Libra: To support the termination of old life patterns and true personal transformation. *Cayenne* as catalyst to help break free of habits. *Walnut* for protection, support in making profound changes.

Scorpio: To function with awareness of others versus personal gratification. *Yellow Star Tulip* to clarify why others are in your life. *Evening Primrose* to release old wounds affecting your ability to form intimate bonds.

Sagittarius: For discipline and organization in everyday life. *Vervain* for grounding in the body and harmonizing of spiritual forces. *Madia* to discipline attention and concentration.

Capricorn: To develop a channel for creativity to flow in profound ways. *Iris* for inspiration and transcending limitations to creativity. *Pomegranate* to clarify form, focus of creative urges.

Aquarius: To establish a secure base of operations for long-term ambitions. *Blackberry* to create foundations for expression. *Sweet Pea* for finding a sense of belonging to place, community.

Pisces: To deepen your thinking and communicate more effectively. *Trumpet Vine* to help express ideas with vitality and conviction. *Cosmos* to express your spiritual wisdom through words.

The sun pours out its energy through each sign's filter for one month a year. We feel its pulse in our daily life. The sun's sign influences our energy and colors our conscious world. Each of us holds our sun sign's medicine for the world.

Fire Magic Woman
□ *Lucy Kemp1999*

Aries (March 20– April 19): While the sun is in Aries we return to our Self, then reach for new beginnings. We have the courage to start over; in the process we may be headstrong and miss the subtleties. Decide what seeds to plant for this turn of the wheel.

An Aries embodies spring fire; she is erotic and independent, a primal rebel with revolutionary thought. She teaches us to stay centered and listen to our own calling.

Taurus (April 19–May 20): The Taurus sun sprouts the seed. Our ideas and creations begin to become solid and durable. This is a time to celebrate your body and the body of the Mother as we garden, sing, touch, make love, strengthen.

The Taurus womon embodies the strength to be soft and the heartbeat of the earth Mother. She makes her beliefs tangible. Comfort is her ritual. The Taurus challenge is to keep the material a sacred vessel, not an end in itself.

Gemini (May 20–June 21): While the sun traverses Gemini we learn the magic of communication as we cross-pollinate ideas and crops. Words weave connection. We search for inspiration.

Gemini eyes and nerves sing with electricity. She translates—from one friend to another or from one culture to another. Gemini challenges are to keep heart and nerves connected and to see through a problem, not just change the subject.

Cancer (June 21–July 22): While the sun swims through moon-ruled Cancer we learn the grounding magic of our home, our shell, our temple's hearth. To nourish body and soul we explore work with our chosen family, homeland and what makes us feel safe in the world.

Our moon woman is the guardian of the hearth, heart and culture. Their good minds and unusual memory all work as servant to the heart, their moods a source of wisdom. The Cancer challenge can be to let go, compost, explore.

Leo (July 22–Aug. 22): Life is a circus while the sun is at home in Leo—celebrate the ripening of the fruits of your plants and your creativity, passion and plans.

Leo can make a celebration out of any situation—why live a boring life. We gather around her as we gather around a bonfire. In that golden glow, all comes alive. Her challenge is to listen deeply and call people together for good reason.

Virgo (Aug. 22–Sept. 22): While the sun works its way through Virgo we bring in the harvest. It is time to sort our life, listen for new patterns and draw blueprints. Our thoughts turn inward and practical as we plan how to manifest the next stage of our dream.

Virgo harvests and sorts the wheat from the chaff. She is a healing force as long as she trains her vision to the harvest. Her challenge is to not get stuck on the chaff.

Libra (Sept. 22–Oct. 23): While the sun dances through Libra, meditate on relatedness; bring your life and loves into balance. Infuse beauty into your world. It's time to explore the Libran principle—where there is justice, there is peace.

Libra looks for engagement with equals. She offers kind respect, a steady eye and wants to bring balance to our world and all our relations. Her challenge is to seek internal balance.

Scorpio (Oct. 23–Nov. 21): While the sun burrows into Scorpio we prepare for winter's hibernation. It is time to bring our focus inward, concentrate on the mysteries and grow stronger as we face our fears.

A Scorpio is a deep well, a mystery and a detective. She knows nothing is simple. She is more interested in transformation than security. Sexuality is powerful magic to Scorpio. Her challenge is to balance her formidable focus with a broader horizon.

Sagittarius (Nov. 21–Dec. 21): While the sun travels through Sagittarius it's time to give thanks for the harvest. Let your restlessness take you anywhere unexplored—new friends, unfamiliar ideas or foreign soil.

Sagittarians live in the big picture. "Don't fence me in" is their theme song. They can speak to anyone. The Sagittarian challenges can be patience with slower mortals and learning to trust connection rather than a geographic cure.

Capricorn (Dec. 21–Jan. 20): With the sun in Capricorn, we are renewed by tradition and set our intentions for the year ahead. The Capricorn symbol is a sea-goat: she takes vision from the bottom of the oceanic dreamworld and walks it to the mountaintop.

Capricorns have backbone and help us see structure, form and practicality. She benefits from time alone, but without isolation. She needs goals she believes in—mountain goats aren't comfortable on flat land.

Aquarius (Jan. 19–Feb. 18): While the sun moves through Aquarius we dance with our politics and dialogue with our culture. It is time to find like minds and build strange alliances.

The Aquarian understands community. She holds the circle open for us. Innovation is her magic. She can be hypersensitive to the rules—breaking some and unusually bound by others. Her challenge is to build intimacy with herself first and then others.

Pisces (Feb. 18–March 20): While the sun courses through Pisces we soak it all up, listen to our dreams and ask where compassion will summon our actions in the year ahead.

The Pisces woman feels the web that interconnects all life. Her dreams can hold the vision for all of us and our potential. Pisces are compassionate, intuitive mystics. Her challenge is to build a sound container to hold her dreams and keep her sensitivities intact.

MOON SIGN AND TRANSITS

The moon speaks directly to our spirit. It describes the daily pulse and the emotional matrix we walk through. As the moon changes sign every 2½ days, the filters on our inner world change. Let the garden be a metaphor for any project you want to nourish. Our own moon sign indicates our personal, spiritual lineage and our emotional prime-directive.

The **Moon in Aries** asks us to wake up and remember who we truly are, even if it bothers those we love or work for. Tempers, tears and passions run hot. It's a great time for digging new beds, moving boulders, weeding or pest removal, but put a hold on planting. The Moon in Aries womon searches for fire, fierce independence, and her own voice. She may need to learn patience and cooperation. She appreciates our fire.

The **Moon in Taurus** asks us to discover what nurtures us and how to grow deeper roots. We can almost feel the mud oozing between our toes, awakening our senses and sensuality, and growing our stubbornness. It is time to cultivate our material resources, our homes and our body. Plant anything you want to grow strong and fertile. The Moon in Taurus womon searches for stability and sensuality. She may need to learn mobility. She offers us comfort, beauty and solid presence.

□ *May Trillium 2000*

The **Moon in Gemini** quickens our nervous system. Build a web of understanding—network, absorb new information. Speak to your plants, trim, but avoid planting. The Moon in Gemini womon wants to understand, she lives and breathes communication. She may need to learn to honor stillness and concentration. She translates for us, questions us.

With the **Moon in Cancer** our feelings take the lead. Cancer encourages the wisdom rising out of our oceanic unconscious through moods and feelings. Ground in the magic of our home as a temple. Ask what needs protecting and feeding. Plant, fertilize and water your garden. The Moon in Cancer woman searches for what nurtures her soul and the world's. She may need to learn to carry her security with her. She respects our deepest feelings, eases our past fears.

With the **Moon in Leo** we have the guts to be visible and bring culture to life. In your garden or life, arrange, glorify and weed the extraneous so your star can shine, but don't plant or fertilize. The Moon in Leo woman came here to dramatize and ritualize her world. She may need to learn to find the sacred in the mundane. She offers us celebration and fascination and honors our self-expression.

The **Moon in Virgo** asks us to consider what needs healing, what needs composting. It's time to study, learn, train, organize and turn our compassion into pragmatic action. Don't get stuck in your head. Weed, prune, ammend your garden with nutrients and companion planting. Plant and care for medicinal herbs. The Moon in Virgo woman came here to diagnose and heal her soul and the world's. She needs to learn to celebrate the beauty in each of us. She offers us practical compassion and ancient wisdom.

Moon in Libra highlights the magic of the dance of inter-relatedness—friendly, romantic, and searching for a way to connect. Libra asks us to treat those around us as equals and make sure our politics and art, our lovemaking and our networks integrate. Tend to the beauty of the garden, cultivate, but don't plant. The Moon in Libra woman came here to feel the beauty in cooperation. She may need to learn to hear her own voice under conflict. She offers us bone-deep kindness, mediation and justice.

With the **Moon in Scorpio**, dig deep. Scorpio weaves the visible and invisible worlds together. We see through and into the roots. Direct this energy away from obsession and towards creation. Sexuality can be potent, musky. Dig in your garden, plant roots, feed the soil and compost. The Moon in Scorpio woman came here to find herself in solitude first and then through transformative action with others. She may need to learn flexibility. She offers us a fearless guide to the inner worlds as she midwifes all transitions.

Moon in Sagittarius brings out our inner-Artemis; we need to roam, to explore in body and in soul. Our curiosity intensifies. Check out untraveled territory and connect with the organic world. Have a long talk with the animals in your garden. Work the soil but hold off on the planting. The Moon in Sagittarius womon came here to explore. She needs to learn to hold still and work through a challenge. She offers us radical acceptance.

Silver Moon
© *Lynn Dewart 1997*

Moon in Capricorn brings planning magic and takes your ideas, giving them form and hope. We can tap into the inner wisewoman—ask how form, ritual, organization or tradition can serve. Trim, prune, plant slow-growing seedlings and make sure you and your garden have enough water. The Moon in Capricorn womon came here to accomplish and understand compassionate leadership. She may need to learn to respect other rhythms and to love herself, not just what she does. She offers us constructive determination and practical support.

The **Moon in Aquarius** expands our circles and offers the magic of collaboration; spirit and politics weave together. We can get too farsighted now and need to stay aware of others' feelings. Let go of assumptions and find new, unusual allies. A time to gather plants, mulch, prune and talk to your garden. The Moon in Aquarius womon came here to understand group dynamics. She may need to learn to be comfortable with emotional intimacy. She offers us a global perspective and collaboration.

With the **Moon in Pisces** we feel the world with compassion, heightened senses and strong imagination. We need quiet time in the temple or back under our covers to deal with sensory overload. A time to vision, listen to inner voices, creative juices and touch each other with new awareness. Plant, transplant, water, fertilize. Moon in Pisces womon came here to feel everything; she may need to filter impressions and find her deep strength. She offers us insight, imagination, and subtle, compassionate medicine while encouraging our vision.

© *Heather Rowntree 2000*

LUNAR RHYTHM

Everything that flows moves in rhythm with the moon. She rules the water element on earth. She pulls on the ocean's tides, the weather, female reproductive cycles, and the life fluids in plants, animals and people. She influences the underground currents in earth energy, the mood swings of mind, body, behavior and emotion. The moon is closer to the earth than any other heavenly body. The earth actually has two primary relationships in the universe: one with the moon who circles around her and one with the sun whom she circles around. Both are equal in her eyes. The phases of the moon reflect the dance of all three: the moon, the sun, and the earth, who together weave the web of light and dark into our lives. No wonder so much of our life on earth is intimately connected with the phases of the moon!

On the following two pages you will find articles about the moon and her cycles that correspond to the chart below.

□ Musawa 2000

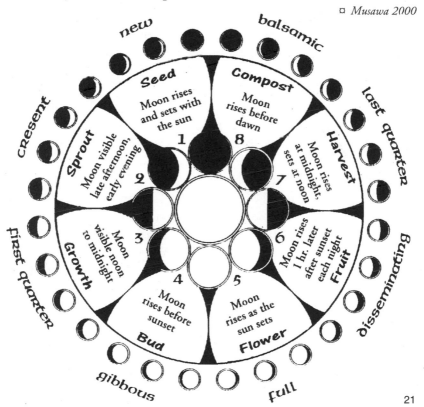

THE EIGHT LUNAR PHASES

As above, so below. Look into the sky and observe which phase the moon is in. Then you will know where you are in the growth cycle of each lunar month. The phase that the moon was in when you were born reflects your purpose, personality and preferences.

The **new moon** is like a SEED planted in the earth. We cannot see her but she is ready to grow, full of potential and energy for her new journey. We'moon born during the new moon are impulsive, passionate and intuitive. They are risk takers and pioneers.

The **crescent moon** is the SPROUT. The seed has broken through the earth and reaches up as she ventures from the dark, moist earth she has known. We'moon born during the crescent moon must break from the past to create their own destiny.

The **first quarter moon** is the GROWTH phase. Roots go deeper, stems shoots up and leaves form as she creates a new strong body. We'moon born during the first quarter moon live a full active life— old structures are cleared away providing room for new development.

The **gibbous moon** is the BUD of the plant, the pulse of life tightly wrapped, wanting to expand. For we'moon born during the gibbous moon, their talents lie in the ability to refine, organize and purify. They are seekers, utilizing spiritual tools as guides on their path.

She opens and blossoms during the **full moon** into the FLOWER, with the desire to share her beauty with others. We'moon born during the full moon enjoy companionship and partnership and desire to merge deeply. Fulfillment and illumination are their goals.

As we go into the darkening phase of the **disseminating moon,** we get the FRUIT of the plant's life cycle—the fruits of wisdom and experience. For we'moon born during the disseminating moon, life must have meaning, purpose. They enjoy sharing their ideas with others.

The **last quarter moon** is the HARVEST phase—the plant gives her life so that others may continue theirs. We'moon born during the last quarter have a powerful internal life of reflection, transformation. They can assume different roles while balancing their internal and external worlds.

The **balsamic moon** is the COMPOST phase, when the nutrients remain in the soil, providing nourishment for the next new seed. We'moon born during the balsamic moon possess the potential to be wise, insightful, understanding and patient. They are prophetic and unique.

□ *Susan Levitt 2000*

WHERE'S THAT MOON ?

Why is the moon sometimes visible during the day? And why does the moon sometimes rise very late at night? The answers lie in what phase the moon is in, which reflects the angle between the sun and moon as seen from Earth. For each of the eight moon phases, the angle between the sun and moon progresses in 45° increments. Each phase lasts approximately 3–4 days of the moon's entire 29½ day cycle.

The **new moon** (or dark moon) rises at sunrise and sets at sunset. Astrologically, the sun and the moon are in *conjunction*. Because the sun's light overpowers the nearby moon in the day, and the moon is on the other side of the earth with the sun at night, she is not visible in the sky at all.

The **crescent moon** (or waxing crescent moon) rises midmorning and sets after sunset. She is the first visible sliver of moon seen in the western sky in the late afternoon and early evening.

The **first quarter moon** (or waxing half moon) rises around noon and sets around midnight. Astrologically, the moon is *square* to the sun. She is visible from the time she rises until she sets.

The **gibbous moon** rises midafternoon and sets before dawn. She is the bulging moon getting ready to be full, visible soon after she rises until she sets.

The **full moon** rises at sunset and sets at sunrise. Astrologically, the sun and moon are in *opposition* (ie., opposite each other in the sky and in opposite signs of the zodiac). She is visible all night long from moonrise to moonset.

The **disseminating moon** is the waning full moon getting visibly smaller. She rises midevening and sets midmorning. She is visible from the time she rises almost until she sets.

The **last quarter moon** (or waning half moon) rises around midnight and sets around noon. Astrologically, the moon is *square* to the sun. She is visible from the time she rises until she sets.

The **balsamic moon** (or waning crescent moon) rises before dawn and sets midafternoon. She is the last sliver of moon seen in the eastern sky in the dawn and in the very early morning.

□ *Susan Levitt, Musawa and Beth Freewoman 2000*

ECLIPSES

Eclipses demonstrate deep processes of transformation. They crack open doors to our true selves. Eclipses remind us that we are indeed not in control of our lives and that our choices manifest in our response to external stimuli. We can either recognize our fantastic natures and grow like wild flowers, or react to our external world with fear of change. We can use the alignment of the sun, moon and earth as a great ally in our own process of deep transformation. Since ancient times, astrologers have used the eclipse as a means of prediction. To determine the effect of a specific eclipse, check your natal chart and find out in what house the eclipse falls. Each house governs a specific activity or area. The effects of an eclipse are felt whether it's visible or not.

A solar eclipse is a conjunction of the Sun and Moon (new moon) and can be either total, partial or annular. A lunar eclipse is an opposition of the Sun and Moon (full moon) and can be either total, partial or appulse. The dates for the 2001 eclipses are Jan. 9, June 21 and July 5, and Dec. 14 and 30. See these particular dates for eclipse types and places from which they are visible.

© *Mari Susan Selby 2000*

RETURN TO SOURCE: MERCURY RETROGRADE ☿R

The cycle of the wing-footed messenger, Mercury, represents our mental and communicative life processes. This companion dancer to the sun (never traveling more than 28° away) inspires mobility and adaptability. Mercury retrogrades three or four times a year, each time in a sign of the same element. During this passage, lasting 20 to 28 days, our attention moves to unfinished business. Since all backward movement symbolizes a return to source, we can use these times to attend to our inner perceptions and reconnect with the spiritual source of our thoughts.

In 2001, Mercury retrogrades three times, in each of the Air Signs, highlighting a strong cycle of mental activity. During Aquarius, from February 3–25 when Mercury reverses, reflect on ideas and look for missing pieces in projects. During Gemini, from June 3–27 when Mercury retreats, find time to play with your inner child, allow journaling or letter writing to access memories and express undercurrents. During Libra, from October 1–22 when Mercury retraces her steps, we may revise and reshape our perspectives, especially in relationships. Allow for inner dialogs to review intentions.

© *Sandra Pastorius 2000*

THE YEAR OF THE SERPENT

The year of the Serpent begins on the new moon of January 24, 2001.* Serpent is the embodiment of wisdom, mystery and sensuality. She is honored for her feminine yin energy and is a symbol of the earth. The Chinese Serpent goddess, Nu Kua, formed the first people from yellow clay from the banks of the Yellow River. In Chinese folk tales, magical Serpent takes the form of Goddesses and heroines who assist women in childbirth and bless children with remarkable talents.

Due to Serpent's wisdom, Serpent year is a time of introspection, planning and seeking answers. It is best to ponder and think before acting. Good taste and elegance will prevail in all the arts. Serpent wisdom influences contributions in the sciences through new technological inventions and discoveries. But this is not an auspicious year for gambling, investing or taking financial risks. Expect political extremes, scandals and the exposing of secrets.

We'moon born in Serpent years (2001, 1989, 1977, 1965, 1953, 1941, 1929, 1917 and 1905) are enchanting, creative, spiritual, attractive and talented. They possess both charm and a mysterious quality. They are very sociable and love making friends, creating contacts and networks. But they can appear cool and aloof at times and won't easily reveal their thoughts to just anyone. If they allow you to get close you will discover that the Serpent is sensitive, caring, compassionate and humorous.

A great observer of human nature, Serpent has keen perceptions. Rarely is she openly aggressive, though she may be secretly plotting her next move. Serpent accomplishes her goals through careful plans and calculations. She has incredible patience to wait silently until the time is right. When she attacks a target she is swift, focused and rarely misses, especially Serpents born in the heat of summer.

A natural philosopher and theologian who likes to coil up and contemplate, Serpent is psychologically complex. She must not let her contemplative nature become overly pensive, brooding or moody.

© Susan Levitt 1999

Snake
© Tarmes 1999

*Asian New Year begins
the second new moon after Winter Solstice.

THE WHEEL OF THE YEAR: HOLY/HOLIDAYS

The seasonal cycle of the year is created by the tilt of the earth's axis, leaning toward or away from the sun, north to south, as the earth orbits the sun. Solstices are the extreme points (like new and full moon in the lunar cycle) when days and nights are longest or shortest. On equinoxes, days and nights are equal (like the light of the half moon). The four cross-quarter days roughly mark the midpoints in between solstices and equinoxes. These natural turning points in the the earth's annual cycle are the holidays we commemorate in **We'Moon**. We use the dates in the ancient Celtic calendar because it most closely approximates the eight spokes of the wheel of the year. As the wheel of this year turns, **We'Moon** features Colette Gardiner's interpretation of the Celtic holydays (names and dates in bold as follows). The holy/holiday celebrations of many other cultures cluster around these same times with similar universal themes:

Dec. 21: Solstice/Winter: the dwindling and return of the light—Kwanzaa (African-American), Soyal (Hopi), Santa Lucia (Scandanavian), Cassave/Dreaming (Taino), Chanukah (Jewish).

Feb. 2: Imbolc/Mid-Winter: celebrations, prophecy, purification, initiation—Candlemas (Christian), New Years (Tibetan, Chinese, Iroquois), Ground Hog's Day (American), Tu Bi-Shevat (Jewish).

Mar. 19: Equinox/Spring: rebirth, fertility, eggs, resurrection—Passover (Jewish), Easter (Christian), Festivals of the Goddess: Eostare (German), Astarte (Semite), Persephone (Greek).

May 1: Beltane/Mid-Spring: blossoms, planting, fertility, sexuality—May Day (Euro-American), Root Festival (Yakima), Ching Ming (Chinese), Whitsuntide (Dutch).

June 20: Solstice/Summer: sun, fire festivals—Niman Kachina (Hopi), Sundance (Lakota), Goddess festivals: Isis (Egypt), Litha (N. Africa), Yellow Corn Mother (Taino), Ishtar (Babylonian).

Aug. 2: Lammas/Mid-Summer: first harvest, breaking bread, goddesses of abundance: Green Corn Ceremony (Creek), Corn Mother (Hopi), Amaterasu (Japan), Hatshepsut's Day (Egypt).

Sept. 22: Equinox/Fall: gather and store, ripeness, goddesses: Tari Pennu (Bengal), Old Woman Who Never Dies (Mandan), Chicomecoatl (Aztec), Black Bean Mother (Taino).

Oct. 31: Samhain/Mid-Fall: underworld journey, ancestor spirits, Hallowmas/Halloween/Festivals of the Dead around the world, Sukkoth (Jewish harvest/wine festival).   □ *Musawa and Nell Stone 2000*

Sources: *The Grandmother of Time* by Zsuzsanna E. Budapest, 1989; *Celestially Auspicious Occasions* by Donna Henes, 1996; and *Songs of Bleeding* by Spider, 1992

INTRODUCTION TO THE THEME: MAGIC

Do you believe in magic? Magic happens, whether we believe in it or not. But have you ever noticed that when you are open to it, it seems to happen a lot more?

Human life has been guided by magical worldviews from the beginning of human consciousness. People living close to the earth have maintained the sacred web of life by understanding that we are participants in magic: mystery greater than we can fathom or control. Ancient spiritual traditions of every culture pass on teachings, often in coded form, with keys to the magical workings of life. The Tarot is one such ancient set of keys which we now use to divine the themes of each year's **We'Moon**. We took our cue for **We'Moon '01** from The Magician card, number one (I) in the Major Arcana (the 22 archetypal images in Tarot that embody aspects of spiritual empowerment).

Magician

© Motherpeace, a psuedonym for Vicki Noble and Karen Vogel 1981   27

Over the last thousand years, magic itself became a disappearing act, unless sanctioned by ruling patriarchal institutions. Folk magic was forbidden. Powerful wise women, midwives and healers were burned as witches. Indigenous people, cultures and lands were taken over. Esoteric traditions went underground. Tarot, for instance, became an ordinary deck of playing cards, with its four suits dimly reminiscent of the original symbols representing the four elements and the Major Arcana reduced to Jokers. Magic became associated with trickery. Reason and empirical science became contemporary culture's means towards truth.

By the beginning of this millennium (technically January 2001), magic has come full circle. The ever-new wonders of technology have us spell bound; even the complexity of machines we use every day is mystifying to most people. Scientists go between the worlds of inner and outer space, where the stuff of reality is neither particles or waves but both, and the keys to mystery are now terms like quarks, quantum leaps, black holes, super strings. Yet technology can only imitate nature, not replace her. The genetic code may be cracked but the life force remains a mystery. Mother Nature is the greatest Magician of all—we may learn some tricks from Her, but She always has another card up Her sleeve.

Witchy wizard, bruja brew
Mystic, medium, source-erer, too
Mystery, miracle, ritual, spell
Coven, altar, circle, well
Alter, healer, familiar, muse
Affirmation, charm, power to choose . . .

In our Call for Contributions, we conjured great magic that appears in the art and writing on the calendar pages. But somehow when it came to writing this introduction we (Bethroot and Musawa) had a hard time getting into magic ourselves. Why? We are both lucky to work with creating the **We'Moon** and to live in women's land communities where magic is supported in everyday life. So what's the problem? The problem is the language of magic is more experiential than explanatory. We are very busy, like everyone else, hooked up by email and telephone over thousands of miles. We feel stuck behind the magic doorway to this writing until we discover the oldest magic of all—the art of turning obstacles into openings. We explore the stuck place with some here and now magical work. The common dilemma of *how* to connect with magic shifts the focus, *becomes* our focus. We each have a tale to tell about breakthrough:

BETHROOT (Musing on some definitions of magic quoted in our Call for Contributions): Where are the magic words? I am a witch and a word priestess. Can't I just light a candle, be still, tune into my magic, and channel some imaginative paragraphs? *Magic: An extraordinary power or influence seemingly from a supernatural source* (Webster's Dictionary). Be still. Wait. It is not just up to me. There is supernatural source. Deva, Fairy, Spirit, Muse, Angel, Goddess . . . She waves the magic wand, and Poof! The humdrum sentence sparkles with fairy dust. But Magic is elusive: now you see Her, now you don't. If She is not ready to inspire, then so be it. Yes, but *Magic is the art of changing consciousness at will* (Dion Fortune). I do have agency here. *Ask, Believe, Receive.* There are affirmations to focus, invocations to sing, prayers to offer. Have to get past my boredom with glib formulas that make magical work sound so easy. It's an effort to conjure up my out-of-ordinary power. Musawa and I persevere. We align our intentions for magical work.

MUSAWA (Attending a Trauma Training, in Hakomi Integrative Somatics while writing this): I'm thinking of magic as a missing resource in this culture. Do we still carry collective and cellular memory of the burning times? Inner body sensations, thoughts and feelings get dissociated in order to survive trauma—that's what we need to reconnect with. The ancient Hawaiian healing tradition of *Ho'opono'pono* focuses on these same three channels of inner knowing: *Mana'o*, thoughts and beliefs, *Pu'uwai*, heart and feelings and *Na'au*, gut knowing. When we are in touch with them, here and now, we are *pono*: a balanced state of being that allows *uhane*, our natural "spirit greatness" to flow through. That's when magic happens. Opening our "ordinary" channels of inner experience, our "extra-ordinary" perceptions come alive.

I want to ask our minds, hearts, bodies what comes up for us in trying to write about magic. Bethroot records responses, as I dive into stream-of-consciousness. *Mana'o* (Head/Thinking Mode)— mind by itself gets stuck, cut off from magic. One part rules from the top down. Magic is not heard when head rules. Doesn't work that way. Has its own language. Magic comes from a deep connected place. Is how everything unfolds. Going to the Source, sorcery. *Pu'uwai* (Heart/Feeling Mode)—when magic gets stuck inside, I feel small. Feel a loss. Frustration, sadness, anger. Magic has been co-opted, squashed. When I am feeling my magic, there is a current running through me. No part of me is left out. I feel connected, open. My heart is getting bigger, expanding. Feels good! *Na'au* (Body/ Physical Mode)—hearing the word "magic", just now, sounds a "ding" inside my heart. Like a wand got waved. My body feels light and spacious and open and alive inside. Cells squishing and touching, juices flowing. I'm stretching my back and shoulders, sitting up straight. Making room for magic in my body. My voice deepens, senses awaken. I breathe deeper, slow down, open. My body *is* magic. Energy sparking, moving me.

Feeling magic literally moving inside me melts my resistance—breakthrough, releasing my words. Later a dream comes and pulls these strands together. I dream about the magic of flying. My body knows how, naturally, but my conditioned mind thinks I need something external to hold on to, and the heart of my inner survivor-witch fears flying too high. I am cautioned not to get distracted by the heavy machinery of mind or matter. This is dream magic's gift: spontaneous heart/mind/body connection in the spirit realm.

BETHROOT (Exploring mind-heart-body depths, I am word-riffing): I joke about how many bunnies there can be on the head of a pin. Musawa is typing my words and exclaims with surprise as her computer takes off with a mind of its own and types *mamanymany bunnies*; at the same moment an office machine next to me gives a beep and starts displaying numbers on its own. I am laughing with delight. There She is! Magic! The elusive one has paid us an electronic visit. Breakthrough for me. This warming laughter is the elixir, and I am joyful to imagine the surprise intervention of another presence, whom we called in with our focused search and our willingness to perceive Her activity in the mundane wonders of the moment. How could I have doubted? She has been with us all along in our process. At this year's final Weaving Circle, in which we make semi-final selections for the **We'Moon**, a perfectly intact, just-dead little bat turned up outside the door—a witchy blessing for our witchy tasks.

To practice magic is to bear the responsibility for having a vision, for we work magic by envisioning what we want to create, clearing the obstacles in our way, and then directing energy through that vision (Starhawk). As we create the **We'Moon**, we consciously invoke the spirit of magic in our working sessions. Candles, silence, song, intention help us to create sacred space. We are guided—now to this image, now to those words—layering a tapestry of beauty, which will go out into the world and accompany women through the year. For the second year, we have chosen not to name a sub-theme for each of the 13 Moons, but to weave thematic concepts throughout the calendar.

Magic roams through the wheel of the year in many different guises. There are spells and meditations, rituals and blessings. We visit ancient holy sites and invoke ancestral magic. Angel, witch, fairy, psychic, dybbuk, shaman appear as mediums and agents

Renaissance Phoenix
© *Trace Ashleigh 1999*

of magical energy. Transformation resonates from Moon to Moon as we'moon describe powerful acts of magic they have experienced, as activists, gardeners, healers, artists. They share with us the soft magic of loving relationship, the everyday magic of kitchen and hearth, the cellular magic of bodily changes. We are reminded of the magical animals who inhabit our world and our imaginations. We are invited to witness the fact that conscious intention, put forward with sacred purpose, makes *change* whether focused in group ceremony or private affirmation, in acts of devotion or personal creativity. Magic circles the globe, and the calendar pages are rich with words and images which reflect Her activity among women of many cultures, including Asian, British, Native American, Jewish, African, Scandinavian.

Read between the lines and go between the worlds . . .We begin and end this **We'Moon** calendar with images of a child invoking magic. Children live in a world of everyday miracles. The veil is always thin between seen and unseen, make-believe and just-so. Ritual is child's play. Spontaneity raises energy. May the innocence and wonder of childhood magic open our hearts and tender the world.

With this **We'Moon** we cast a circle around the earth; as the wheel turns, we turn the pages together. Join in the magic with other we'moon, as we stir the cauldron of transformation with our dreams and visions.

◻ *Musawa and Bethroot 2000*

Dewi IV
¤ *Gyps Curmi 1998*

December

ᴰᴰᴰ   lundo

♎︎

Monday
18

☽△♃	5:13 am	☉⚹♂	9:08 am
⚷ApG	5:31 am	☽△♀	9:23 pm
☽△♆	7:39 am	☽⚹♀	10:42 pm

♂♂♂   mardo

♎︎

Tuesday
19

☽△♅	7:22 am
♀⚹♀	1:07 pm
☿⚻♄	5:15 pm
☽⚹♅	8:48 pm

☿☿☿   merkredo

♎︎ ♏︎

Wednesday
20

☽♂♂	1:41 am	
☉⚹☽	3:07 am	v/c
☽→♏︎	5:12 am	
☽□♆	2:24 pm	

♃♃♃   jaŭdo

♏︎

Thursday
21

☉→♑︎	5:37 am
☽□♀	10:09 am
☽□♅	3:19 pm

Solstice

♑︎

Sun in Capricorn 5:37 am PST

♀♀♀   vendredo

♏︎ ♐︎

Friday
22

		☽→♐︎	1:57 pm
☽⚻♄	4:28 am	v/c	☿→♑︎	6:03 pm
☿ApG	4:51 am	☽⚻♃	7:46 pm
☿⚹♂	10:31 am	☽⚹♆	11:42 pm

♄♄♄   sabato

♐︎

Saturday
23

♂→♏︎	6:37 am
☽♂♀	4:11 pm
♀♂♅	9:52 pm

☉☉☉   dimanĉo

♐︎

Sunday
24

☉⚻♃	1:31 am	
☽⚹♅	1:40 am	
☽⚹♀	2:03 am	v/c
☿⚻♃	12:58 pm	

33

Magic

At the core of magic lies the essence of mystery. It is beguiling, it is mystical and it is wondrous. For eons, magic has confounded and baffled many. Magic has been feared. It has been threatening to many. Through the ages, magic has been vilified, even outlawed. Yet, magic is pervasive, it is undeniable. Magic endures. For magic is a purely natural force within our universe. Magic is evident everywhere we look, from the spin of an electron about an atom's nucleus to the revolution of our lovely Mother Earth about our Sun. We see it in each blade of grass, every petal of each flower, in the leaves upon the trees. We see it in the ecological dance of flora and fauna, in the energetic interplay of the elements, wind and water, sunlight and earth. We see it when we look into the night sky and bear witness to the wheeling of massive galaxies across the infinity of the cosmos.

We see magic when we are basking in the light of love. For the human heart is a crucible. Within our hearts lies the greatest potential for transformation, for transmutation and for evolution. In a compassionate heart we may find our greatest opportunity for growth, for expansion and for embodying our truest purpose as a human being.

In its deepest context, magic may simply be our innate human ability to allow the flow of love, the flow of creativity, and joy, peace, wonder, gratitude and humility that pervades the universe to pass through us. Magic may just be about allowing, blessing, and honoring All That Is, and serving as a conduit for the beauty and grace of the cosmos. It is about opening ourselves to let its magnificence stream through our beings, to find its divine expression of embodiment into the physical plane, through us.

We are the magicians. *We* are the wizards. We own the power of alchemical transmutation . . . the power to hone our craft, the art of co-creativity by embodying the essence of the truest magic there is, pure love.

□ *Linda Zurich 1999*

MOON I

Moon I: December 25–January 24

New Moon in ♑ Capricorn: Dec. 25; Full Moon in ♋ Cancer: Jan. 9; Sun in ♒ Aquarius: Jan. 19

Kuan-Yin: Goddess of Compassion

December
Desemba

☽☽☽ Jumatatu

♐
♑

Monday
25

☽→♑ 12:54 am
☽⚹♂ 3:05 am
☽☌☿ 9:15 am
☉☌☽ 9:22 am
☉☌☿ 11:23 am

New Moon in ♑ Capricorn 9:22 am PST
Partial Solar Eclipse 9:35 am PST (0.723 mag.)
Eclipse visible from North and Central America

♂♂♂ Jumanne

♑

Tuesday
26

☿☿☿ Jumatano

♑
♒

Wednesday
27

☽△♄ 2:52 am v/c
♀⚹⚷ 5:42 am
☽→♒ 1:25 pm
♂⚻♃ 2:00 pm
☽△♃ 6:34 pm
☽□♂ 6:50 pm

♃♃♃ Alhamisi

♒

Thursday
28

☽☌♆ 12:00 am
☽ApG 7:05 am
☽⚹♇ 5:15 pm

♀♀♀ Ijumaa

♒

Friday
29

☽☌♅ 3:09 am
♀□♄ 2:35 pm
☽□♄ 3:40 pm
☽☌♀ 3:47 pm v/c

My First We'Moon

it came as a Gift

on a Yule with no moon

like Hope on a stick

dangled over the quicksand pit

tangible proof that Sisters exist

inside was a portal

to a Healing Spell

We'Moon Magic

made me well

□ *Pam Fox 1999*

Life
□ *Lori Nicolosi 1993*

♒
♓

Saturday
30

☽→♓ 2:27 am
☽□♃ 7:07 am
☽△♂ 11:00 am
☉⚹☽ 10:23 pm

♓

Sunday
31

☽⚹♅ 5:47 am
☽□♀ 6:08 am

January
Januar

2001

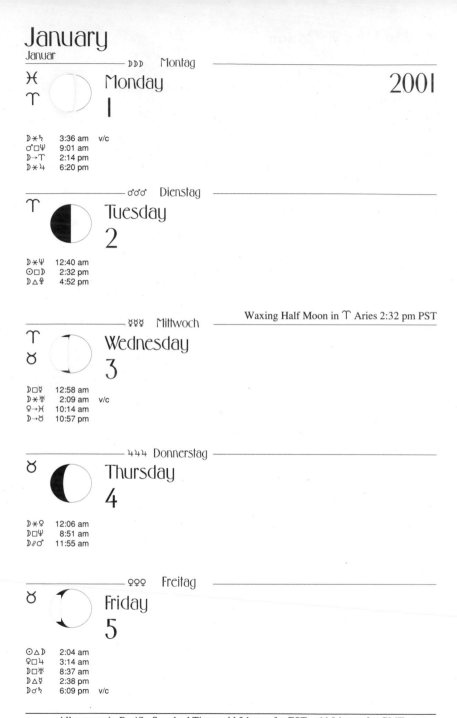

———— ⅅⅅⅅ Montag ————

♓
♈

Monday
1

☽⚹♄	3:36 am	v/c
♂□♆	9:01 am	
☽→♈	2:14 pm	
☽⚹♃	6:20 pm	

———— ♂♂♂ Dienstag ————

♈

Tuesday
2

☽⚹♆	12:40 am
☉□☽	2:32 pm
☽△♀	4:52 pm

———— ☿☿☿ Mittwoch ————

Waxing Half Moon in ♈ Aries 2:32 pm PST

♈
♉

Wednesday
3

☽□☿	12:58 am	
☽⚹♅	2:09 am	v/c
♀→♓	10:14 am	
☽→♉	10:57 pm	

———— ♃♃♃ Donnerstag ————

♉

Thursday
4

☽⚹♀	12:06 am
☽□♆	8:51 am
☽☍♂	11:55 am

———— ♀♀♀ Freitag ————

♉

Friday
5

☉△☽	2:04 am	
♀□♃	3:14 am	
☽□♅	8:37 am	
☽△☿	2:38 pm	
☽♂♄	6:09 pm	v/c

All aspects in Pacific Standard Time; add 3 hours for EST; add 8 hours for GMT

Her Magic

Are you bathed in Her beam?
Are you dazed in Her glance?
Are you drunk in Her scent?
Are you shocked in Her chant?
Are you thrilled in Her cry?
Are you crushed in Her dance?
Are you cooked in Her fire?
Are you wrecked in Her storm?
Are you lost in Her game?
Are you freed in Her joy?
Are you drowned in Her sea?
Are you cleansed in Her peace?
Are you healed in Her arms?
Are you saved in Her grace?
Are you waked in Her love?
Are you found in Her light?

© Janine Canan 1999

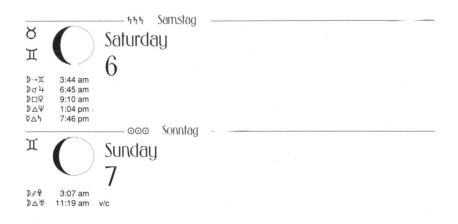

ㅎㅎㅎ   Samstag
♉   **Saturday**
♊
       6

☽→♊   3:44 am
☽☌♃   6:45 am
☽□♀   9:10 am
☽△♆   1:04 pm
♉△♄   7:46 pm

☉☉☉   Sonntag
♊   **Sunday**
       7

☽☍♀   3:07 am
☽△♅   11:19 am   v/c

January
'Ianuali

— ⅅⅅⅅ   Pō'akahi —

♊
♋ 🌑 Monday
8

ⅅ→♋   5:09 am
ⅅ△♀   2:05 pm
ⅅ△♂   8:38 pm

Procession
□ *Miranda 1989*

— ♂♂♂   Pō'alua —

♋ 🌕 Tuesday
9

☉☍ⅅ   12:24 pm
ⅅ⚹♄   7:41 pm

Total Lunar Eclipse 12:22 pm PST (1.189 mag.)
Eclipse visible from Africa, Europe, Asia, Australia and eastern Americas
Full Moon in ♋ Cancer 12:24 pm PST

— ☿☿☿   Pō'akolu —

♋
♌ 🌕 Wednesday
10

ⅅPrG   12:56 am
ⅅ☍♅   4:39 am   v/c
ⅅ→♌   4:44 am
☿→♒   5:26 am
ⅅ⚹♃   7:11 am
ⅅ☍♆   1:42 pm
ⅅ□♂   9:55 pm

— ♃♃♃   Pō'ahā —

♌ 🌖 Thursday
11

ⅅ△♀   3:03 am
☿△♃   3:21 am
ⅅ☍♅   11:07 am
ⅅ□♄   7:08 pm   v/c

— ♀♀♀   Pō'alima —

♌
♍ 🌗 Friday
12

ⅅ→♍   4:26 am
ⅅ□♃   6:48 am
ⅅ☍♀   8:51 pm

All aspects in Pacific Standard Time; add 3 hours for EST; add 8 hours for GMT

Full Moon in Africa

We are sitting in circle
in the orchard
next to the train tracks.
Seven women gathered
for Full Moon Ceremony.

Candles, prayers, stories—
and in the midst of my story
a train goes by
screaming in our ears,
shaking the ground we sit on,
so loud, so disruptive,
so intrusive to our ritual

until Christine laughs
and tells us that it sounds
like a herd of elephants running by
and suddenly
we are all transported to Africa.

Seven women sitting in circle
gathered in the jungle
next to the elephant herd
for Full Moon Ceremony.

◻ *Annalisa Cunningham 1999*

──────── ᚻᚻᚻ   Pōʻaono ────────

♍ Saturday
13

☽✶♂	12:06 am
☽□♀	3:34 am
☿♂♆	5:10 pm
☉△☽	8:00 pm
☽△♄	8:12 pm v/c
☉△♄	10:49 pm

──────── ☉☉☉   Lāpule ────────

♍
♎ Sunday
14

☽→♎	6:05 am
☽△♃	8:27 am
☽△♆	4:06 pm
☽△☿	7:09 pm

January
Januaro

ᗞᗞᗞ lundo ------------------

♎︎

Monday
15

D ✶ ♀ 6:47 am
♄ ⊼ ♇ 11:25 am
D △ ♅ 3:57 pm

formless:
the form of the moment;
shape of bottle, sink
cupped hands,
teapot,
pond, river

*excerpt ▢ Jacqueline
Elizabeth Letalien 1999*

------------------ ♂♂♂ mardo ------------------

♎︎
♏︎

Tuesday
16

☉ ☐ D 4:35 am v/c
D → ♏︎ 11:02 am
D ☐ ♆ 9:56 pm
♀ ☐ ♀ 10:35 pm
♀ △ ♂ 11:58 pm

Waning Half Moon in ♎︎ Libra 4:35 am PST

------------------ ☿☿☿ merkredo ------------------

♏︎

Wednesday
17

D ☐ ♅ 8:55 am
D ♂ ♂ 2:20 pm
D △ ♀ 2:53 pm
D ☐ ♅ 11:31 pm

------------------ ♃♃♃ ĵaŭdo ------------------

♏︎
♐︎

Thursday
18

D ☍ ♄ 8:12 am
☉ ✶ D 5:44 pm v/c
D → ♐︎ 7:35 pm
D ☍ ♃ 10:01 pm
☿ ✶ ♀ 10:53 pm

------------------ ♀♀♀ vendredo ------------------

♐︎

Friday
19

D ✶ ♆ 7:18 am
☉ → ♒︎ 4:16 pm
D ☐ ♀ 11:48 pm

Sun in Aquarius 4:16 pm PST

All aspects in Pacific Standard Time; add 3 hours for EST; add 8 hours for GMT

Year at a Glance for ♒ AQUARIUS (Jan. 19–Feb. 18)

The persona or mask the world sees of you is swiftly shifting these days. You are a chameleon as you seek the perfect vessel for the restless energy permeating your body. You take inspiration from figures in literature or from your own private fantasy worlds, trying to express the changes that are occurring internally. What is your fairy tale today?

After April, the time and effort you have been putting into making your home life support your emerging self should begin to pay off. However, plan for a slow start. The most dependable stability lies within you and all action must emerge from your own redefined, restructured inner self. Interfacing with the world can be tricky—your persona is still emerging.

The answer may be to act as if. Act as if you have figured everything out. Trust that you are the perfect conduit, for the goddesses' divine plan, to move the world forward. You will find playmates with whom you feel very vital and alive, especially through June.

Later in the year, you may experience some intense and difficult emotional encounters. This is happening because you are ready to confront new dimensions of yourself. People you are now meeting are not casual encounters—they are showing up to help you in your individual development.

The radical changes you continue to experience may plunge you into entirely new social circles. Use some discrimination, you are still forming and may be too easily swayed. Avoid giant, irrevocable steps. Although you may not feel it, you are already moving along just fine.   *Gretchen Lawlor 2000*

© *Sequoia 1998*

———— ♄♄♄   sàbato ————

♐ ● **Sàturdau**
   20

♉□♂	1:05 am	
☽✶♉	3:28 am	
☽□♀	6:15 am	
☽✶♅	10:18 am	v/c
☉△♃	8:58 pm	

———— ☉☉☉   dimanĉo ————

♐ ● **Sundau**
♑   **21**

☽→♑   6:57 am

Inside the Psychic's Tent
© *Cynthia Ré Robbins 1996*

MOON II

Moon II: January 24–February 23

New Moon in ♒ Aquarius: Jan. 24; Full Moon in ♌ Leo: Feb. 7; Sun in ♓ Pisces: Feb. 18

The Psychic's Tent
© *Cynthia Ré Robbins 1996*

January
Januari

Witch by Moonlight
© *Kim Antieau 1999*

〰 ♌♌♌ Jumatatu ───────

♑

Monday
22

☿☌♅ 11:35 am
☽⚹♂ 6:35 pm

♂♂♂ Jumanne ───────

♑
♒

Tuesday
23

☽⚹♀ 12:06 am
☽△♄ 7:38 am   v/c
☽→♒ 7:43 pm
☽△♃ 10:09 pm

☿☿☿ Jumatano ───────

♒

Wednesday
24

☉☌☽ 5:07 am
☽☌♆ 8:21 am
☽ApG 10:59 am
♄sD 4:24 pm

Lunar Imbolc
New Moon in ♒ Aquarius 5:07 am PST

♃♃♃ Alhamisi ───────

♒

Thursday
25

♃sD 12:38 am
☽⚹♀ 1:18 am
☽□♂ 10:37 am
☽☌♅ 12:20 pm
☿□♄ 1:35 pm
☉☌♆ 7:55 pm
☽□♄ 8:37 pm
☽☌☿ 9:28 pm   v/c

♀♀♀ Ijumaa ───────

♒
♓

Friday
26

♆ApG 2:15 am
☽→♓ 8:39 am
☽□♃ 11:03 am
☿⚹♄ 12:35 pm
♀⚹♄ 9:25 pm

All aspects in Pacific Standard Time; add 3 hours for EST; add 8 hours for GMT

Synchronicity's Kiss

Car on the highway, mind in a crossroads. Needed a guide, asked for a sign.

That's when I spotted someone over on the access road. She was walking against traffic, bent far forward, hands on straps, an enormous parcel on her back.

Getting closer I could see it was an old woman. Sun-faded clothes, plain brown shoes, grey hair hung long and loose beneath an old felt Stetson, brim laid flat.

The pack was no traveler's fare, but a home-made rig of many clothed-wrapped bundles tied together. Piled high with all she owned, her steps strong, deliberately slow. A practiced, balanced load. She was moving and had moved before. Something sane was in her eye.

Caught all this while whizzing by, still wondering if . . .

Then my heart almost stopped. Stuck through the straps at the very top—was her Broom.

¤ Pam Fox 1999

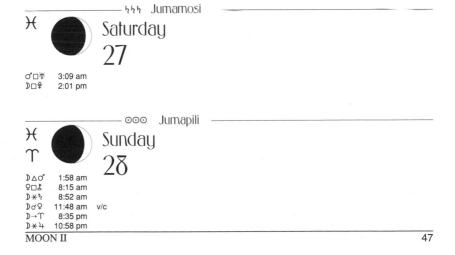

January
Januar

♈ **Monday**
29

D ⚹ Ψ   9:07 am
☉ ⚹ D   4:29 pm

♈ **Tuesday**
30

D △ ♀   1:11 am
D ⚹ ♅   11:54 am

♈
♉   **Wednesday**
31

D ⚹ ♅   5:36 am   v/c
D → ♉   6:21 am
D □ Ψ   6:27 pm
☿ → ♓   11:09 pm

♉ **Thursday**   **February**
1

☉ □ D   6:02 am
D □ ♅   7:50 pm

Waxing Half Moon in ♉ Taurus 6:02 am PST

Imbolc/Candlemas

♉
♊ **Friday**
2

D ☍ ♂   1:05 am
D ☌ ♄   2:31 am   v/c
♀ → ♈   11:14 am
D → ♊   12:56 pm
D ⚹ ♀   1:02 pm
D □ ♉   1:56 pm
D ☌ ♃   3:14 pm

All aspects in Pacific Standard Time; add 3 hours for EST; add 8 hours for GMT

© Monica Sjöö 1990

Imbolc

At Imbolc in the Northern Hemisphere, the days lengthen just enough for growth to quietly resume. In many countries the focus moves away from the indoor hearth to early field preparations. Sap rises, buds swell and spring greens abound. Serpent power stirs in underground rivers, sacred wells are awakened by fires and magical healing is possible.

Imbolc is traditionally a time to work on initiations and commitments for the coming year and a ritual bath can be a good place to consider those commitments. You can create your own healing waters by adding herbs such as Fennel (*Foeniculum vulgare*). Harvest early Fennel shoots or use the dried leaf or seed if fresh isn't available and make a gallon of strong tea. Pour the Fennel tea into bath water for ritual purification and healing. Or simply place fresh shoots in bath water and gently use them as a scrub. Since Fennel essential oils are mild vasodilators for the lungs, it can give you more wind power to speak your truth. Harvest additional early Fennel shoots as they appear and hang them in your doorways as a reminder of what you are committed to and to provide protection. Imbolc is a powerful time to be re-inspired as activists in whatever field we work in.

© Colette Gardiner 2000

Magic
on the Walk from Silbury Hill to Stonehenge

Four days and nights we trek across military bases in the heart of England, from one Sacred Site to another, (inspired by Greenham ♀, Mary Millington). 150 ♀, children, babies, dogs, instruments. Mostly Greenham Common ♀'s Peace Camp ♀/lesbians and others, some from different lands—Japan, Australia, U.S.A., France, Sweden and more. Hiro, Zohl, Musawa, Monica Sjöö, Starhawk. All walking for Peace on our Mother Earth.

Second night, we camp next to a military base; wake to tanks firing, soldiers and police barring our way. Too much for some ♀. Some of us deeply determined we can do it, as we have done before in other places—we decide to walk through, not around.

We pass from hand to hand a Sacred Stick, dark brown, smooth and carved, given to Zohl in trust by Aboriginal Elders in Australia—"It's time," they say, "for this to travel around the world."

Suddenly, amazed, I *see* a very powerful clear river of energy pouring down the road from behind us into the base. Nudging Katrina, next to me, I say with total certainty, "We're going through today."

Spiral, snake dancing into the base, soldiers, police and dogs unable to contain us, Hiro and I spin free, race down the track between land mines and firing tanks. A Landrover screeches to a halt in front of us; we are confronted by a soldier, he is shaken by his inability to control us inside the firing zone.

I tell him, calmly, with utter conviction, "get on that little machine of yours and tell them to stop. We're coming through today."

And so we did—Helped by Spirits—following a Magic River.

Blessed be.

□ *Boand 1999*

© Marie Perret 1993

Old Kali came bustin' round my doorstep the other day.
You know who I mean, the Great Black Mother who knows
how to change things.
Powerful Woman!

excerpt © Suzy Coffee 1999

ካካካ Samstag

♊

Saturday
3

☽△♆	12:24 am
☉⚹♀	5:05 am
♂☍♄	1:33 pm
☽☍♀	2:30 pm
☉△☽	3:13 pm
☿sR	5:58 pm

☉☉☉ Sonntag

♊
♋

Sunday
4

☽△♅	12:12 am	v/c
♀⚹♃	1:26 am	
☽→♋	4:00 pm	
☽△♉	5:00 pm	
☽□♀	7:16 pm	

February
Pēpēluali

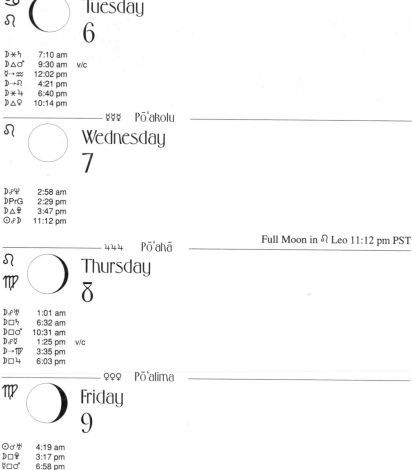

Back of the bread is the flour
And back of the flour is the mill
And back of the mill
is the wind and the rain
And the Mother's will.
  ❑ *food blessing song of unknown origin*

————))) Pōʻakahi ————

♋

Monday
5

———— ♂♂♂ Pōʻalua ————

♋
♌

Tuesday
6

☽✶♄	7:10 am	
☽△♂	9:30 am	v/c
☿→♒	12:02 pm	
☽→♌	4:21 pm	
☽✶♃	6:40 pm	
☽△♀	10:14 pm	

———— ☿☿☿ Pōʻakolu ————

♌

Wednesday
7

☽☍♆	2:58 am	
☽PrG	2:29 pm	
☽△♀	3:47 pm	
☉☍☽	11:12 pm	

———— ♃♃♃ Pōʻahā ————

Full Moon in ♌ Leo 11:12 pm PST

♌
♍

Thursday
8

☽☍♅	1:01 am	
☽□♄	6:32 am	
☽□♂	10:31 am	
☽☍♅	1:25 pm	v/c
☽→♍	3:35 pm	
☽□♃	6:03 pm	

———— ♀♀♀ Pōʻalima ————

♍

Friday
9

☉♂♅	4:19 am	
☽□♀	3:17 pm	
☿□♂	6:58 pm	

———

All aspects in Pacific Standard Time; add 3 hours for EST; add 8 hours for GMT

Magic Bread

Goddess taught me how to bake bread.
She gave me the song to Invoke Spirits of Earth's Bounty.
Grain seeds nuts fruit yeast.
Harvesting the Full Moon water.
Singing my thanks as I knead.
Wait quietly, patiently inviting Air,
Watch this Magical dough inhale and rise.
On the exhale, She taught me to let go.
Pushing out every bubble of stress, ache, apathy & fear.
My intentions I whisper to the seeds
& sprinkle inside the sacred spiral
to roll into a living loaf.
Welcome Fire Spirit, bring my intentions & love
to harvest. The hearty smells of my spells
dance through my kitchen out windows & doors
calling our tribe to gather.
This year She taught me the awesome power of
humble subtle ceremony.

□ *Kara Mathiason 1999*

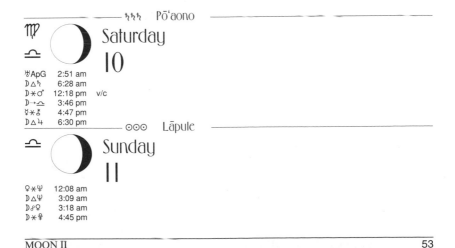

ħħħ Pō'aono

♍
♎ Saturday
10

♅ApG	2:51 am	
☽△♄	6:28 am	
☽✳♂	12:18 pm	v/c
☽→♎	3:46 pm	
☿✳⚷	4:47 pm	
☽△♃	6:30 pm	

☉☉☉ Lāpule

♎ Sunday
11

♀✳♆	12:08 am
☽△♆	3:09 am
☽☍♀	3:18 am
☽✳⚷	4:45 pm

February
Februaro

─── ☽☽☽　lundo ───────────

♎︎
♏︎ **Monday**
12

☽△♅	3:06 am	
☉△☽	8:22 am	
☽△☿	9:31 am	v/c
☿□♄	3:25 pm	
☉♂☿	4:17 pm	
☉□♄	5:21 pm	
☽→♏︎	6:51 pm	

□ *May Trillium 1999*

─── ♂♂♂　mardo ───────────

♏︎ **Tuesday**
13

| ☽□♆ | 7:16 am |

─── ☿☿☿　merkredo ───────────

♏︎ **Wednesday**
14

☽□♅	9:15 am	
☽□☿	11:24 am	
♂→♐	12:06 pm	
☽☍♄	3:33 pm	
☉□☽	7:23 pm	v/c
☿PrG	9:04 pm	

Waning Half Moon in ♏︎ Scorpio 7:23 pm PST

─── ♃♃♃　ĵaŭdo ───────────

♏︎
♐ **Thursday**
15

☽→♐	2:02 am
☽♂♂	2:38 am
☉⚹♃	5:24 am
☽☍♃	5:45 am
☿♂♅	10:38 am
☽⚹♆	3:34 pm
☽△♀	9:51 pm

─── ♀♀♀　vendredo ───────────

♐ **Friday**
16

☽♂♀	7:11 am
☽⚹☿	4:43 pm
☽⚹♅	7:30 pm

All aspects in Pacific Standard Time; add 3 hours for EST; add 8 hours for GMT

Year at a Glance for ♓ PISCES (Feb. 18–March 20)

Before May, do your best to clear unresolved issues isolating you from people in your family or community. By doing so, you will realize you have become more confident and capable of expressing yourself. In the next few years you will really appreciate the steady companionship of a well-knit circle of reliable friends.

This is a good year to periodically withdraw from your busy life to develop solidity and order in your home environment. Professional obligations may make this very difficult. A desire to be more powerful can lead you to neglect your home and inner needs. However, it is a very good time to put down roots. This may require renovations on your home or even relocating to a situation that better suits you. The work you do this year to improve the security of your personal life will comfort and support you in the future when you'll need it.

Plan a retreat early in the year for clarity on what feeds your sensitive soul. Create an altar/meditation room in your home. You may find comfort in the cultural or spiritual traditions of your childhood.

A vague restlessness reflects changes deep in your subconscious. Circumstances beyond your control break you open, help you see what you do to keep yourself stuck. Indulge a few wild urges, even small ones.

In a couple of years your life will change phenomenally. This year, you are capable of confronting truths about yourself you are normally reluctant to face and can handle them once and for all. This frees your spirit and prepares you to respond to the possibilities soon to appear on your horizon.

© *Gretchen Lawlor 2000*

--- ♄♄♄ sabato ---

♐
♑

Saturday
17

☉＊☽ 11:22 am   v/c
☽→♑ 12:59 pm

Queen of Cups
© *Lynn Dewart 1998*

--- ☉☉☉ dimanĉo ---

♑

Sunday
18

☉→♓ 6:27 am
☽□♀ 1:00 pm
♂☍♃ 5:57 pm

♓

Sun in Pisces 6:27 am PST

February
Februari

♑ Monday
19

☽△♄   3:03 pm   v/c

♑
♒ Tuesday
20

☽→♒   1:53 am
☽△♃   6:39 am
☽⚹♂   8:03 am
☽ApG   1:39 pm
☉□♃   2:39 pm
☽☌♆   4:36 pm

♒ Wednesday
21

☽⚹♀   5:06 am
☽⚹♇   8:39 am
☽☌☿   11:02 am
☽☌♅   9:42 pm

♒
♓ Thursday
22

☽□♄   4:18 am   v/c
☉□♂   5:11 am
☽→♓   2:45 pm
☽□♃   7:53 pm
☽□♂   11:31 pm

♓ Friday
23

☉☌☽   12:21 am
☽□♀   9:01 pm

New Moon in ♓ Pisces 12:21 am PST

All aspects in Pacific Standard Time; add 3 hours for EST; add 8 hours for GMT

Libations

when there are no answers,
I go to the water;
she offers me her wisdom

when I am hurt, in pain
I go to the water;
she heals me with her power

Communion
© *Lilian de Mello 1999*

when there are no feelings,
I go to the water;
she opens me to my heart

when I am stuck, in mud
I go to the water;
she moves me with her passion

◻ *Jacqueline Elizabeth Letalien 1999*

--- ♄♄♄ Jumamosi ---

♓

Saturday
24

☽✶♄   4:25 pm   v/c

--- ☉☉☉ Jumapili ---

♓
♈

Sunday
25

♀△♀	12:30 am	☽△♂	1:22 pm
☽→♈	2:20 am	☿✶♀	3:50 pm
♀sD	7:41 am	☽✶♆	4:44 pm
☽✶♃	7:48 am		

Bird Mother Calls

In the gray between
She takes me to a field of dry grasses
brittle after a long winter
and chooses only those hollow stalks
the narrow-lipped wind whistles through.

Into the lucent bowl of sky
She dips each stem
canary dawn and beryl noon
a dab of robin's egg blue
and a speck of henna from evanescent sunset.

As a final touch
She brushes one opal stroke
from the albedo of the moon
until the stalks grow radiant as rush-light.

Then She places them
one against the other
like fringes of eyelash
until She has a feather.

By gathering the air into a dark circle
between arched palms
She forms the breast and backbone
of a small round body.

She presses her lips
to the cupped opening
between her thumbs
exhaling until her breath
becomes a whistle, a warble, a hoot
a trembling hum.

Then She lets her hands leap forward
releasing wings to the wind
and calls down to me
as the flock sails higher,
Wherever you go from now on
It will be in the company of birds.

¤ *Ann Megisikwe Filemyr 1999*

MOON III

Moon III: February 23–March 24

New Moon in ♓ Pisces: Feb. 23; Full Moon in ♍ Virgo: March 9; Sun in ♈ Aries: March 20

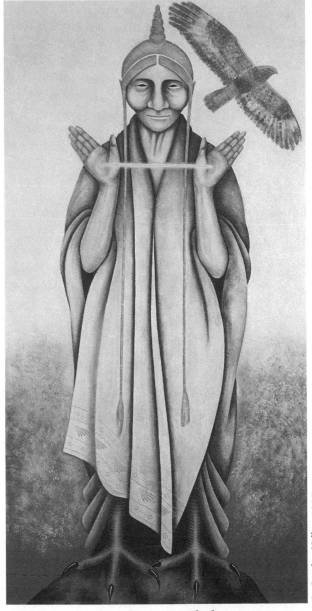

© *Carolyn Hillyer 1997*

Vwalā: Long Flight

February
Februar

Pinning us to the cloak of dreams
night filters in through unlatched windows.
excerpt © Nancy Bennett 1999

☽☽☽ Montag

♈

Monday 26

☽△♇ 7:47 am
☽✶☿ 8:22 am
☽☌♀ 8:47 am
☽✶♅ 8:34 pm v/c

♂♂♂ Dienstag

♈ ♉

Tuesday 27

☽→♉ 12:06 pm

☿☿☿ Mittwoch

♉

Wednesday 28

☽□♆ 2:09 am
☉✶☽ 7:02 am
☽□☿ 6:04 pm

♃♃♃ Donnerstag

♉ ♊

Thursday 1

March

☽□♅ 4:59 am
♂✶♆ 7:32 am
☽☌♄ 10:57 am v/c
☽→♊ 7:36 pm

♀♀♀ Freitag

♊

Friday 2

☽☌♃ 1:33 am
☽△♆ 9:09 am
☽☍♂ 10:03 am
☉□☽ 6:03 pm
☽☍♇ 10:44 pm

Waxing Half Moon in ♊ Gemini 6:03 pm PST

All aspects in Pacific Standard Time; add 3 hours for EST; add 8 hours for GMT

© Roxi 1995

Magic of the Night

Each night I lower myself down
Into the magic depths of sleep
Oblivious to that embracing
Moment when it takes me deep
Into the silent world of nowhere
There, with others, animals and insects,
Even flowers
I live the other side of life that sleeps by day.

© Marguerite Bartley 1999

ħħħ   Samstag ────────

♊

Saturday
3

☽△♅   1:59 am
☽⚹♀   2:03 am
♅⚹♀   4:36 am
☽△♅   10:45 am   v/c

⊙⊙⊙   Sonntag ────────

♊
♋

Sunday
4

☽→♋   12:24 am

March
Malaki

☽☽☽ Pō'akahi

♋ Monday 5

☉△☽ 1:33 am
☽□♀ 5:54 am
☉□♇ 10:11 am
☽✶♄ 7:10 pm v/c

© Meghan Lewis 1998

Morgain's Moon

♂♂♂ Pō'alua

♋ ♌ Tuesday 6

☽→♌ 2:30 am
☽✶♃ 8:41 am
☽☍♆ 2:58 pm
☽△♂ 6:56 pm

☿☿☿ Pō'akolu

♌ Wednesday 7

☽△♇ 3:09 am
☽△♀ 7:04 am
☽☍☿ 10:55 am
☽☍♅ 2:28 pm
☽□♄ 7:50 pm v/c

♃♃♃ Pō'ahā

♌ ♍ Thursday 8

☽PrG 12:49 am
☽→♍ 2:44 am
☽□♃ 9:12 am
♀sR 5:07 pm
☽□♂ 8:26 pm

♀♀♀ Pō'alima

♍ Friday 9

☽□♇ 3:04 am
☉☍☽ 9:23 am
☽△♄ 8:01 pm v/c

Full Moon in ♍ Virgo 9:23 am PST

All aspects in Pacific Standard Time; add 3 hours for EST; add 8 hours for GMT

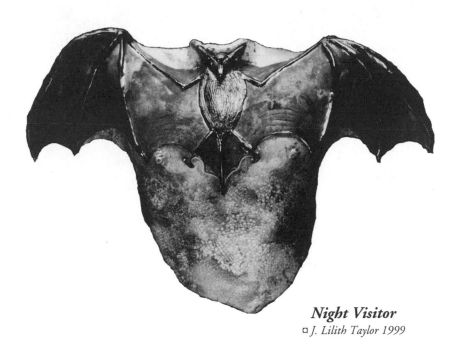

Night Visitor
¤ *J. Lilith Taylor 1999*

♍
♎

Saturday
10

♉♂♅	1:50 am
☽→♎	2:47 am
☽△♃	9:49 am
☽△♆	3:31 pm
☽⚹♂	10:32 pm

♎

Sunday
11

☽⚹♀	3:50 am	
☽☍♀	7:42 am	
☽△♅	3:59 pm	
☽△☿	6:44 pm	v/c

March
Marto

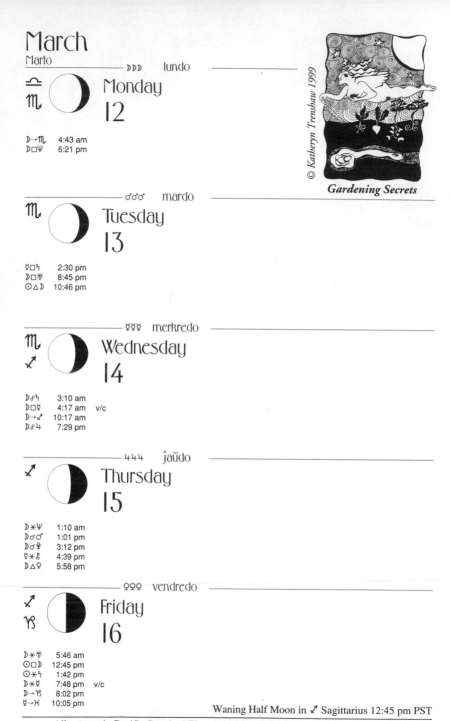

Gardening Secrets

𝄇𝄇𝄇   lundo

Monday
12

☊ ♎
♏

☽→♏	4:43 am
☽□♆	6:21 pm

♂♂♂   mardo

♏

Tuesday
13

♉□♄	2:30 pm
☽□♅	8:45 pm
☉△☽	10:46 pm

☿☿☿   merkredo

♏
♐

Wednesday
14

☽☍♄	3:10 am	
☽□☿	4:17 am	v/c
☽→♐	10:17 am	
☽☍♃	7:29 pm	

♃♃♃   ĵaŭdo

♐

Thursday
15

☽⚹♆	1:10 am
☽☌♂	1:01 pm
☽☌♀	3:12 pm
☿⚹♇	4:39 pm
☽△♀	5:58 pm

♀♀♀   vendredo

♐
♑

Friday
16

☽⚹♅	5:46 am	
☉□☽	12:45 pm	
☉⚹♄	1:42 pm	
☽⚹♉	7:48 pm	v/c
☽→♑	8:02 pm	
☿→♓	10:05 pm	

Waning Half Moon in ♐ Sagittarius 12:45 pm PST

All aspects in Pacific Standard Time; add 3 hours for EST; add 8 hours for GMT

Raising Power, Inviting Life

I dismantled the crumbling, blackened cinder-block firepit, waist high with years-old toxic ashes, broken glass, disintegrating aluminum, rusted barbed wire, remnants of aerosol cans, paint thinner, acetate, and goddess knows what else had long been seeping into her soil, our new home.

The cleansing process was lengthy, progress slow, my shovel hitting buried pipes and bricks and wire. Not one bug or worm squirmed. I saw absolutely no life in this lethal mess, stinking like a garbage truck leaking trash juice. Finally, the ground was clear and raked smooth. Yet it did not feel purified.

A few days later at our Spring Equinox gathering, individuals colored eggs with symbols of dreams they wished to manifest. I called a circle and dug a spiral in the center of what had been the firepit. I arranged the eggs in a spiral, burying these small gifts, asking Mother Earth to feel our dreams embodied within these powerful eggs.

I felt my energy rise. Songs fluently tumbled from my lips as I tossed manure on the spiral, thanking the universe. The following morning, a flock of thirty birds was pecking and chirping, all crowded together exactly on the spiral! A few days later, I scooped soil from the spiral with my hands. It was writhing and alive with earthworms! Blessed Be!

© *Diana Tigerlily 1999*

♑ ꜛꜛꜛ sabato

Saturday
17

♀sR   6:36 pm

♑ ☉☉☉ dimanĉo

Sunday
18

♂☌♀   3:45 am
☽□♀   3:55 am
☉□♅   8:16 pm
♀△♂   9:30 pm

Speaking Lightning

Bring your spirit up, bring it to the mountain and the wind and
The flames.
Creep, fly, crawl, sing, stomp, fight, to this, the place.
The Place.
Bring your feet to the ocean and wash chains away from your
Strong ankles.
Do not fear the current too much.
Make it this far, then, make it farther.
Cloak your shoulders in a mantle of soil—earth, proclaim
Yourself Goddess of statues and icons and young, pregnant
Bellies.
Sing Afraid as a song of joy.
"LA LA LA Afraid Afraid Afraid LA LA LA."
Refuse to allow your blood to escape you when you are not
Brave.
Sit in the quiet and listen for the voice of your low mouth.
Your cunt is wise but it speaks to angels, devils and the
Listening only, and it does not like to be interrupted.
Flick your whip, smack your hands together and then, STRUT.
I have been, will be, am always.
To speak in electricity, as we now do, is a familiarity that I
Pretend to believe in.
Think about speaking lightning again, like old countries and
Two dimensions.
Break up your bones and hand the pieces to your spirit, one
By one.
It will know what to do.
Touch each other.

Oya
© *Sandra Stanton 1999*

Spring Equinox

At Spring Equinox, above the Equator, the world is full of new growth beckoning us out of winter's closet. Our creative side is called forth by the burgeoning fertility and promise of early blooms. During this time of balance, assess potential for creativity and growth.

Cinquefoil (*Potentilla spp.*) is considered a lucky or expansive herb to use magically during this season. Place its bright yellow flowers on your Spring Equinox altar to welcome the increasing light and to honor your ability to grow and expand. One of Cinquefoil's old names is Five Finger Grass. The five petals are said to symbolize love, power, wisdom, health and abundance. The foliage can be used in baths prior to ritual or ceremony for purification. Cinquefoil is a skin purifier. Put 1/4 cup of dried leaf or flowers in a sock or draw string bag and place it in the tub. You can also brew up a batch of tea to add to the bath. Offer bouquets of Cinquefoil tied with a bright green ribbon to friends as a good luck aid.

© *Colette Gardiner 2000*

March
Machi

───── ☽☽☽ Jumatatu ─────────────────

♑
♒

Monday
19

☽△♄ 1:38 am
☉✶☽ 6:40 am v/c
☽→♒ 8:36 am
♀△♀ 3:31 pm
☽△♃ 8:09 pm

───── ♂♂♂ Jumanne ─────────────────

♒

Tuesday
20

☽♂♆ 1:03 am
☽ApG 3:24 am
☉→♈ 5:31 am
☽✶♀ 2:49 pm
☽✶♀ 3:43 pm
☽✶♂ 5:57 pm

Equinox

♈

Sun in Aries 5:31 am PST

───── ☿☿☿ Jumatano ─────────────────

♒
♓

Wednesday
21

☽♂♅ 7:24 am
♅□♃ 11:41 am
☽□♄ 3:03 pm v/c
☽→♓ 9:28 pm

───── ♃♃♃ Alhamisi ─────────────────

♓

Thursday
22

☽□♃ 9:37 am
☽♂♅ 12:08 pm

───── ♀♀♀ Ijumaa ─────────────────

♓

Friday
23

☽□♀ 3:53 am
☽□♂ 8:12 am

All aspects in Pacific Standard Time; add 3 hours for EST; add 8 hours for GMT

Year at a Glance for ♈ ARIES (March 20–April 19)

Necessity spurred you to lay the groundwork for future security and stability in 2000. A pragmatic appraisal of your gifts clarified both your resources and values. You now should be experiencing some consolidation in your finances. What you establish by the end of April will serve you well for years.

Millennial tensions challenged each of us to identify what we could contribute to the birth of a bold, new world. Always the pioneer, courageously exploring the furthest edge, this year you link your efforts with others for joint expeditions into the future. This is not a solitary time; you won't need to look far to find companions who share your ideals.

A movement that works for spiritual or compassionate causes needs your infectious enthusiasm. Consider further training to learn how to express yourself past that initial enthusiasm. Be open to experimenting and adapting your communication style to the requirements of different audiences.

By mid-year you experience a fresh burst of inner confidence. You can see yourself and your issues in a clear dispassionate light, making it easier for you to live up to your potential.

The second half of the year you may experience some opposition to your ideas. If so, you will be most successful if you do all you can to cooperate for the good of the whole. Emphasize any win-win potential. Your view of the world and your own place in it is undergoing a profound revolution and it does not always serve to hold to your convictions. Let yourself be moved by the currents of the collective tide, though be careful not to martyr yourself. © *Gretchen Lawlor 2000*

Flames Within
□ *Danielle Diamond 1998*
New Moon in ♈ Aries 5:21 pm PST

——— ♄♄♄ Jumamosi ———

♓
♈

Saturday
24

☽⚹♄	2:58 am	v/c
☽→♈	8:43 am	
☉☌☽	5:21 pm	
☽⚹♃	9:13 pm	

——— ☉☉☉ Jumapili ———

♈

Sunday
25

☽⚹♆	12:32 am
☽☌♀	8:24 am
☽△♇	2:02 pm
☽△♂	8:06 pm

Be Coming Magickal: A Blackwomyn's Journey
(Or: How to Become a Witch
When All Your Teachers Are White)

1. Age 3: Touch the ground with your palm, saying, "The earth is my mother."

2. Age 6: Predict to your mother the day of your baby brother's birth. Correctly.

3. Age 17: Discover Wicca. Find a coven.

4. Read literature and when you discover that maiden, mother, crone are all white and "beautiful," leave.

5. Age 18: Discover Cabot's *Power of the Witch*. Worship it as your new dictionary (you rarely read the bible).

6. Try weakly to memorize the Holy Days. Wear a pentacle and say, "Blessed Be." Feel part of a family.

7. Look for brown faces. Find none. Still, feel like you belong.

8. Meet with your white sisters for ritual, worship and plain old fun, in the woods, skyclad. Accept the absence of your kind as temporary, visualizing more diversity in the future.

9. Read Starhawk, Budapest, Valiente. Finally locate a magickal guide written by a blackwomyn. Don't relate to sweeping floors with urine. Respectfully move on.

10. Decide to become solitary, undeclared, non-denominational.

11. Listen to urges, or innate "instructions," to pour a protective circle of salt outside your house and hang herbs and plants all about. Ancient callings, heeded.

12. Live with several familiars. Learn to communicate and be guided by them.

13. Create and practice your own Craft. Continue to practice your ESP, use visualization, positive thinking and ritual. Use these to find others like you. Succeed.

¤ *Cassendre Xavier 1999*

MOON IV

Moon IV: March 24–April 23

New Moon in ♈ Aries: March 24; Full Moon in ♎ Libra: April 7; Sun in ♉ Taurus: April 19

Magic Woman
© *Tamara Thiebaux 1993*

March
März

☽☽☽ Montag

♈ ♉

Monday
26

☽✶♅ 5:10 am v/c
☽→♉ 5:50 pm

♂♂♂ Dienstag

♉

Tuesday
27

☉✶♃ 2:57 am
☽□♆ 9:12 am
☽✶☿ 10:04 pm
☿□♇ 10:28 pm

☿☿☿ Mittwoch

♉

Wednesday
28

☽□♅ 12:57 pm
☉✶♆ 1:55 pm
☽☌♄ 8:29 pm v/c

♃♃♃ Donnerstag

♉ ♊

Thursday
29

☽→♊ 1:01 am
☽☌♃ 2:05 pm
♀PrG 2:26 pm
☽△♆ 3:58 pm
☉✶☽ 6:00 pm
☽✶♀ 6:15 pm
☉☌♀ 8:16 pm

♀♀♀ Freitag

♊

Friday
30

☽☍♇ 4:21 am
☽□☿ 11:23 am
☽☍♂ 1:16 pm
☽△♅ 6:54 pm v/c

Bone Mass

My body spoke to me of creation.
But how can I tell you about the geese in the night,
flying North at new moon in a March sky?
And how something in me quickens
when I hear them overhead?

Someone once told me that their bones are hollow.
I know the feeling of hollow bones—
poems leaving my body like fireflies,
lifting me into the night,
my huge wings shining in the dark.

excerpt © Anne Renarde 1999

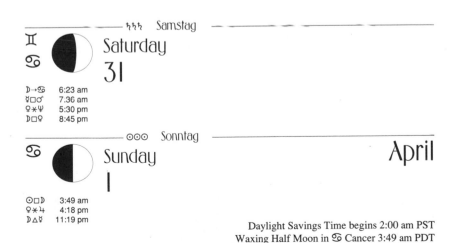

♄♄♄ Samstag

♊
♋

Saturday
31

☽→♋	6:23 am
♀□♂	7:36 am
♀⚹♆	5:30 pm
☽□♀	8:45 pm

☉☉☉ Sonntag

♋

Sunday
1

April

☉□☽	3:49 am
♀⚹♃	4:18 pm
☽△♅	11:19 pm

Daylight Savings Time begins 2:00 am PST
Waxing Half Moon in ♋ Cancer 3:49 am PDT

April
'Apelila

♋

♌

Monday
2

☽✶♄   7:26 am   v/c
☽→♌   10:54 am
☽△♀   10:42 pm

The Journey Home
© *Mara Friedman 1999*

♌

Tuesday
3

☽✶♃   12:22 am
☽☌♆   12:59 am
☉△☽   10:22 am
☽△♀   12:20 pm
☽△♂   11:19 pm

♌
♍

Wednesday
4

☽☌♅   2:18 am
☽□♄   9:46 am   v/c
☽→♍   12:46 pm
☉△♀   3:02 pm
☿✶♄   11:40 pm

♍

Thursday
5

☽□♃   2:33 am
☽PrG   3:02 am
♃△♆   7:26 am
☿□☊   9:17 am
☽□♀   1:39 pm

♍
♎

Friday
6

☿→♈   12:14 am
☽□♂   1:42 am
☽△♄   11:18 am   v/c
☽→♎   1:57 pm
☽☌♅   3:49 pm
☽☌♀   9:54 pm

All aspects in Pacific Daylight Time; add 3 hours for EDT; add 7 hours for GMT

At Passover this year
I thought I might be an angel.
A wandering Jew
hid a piece of the Afikomen*
down the back of my shirt,
it was never found
and dry crumbs lodged
throughout the ritual
making a home in some part of my body;
maddening,
would not be shrugged away.
Reaching behind with a hand
down my own back
my fingers touched a trace of wings,
soft new bristles sprouting
above my shoulder blades,
one each side of my spine.

I wondered if I should
fly now
away to Heaven,
or if it was a sign
that I should stay.

© Berta R. Freistadt 1998

*The Afikomen is the piece of matzoh hidden during the Passover ritual for the children to find. (editor's note)

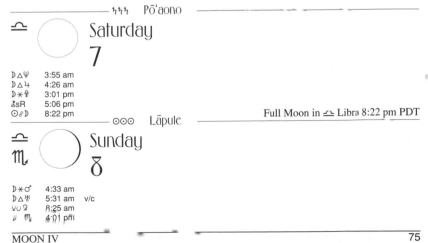

———————————— ♄♄♄ Pōʻaono ————— —   ———

♎ Saturday
7

☽△♆	3:55 am
☽△♃	4:26 am
☽⚹♀	3:01 pm
♄sR	5:06 pm
☉☍☽	8:22 pm

Full Moon in ♎ Libra 8:22 pm PDT

———————————— ⊙⊙⊙ Lāpule ————————————

♎
♏ Sunday
8

☽⚹♂	4:33 am	
☽△♅	5:31 am	v/c
♀∪☊	8:25 am	
☽ ♏	4:01 pm	

April
Aprilo

♏︎ ▷▷▷ lundo

Raven Calls Her
© Michelle Waters 1997

♏︎ ☽

Monday
9

☽□♆ 6:39 am

♏︎ ☽ ♂♂♂ mardo
♐︎

Tuesday
10

♂⚹♅ 6:27 am
☽□♅ 9:44 am
☿⚹♆ 6:02 pm
☽☍♄ 6:43 pm v/c
☽→♐︎ 8:47 pm

♐︎ ☽ ☿☿☿ merkredo

Wednesday
11

☽△♀ 2:19 am
♄⚻♇ 5:20 am
☿⚹♃ 7:13 am
☽⚹♆ 12:30 pm
☽☍♃ 2:29 pm
☽△♅ 3:36 pm

♐︎ ☽ ♃♃♃ ĵaŭdo

Thursday
12

☽☌♇ 12:46 am
☉△☽ 3:58 pm
☽⚹♅ 5:40 pm
☽☌♂ 6:56 pm v/c

♐︎ ☽ ♀♀♀ vendredo
♑︎

Friday
13

☽→♑︎ 5:21 am
☽□♀ 9:51 am
☉⚹♅ 2:24 pm

All aspects in Pacific Daylight Time; add 3 hours for EDT; add 7 hours for GMT

Spirit
⌑ *Penny Sisto 1999*

♑ Saturday
14

♉△♀ 4:37 am
☽□♉ 12:23 pm
☉△♂ 7:31 pm

⊙⊙⊙ dimanĉo

♑
♒ Sunday
15

☉□☽ 8:31 am
☽△ħ 4:00 pm v/c
☽→♒ 5:11 pm
☽⚹♀ 8:48 pm

Waning Half Moon in ♑ Capricorn 8:31 am PDT

April
Aprili

♒

Monday
16

☽☌♆	10:40 am
☽△♃	2:41 pm
☽ApG	11:00 pm
☽⚹♀	11:43 pm

♒

Tuesday
17

☽⚹☿	1:20 pm
☽☌♅	6:11 pm
☽⚹♂	9:55 pm

♒
♓

Wednesday
18

☉⚹☽	2:49 am	
☽☐♄	5:26 am	v/c
☽→♓	6:00 am	
☉△♇	12:52 pm	
☿⚹♅	5:53 pm	

♓

Thursday
19

☽☐♃	4:13 am
☽☐♀	11:56 am
☉→♉	5:36 pm
☿△♂	8:21 pm
♀sD	9:34 pm
☿ApG	11:36 pm

Sun in Taurus 5:36 pm PDT

♉

♓
♈

Friday
20

☽☐♂	10:40 am	v/c
♄→♊	2:59 pm	
☽→♈	5:18 pm	
☽⚹♄	5:19 pm	
☽☌♀	8:09 pm	
☿△♇	11:14 pm	

All aspects in Pacific Daylight Time; add 3 hours for EDT; add 7 hours for GMT

Year at a Glance for ♉ TAURUS (April 19–May 20)

The May 2000 configuration of all eight visible planets in Taurus handed you an armload of projects and your life took off. With upbeat confidence you are now moving beyond your prior limits and your abilities as a "resourceress" are becoming increasingly more obvious. You have opportunities to use your material and/or psychological assets consciously and responsibly to initiate progressive social change.

Many Taureans will start new businesses this year; plans should emphasize simplicity and economy of effort as well as product. It is critical that whatever you do be in a spirit of helping others. You are more likely to be recognized through your association with a progressive group or ideal than as a self-serving individual. Stand on your principles.

Health issues or a general lack of vitality experienced in the last couple of years have served two purposes: to keep you from responding in old habitual ways and to give you time out to ponder your accomplishments. You will feel much more energetic by May after Saturn leaves your sign.

In the early months of this year, weed out projects that do not reflect your new personality. Be alert for deceptive practices amongst associates. It is not a good year to go deeply into debt. Not only is the anxiety not worth it but plans could be blocked by the loaner.

Emotional involvements with intimates are transformative and intense and tend towards crisis from August–November. Ultimately you discover strengths and talents now ready to be used. Sexual intimacy reaches new heights if you can break through subconscious defenses to really relax and let yourself go.

© *Gretchen Lawlor 2000*

Powers of the North
© *Loes Raymakers 1998*

--- ♄♄♄ Jumamosi ---

♈

Saturday
21

☽✶♆	9:57 am
♀→♉	1:08 pm
☽✶♃	3:31 pm
☽△♀	9:52 pm

--- ☉☉☉ Jumapili ---

♈

Sunday
22

☽✶♅	3:22 pm	
☽△♂	8:34 pm	v/c

Merry Maidens

Women dancing through long grass
sss sss sss
snaking between stones
silent and breathing
stepping softly
Running shoes, strappy sandals
sensible boots, bare toes
reaching down like dowsing rods
for the water of the deep stream
sss sss sss
We coil and pass
meet eyes and sigh
tilt the moons of our faces
toward the sun soaked dome
Clouds dance a spiral in the sky mirror
Stones lean toward us
as a wave of song rises and crests
sinks us to center
Salt wind tones it's own satisfaction
across the moors
sss sss sss
We have come from so far
to circle here
entwined and unknown
mapless, at lands end
in a field that might be any field
if these guardians hadn't watched
so long
waiting for us, only us
sss sss sss
We drop tears into the center
precious offering
speak prayers to the earth
huddled and humming
Then drift away in loose groups
suddenly strangers again

MOON V

Moon V: April 23–May 22

New Moon in ♉ Taurus: April 23; Full Moon in ♏ Scorpio: May 7; Sun in ♊ Gemini: May 20

Ancient Memories
© *Melissa Harris 1997*

And tuck this time into the soul's
deep pocket
where it weighs just enough
to surprise us later
Riding the bus
Waiting in a café
Swimming up from sleep
We will brush against it
in quiet moments
sss sss sss
We find the stones again
dancing silently, reunited
believing
beloved and
blessed   ¤ *Jessica Montgomery 1999*

April
April

April

――――))) Montag ――――

♈
♉

Monday
23

☽→♉	1:56 am
☉♂♉	2:24 am
☉♂☽	8:26 am
☽♂♉	9:04 am
☽□♆	5:53 pm

©Marja de Vries 1999

Magic Clogs

New Moon in ♉ Taurus 8:26 am PDT

―――― ♂♂♂ Dienstag ――――

♉

Tuesday
24

☽□♅	10:08 pm	v/c

―――― ☿☿☿ Mittwoch ――――

♉
♊

Wednesday
25

☽→♊	8:11 am
☽♂♄	9:12 am
☽✳♀	11:50 am
♉□♆	3:23 pm
☽△♆	11:37 pm

―――― ♃♃♃ Donnerstag ――――

♊

Thursday
26

☽♂♃	6:22 am
☽♂♀	10:26 am

―――― ♀♀♀ Freitag ――――

♊
♋

Friday
27

☽△♅	3:07 am	
☽♂♂	9:12 am	v/c
☽→♋	12:49 pm	
☽□♀	5:20 pm	

All aspects in Pacific Daylight Time; add 3 hours for EDT; add 7 hours for GMT

Little Pitcher

© *Alice Lynn Greenwood 1998*

There are fairies underfoot—
be careful not to squish them!
They sprinkle hearts & crescent moons
along the path—
glitter everywhere!

excerpt © Phyllis J. Hanniver 1997

───── ♄♄♄ Samstag ─────

♋

Saturday
28

☉⚹☽	2:58 am	
☿⚻♀	11:51 am	
☽⚹♄	2:53 pm	v/c
☉□♆	4:49 pm	

───── ☉☉☉ Sonntag ─────

♋
♌

Sunday
29

☽→♌	4:25 pm
☽⚹♄	6:18 pm
☽△♀	10:02 pm

April
'Apelila

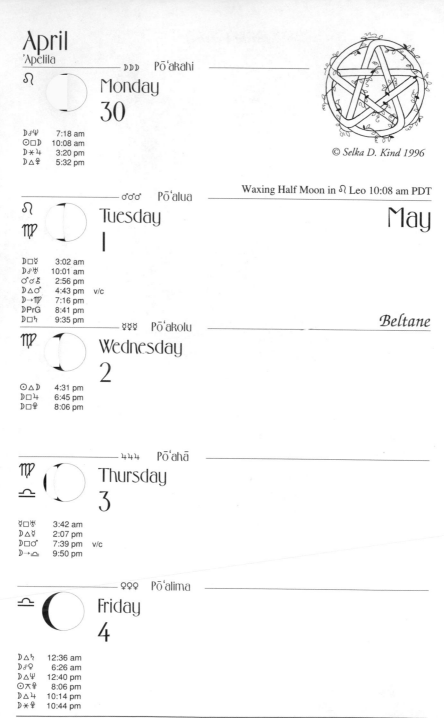

☽☽☽ Pōʻakahi

© Selka D. Kind 1996

♌

Monday 30

☽☍♆ 7:18 am
☉□☽ 10:08 am
☽⚹♃ 3:20 pm
☽△♇ 5:32 pm

Waxing Half Moon in ♌ Leo 10:08 am PDT

♂♂♂ Pōʻalua

May

♌ ♍

Tuesday 1

☽□☿ 3:02 am
☽☍♅ 10:01 am
♂☌⚷ 2:56 pm
☽△♂ 4:43 pm v/c
☽→♍ 7:16 pm
☽PrG 8:41 pm
☽□♄ 9:35 pm

Beltane

☿☿☿ Pōʻakolu

♍

Wednesday 2

☉△☽ 4:31 pm
☽□♃ 6:45 pm
☽□♇ 8:06 pm

♃♃♃ Pōʻahā

♍ ♎

Thursday 3

☿□♅ 3:42 am
☽△☿ 2:07 pm
☽□♂ 7:39 pm v/c
☽→♎ 9:50 pm

♀♀♀ Pōʻalima

♎

Friday 4

☽△♄ 12:36 am
☽☍♀ 6:26 am
☽△♆ 12:40 pm
☉⚻♇ 8:06 pm
☽△♃ 10:14 pm
☽⚹♇ 10:44 pm

All aspects in Pacific Daylight Time; add 3 hours for EDT; add 7 hours for GMT

© Melissa Harris 1999

Beltane

Beltane is one of the great Celtic fire festivals and celebrates the powerful forces of nature that call us to one another. It is a time to banish unhealthy patterns. In many countries there is a tradition of ritually cleansing and renewing livestock and fields in preparation for another cycle of growth and to ensure a plentiful year.

Celebrate the season with Sweet Woodruff * (*Asperula odorata*). The flowers and foliage can be floated in a punch bowl of Mai-Wine. Sweet Woodruff contains coumarins—substances that have a wonderful grassy, vanilla-like scent as they dry. The flavor comes out well when steeped in white wine

Sweet Woodruff is great for making you feel lighter and more optimistic. It makes a great herb for strewing within a ritual circle. Harvest the aboveground parts about 12 hours before a ceremony, then spread it on the ground where it can be walked on and its scent released. Use it to delineate the outer edge of sacred space or the entrance point of the circle. Add rose petals to the mix to invoke love. Sweet Woodruff is a powerful protective herb and its scent reminds us of the sweetness of life. *© Colette Gardiner 2000*

*Sweet Woodruff should be avoided one week prior to surgery or if you are on anticoagulant medications.

Fertility and Choice
© *Jen Shifflet 1998*

Equals Heart

Why carve initials into trees? Lives
are tied and scribed onto bark surfaces,
hatched on termite peels, rough tongues.
Stump's face turns out to sun; uncorked
veins stream inward to decades' rings.
Why cut this protective seal, the crinkled ridges
grown hard against gray winds, yellow breezes that carry
magnolia petals, and red-wine-spilling lovers
on picnic blankets? Tree's advice would be:
scratch love's name into earth, push
back a quarter inch of dirt, centipede-filled.
Tell earthworms and dried remnants of grass
blades, left over from the brown winter,
new sprouts pushing up to the low afternoon
sun. With your love touched
onto earth, the next rain will seep
it into deep soil, trickle it year by year
into sandy and loamy layers, settle it down
through gravel and granite.
Love, run mineral-rich through un-mined
lode, binds cell by cell to bedrock,
held steady now by all earth's time
and movement, a voluminous dance dripped
from a blade of grass.

© *Emily K. Grieves 1997*

— ᚺᚺᚺ   Pó'áoŋo —

♎ ◑ Saturday

5

☿⊼♃	1:29 am
☿⊼♂	7:17 am
☽△♅	3:43 pm
☿→♊	9:53 pm
☽✶♂	11:03 pm	v/c

— ⊙⊙⊙   Lāpule —

♎ ◑
♏

Sunday

6

☽→♏	1:00 am
♃☍♀	3:40 am
☽□♆	4:16 pm
☿♂♄	11:26 pm

May
Majo

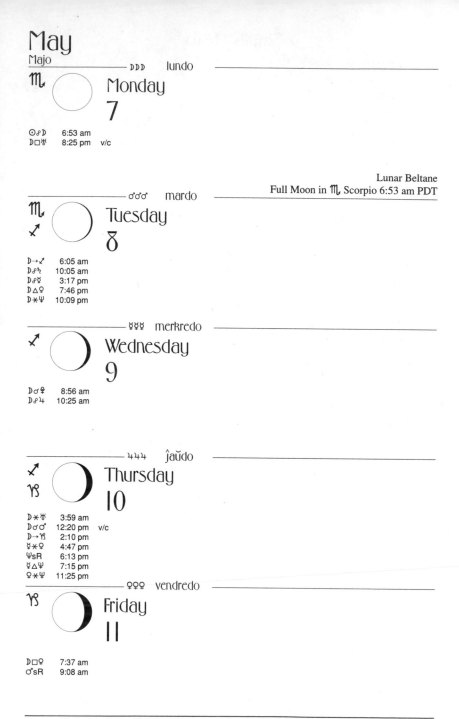

☽☽☽ lundo

♏

Monday
7

☉☍☽ 6:53 am
☽□♅ 8:25 pm v/c

Lunar Beltane
Full Moon in ♏ Scorpio 6:53 am PDT

♂♂♂ mardo

♏
♐

Tuesday
8

☽→♐ 6:05 am
☽☍♄ 10:05 am
☽☍☿ 3:17 pm
☽△♀ 7:46 pm
☽✶♆ 10:09 pm

☿☿☿ merkredo

♐

Wednesday
9

☽☌♇ 8:56 am
☽☍♃ 10:25 am

♃♃♃ ĵaŭdo

♐
♑

Thursday
10

☽✶♅ 3:59 am
☽☌♂ 12:20 pm v/c
☽→♑ 2:10 pm
☿✶♀ 4:47 pm
♆sR 6:13 pm
☿△♆ 7:15 pm
♀✶♆ 11:25 pm

♀♀♀ vendredo

♑

Friday
11

☽□♀ 7:37 am
♂sR 9:08 am

All aspects in Pacific Daylight Time; add 3 hours for EDT; add 7 hours for GMT

A Podful of Dreams

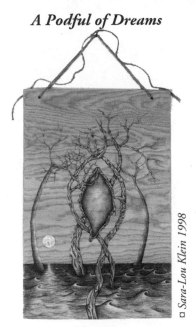

□ *Sara-Lou Klein 1998*

Union
Our union
should have blown the tent to bits,
should have set off sirens, whistles, and bells.
Instead,
there was just a steady glow,
the tent floating in the darkness
like a giant firefly.

□ *Jamie Wright 1999*

— ♄♄♄   sabato —

♑ ◑ **Saturday**
12

☉△☽   9:17 am   v/c

— ⊙⊙⊙   dimancô —

♑
♒ ◐ **Sunday**
13

☽→♒   1:20 am
☽△♄   7:00 am
☽☌♆   7:02 pm
☽✶♀   10:58 pm

MOON V

May

Mei

♒

Monday
14

☽△⛢	5:57 am
☽✳♀	6:34 am
☽△♃	10:39 am
⛢☍♀	10:52 am
☽ApG	6:20 pm

♒
♓

Tuesday
15

☉□☽	3:11 am
☽♂⛢	3:25 am
☉□⛢	6:06 am
☽✳♂	11:53 am v/c
☽→♓	2:01 pm
☽□♄	8:22 pm

Waning Half Moon in ♒ Aquarius 3:11 am PDT

♓

Wednesday
16

⛢♂♃	4:15 am
☽□♀	6:57 pm

♓

Thursday
17

☽□♃	12:14 am
☽□⛢	2:15 am
☉✳☽	8:20 pm
☽□♂	11:18 pm v/c

♓
♈

Friday
18

☽→♈	1:41 am
☉⚼♇	8:08 am
☽✳♄	8:25 am
☽✳♆	6:37 pm
♀△♀	11:56 pm

All aspects in Pacific Daylight Time; add 3 hours for EDT; add 7 hours for GMT

Year at a Glance for ♊ GEMINI (May 20–June 21)

This year, we will all experience contradictions in our lives as both Jupiter (expansion) and Saturn (restriction) travel through Gemini. Gemini born souls will juggle being engaged in two very different directions better than most. Tend to obligations at the same time as you respond to attractive new invitations. To maximize the opportunities you will have to be your twin souls. You may have less energy but more determination. Can you be ostentatious about your belief in yourself while remaining cautious enough to stay within your limits? Delineate a specific arena in which to be adventurous early in the year. Don't make decisions based upon demands from the outside—use your instinct.

Hopefully the last two years have given you opportunities to withdraw from ordinary routines in order to be responsive to the floods of insight. If not, take time for yourself in the first months of this year.

Beloveds continue to resist your growth spurts, though they are unlikely to do so in an overt manner. A crisis will uncover and heal subconscious agendas. You become more of an individual through bumping up against other people's expectations.

If you didn't experience a transformative encounter in 2000, be alert this year. You are more likely to accomplish necessary changes with the input of a mysterious stranger (could be a healer or therapist).

You are growing a new personality from the ground of your being. The last few years may have felt more like a dissolving of everything you knew yourself to be. You are at least half way through the process and beginning to see your new self. Remember the paradox: "In the end is the beginning." © *Gretchen Lawlor 2000*

Seahorse Love
◻ *Candida Sea Blyth 1998*

♄♄♄ Jumamosi

♈ Saturday
19

☽△♀	5:15 am
☽☌♀	5:36 am
☉⊼♂	7:10 am
☽⚹♃	11:26 am
☽⚹♅	6:19 pm

☉☉☉ Jumapili

♈
♉ Sunday
20

☽⚹♅	12:53 am	
☽△♂	7:48 am	v/c
☽→♉	10:29 am	
☉→♊	4:44 pm	

♊

Sun in Gemini 4:44 pm PDT

© *Ildiko Cziglenyi 1999*

Spirit

Eyes closed, I see a lake
rimmed with pine and oak,
breathe until steady, then blow
fear, a black mist, over the water.
An exhale, more fear. Then again.

Eagle flies over the lake
and I feel my body crack open
from my forehead to my pubic bone.
She flies to me, backward steps
into my open body. She turns
shakes her wings down into my arms,
her talons into my feet.
Eagle inside me. Eagle
drapes over me as a head dress.
Eagle over me.
Eagle before me.
Eagle inside me.
Strength to go on.

© *Susan Herport Methvin 1999*

MOON VI

Moon VI: May 22–June 21
New Moon in ♊ Gemini: May 22;
Full Moon in ♐ Sagittarius: June 5;
Sun in ♋ Cancer: June 21

Spiral Dance
© Ildiko Cziglenyi 1998

May
Mai

☽☽☽ Montag

♉

Monday
21

☽□♆ 2:27 am

Peace Owl
© Katheryn Trenshaw 1997

♂♂♂ Dienstag

♉
♊

Tuesday
22

☽□♅ 7:06 am v/c
☽→♊ 4:12 pm
☉☌☽ 7:46 pm
☽☌♄ 11:17 pm

New Moon in ♊ Gemini 7:46 pm PDT

☿☿☿ Mittwoch

♊

Wednesday
23

☽△♆ 7:22 am
☿△♅ 7:56 am
☽☍♇ 4:50 pm
☽✶♀ 11:49 pm

♃♃♃ Donnerstag

♊
♋

Thursday
24

☽☌♃ 12:23 am
☽△♅ 10:56 am
☽☌☿ 12:36 pm
♀✶♃ 12:53 pm
☽☍♂ 4:12 pm v/c
☽→♋ 7:42 pm

♀♀♀ Freitag

♋

Friday
25

☉☌♄ 5:33 am
♄ApG 8:25 am

All aspects in Pacific Daylight Time; add 3 hours for EDT; add 7 hours for GMT

© Sudie Rakusin 1998

Change

Change armory into harmony
Change artillery into art
Change war into worship
Change nuclear into new clear
Invasion into vision
Conquer into concur
Change bombs into bonds
Change end into mend

☐ *Colleen Redman 1999*

──── ♄♄♄ Samstag ────────────────────────

♋
♌

Saturday
26

☽□♀	5:44 am	v/c
♀♂♄	1:01 pm	
☽→♌	10:12 pm	
♀♂♂	11:03 pm	
☽PrG	11:59 pm	

──── ☉☉☉ Sonntag ────────────────────────

♌

Sunday
27

☽⚹♄	5:57 am
☉⚹☽	8:58 am
☽☍♆	12:48 pm
☽△♇	9:53 pm

May
Mei

♌ **Monday**
28

☽⚹♃	7:08 am
☽△♀	11:20 am
☽☊♅	3:55 pm
☽△♂	7:48 pm
☽⚹♅	10:13 pm v/c
♂♂⚷	11:10 pm

Foxy
© Marguerite Bartley 1999

————— ♂♂♂   Pōʻalua —————

♌ ♍ **Tuesday**
29

☽→♍	12:38 am
♅sR	8:11 am
☽□♄	8:54 am
☉□☽	3:09 pm
☉△♆	5:34 pm

————— ☿☿☿   Pōʻakolu —————

Waxing Half Moon in ♍ Virgo 3:09 pm PDT

♍ **Wednesday**
30

☽□♀	12:27 am
☽□♃	10:45 am
☽□♂	9:58 pm

————— ♃♃♃   Pōʻahā —————

♍ ♎ **Thursday**
31

☽□♅	2:40 am v/c
☽→♎	3:41 am
☽△♄	12:36 pm
♀⚹♅	1:12 pm
☽△♆	6:37 pm
☉△☽	10:18 pm

————— ♀♀♀   Pōʻalima —————

♎ **Friday**
1

☽⚹♀	3:53 am
☽△♃	3:25 pm
☽△♅	10:49 pm

June

All aspects in Pacific Daylight Time; add 3 hours for EDT; add 7 hours for GMT

Foxy

Out of the darkness came a discomforting chirping of birds. Alerted, I peered out through my window to see four shining amber lights hanging in the night air. As they moved nearer, the garden sensor light popped on and I was looking into the faces of an adult and a cub fox. Next evening was a repeat procedure except that standing centre stage stood the little red cub fox alone. I felt an excitement rising inside me . . . would it run away again . . . would I frighten it if I opened the half-door . . . what about food? But like a shape-changer it had vanished.

Now four months later I am surrogate mother to this once thin and hungry cub vixen. Her mother never passed this way again. Foxy roams my garden wilderness bringing her magic and her cunning. She is a trickster and likes to play and run off with things and enjoys unearthing my newly planted spring bulbs! She freely eats from my hand.

The fox as totem has touched almost every society. Sadly, in Ireland, it is a hunted enemy. The Indians of Peru had a fox god. The fox was believed to reward those who did it service. Foxy is my cherished reward.

We are two of a kind . . . and as friends and solitary beings, we live in our separate dens in the seclusion of trees and flowers while remaining separate and cautious. I have a deep respect for her . . . She who was given.

© *Marguerite Bartley 1999*

ħħħ   Pōʻaono

♎︎   Saturday
♏︎   2

♀△♂	12:03 am	
☽✶♂	1:07 am	
☽♂♀	1:13 am	
☽△♅	7:41 am	v/c
☽→♏︎	7:56 am	
♀△♄	5:10 pm	
☽□♆	11:16 pm	

☉☉☉   Lāpule

♏︎   Sunday
3

| ♀PrG | 11:54 am |
| ♅sR | 10:22 pm |

June

Junio

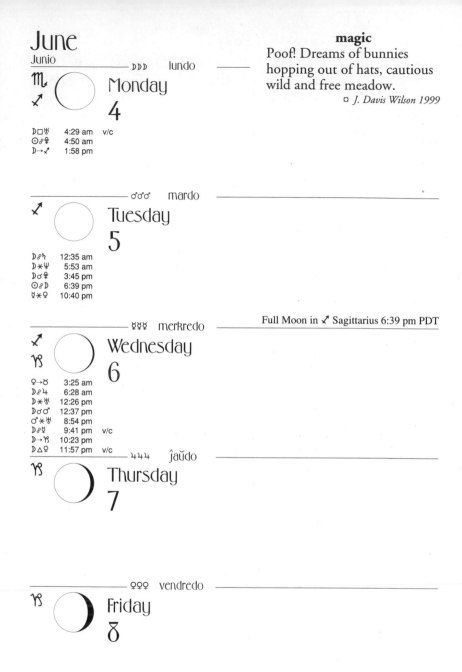

— ☽☽☽ lundo —

♏︎
♐︎ **Monday**

4

☽□♅ 4:29 am   v/c
☉☌♀ 4:50 am
☽→♐︎ 1:58 pm

magic

Poof! Dreams of bunnies
hopping out of hats, cautious
wild and free meadow.

◻ *J. Davis Wilson 1999*

— ♂♂♂ mardo —

♐︎ **Tuesday**

5

☽☍♄ 12:35 am
☽⚹♆ 5:53 am
☽☌♀ 3:45 pm
☉☍☽ 6:39 pm
☿⚹♀ 10:40 pm

Full Moon in ♐︎ Sagittarius 6:39 pm PDT

— ☿☿☿ merkredo —

♐︎
♑︎ **Wednesday**

6

♀→♉︎ 3:25 am
☽☍♃ 6:28 am
☽⚹♅ 12:26 pm
☽☌♂ 12:37 pm
♂⚹♅ 8:54 pm
☽☍♅ 9:41 pm   v/c
☽→♑︎ 10:23 pm
☽△♀ 11:57 pm   v/c

— ♃♃♃ ĵaŭdo —

♑︎ **Thursday**

7

— ♀♀♀ vendredo —

♑︎ **Friday**

8

All aspects in Pacific Daylight Time; add 3 hours for EDT; add 7 hours for GMT

The Moon
¤ *Hariet L. Hunter 1999*

——————— ᚻᚻᚻ   sabato ———————
♑
♒
Saturday
9

☽→♒ 9:20 am
☽□♀ 4:06 pm
☽△♄ 10:08 pm

——————— ☉☉☉ dimanĉo ———————
♒
Sunday
10

☽☌♆ 2:28 am
☽✶♀ 12:59 pm
⚷PrG 3:35 pm

June
Juni

♒︎
♓︎ **Monday**
11

☉△☽	2:42 am
☽△♃	7:23 am
☽✶♂	8:35 am
☽♂♅	11:17 am
☽ApG	12:52 pm
☽△☿	5:38 pm v/c
☽→♓︎	9:53 pm

♂︎♂︎♂︎ Jumanne

♓︎ **Tuesday**
12

♂☍♃	10:01 am
☽✶♀	10:11 am
☽□♄	11:28 am

☿☿☿ Jumatano

♓︎ **Wednesday**
13

☽□♀	1:31 am
☉☍♂	10:46 am
☽□♂	7:28 pm
☉□☽	8:28 pm
☽□♃	9:02 pm

Waning Half Moon in ♓︎ Pisces 8:28 pm PDT

♃♃♃ Alhamisi

♒︎
♈︎ **Thursday**
14

☽□☿	3:26 am v/c
☉♂♃	5:38 am
☽→♈︎	10:03 am
♀□♆	7:46 pm
☽✶♄	11:50 pm

♀♀♀ Ijumaa

♈︎ **Friday**
15

☽✶♆	2:37 am
☿PrG	4:36 am
☿☍♇	9:07 am
☉△♅	11:57 am
☽△♀	12:37 pm

All aspects in Pacific Daylight Time; add 3 hours for EDT; add 7 hours for GMT

Protest Magic in Seattle

What the police were truly unprepared for was the power of nonviolence—not to mention Magic! We were working magic on every level: from rituals we offered before the action to meditation and trance work in our circles, to the WTO spell—an ice sculpture on our altar that melted throughout the ritual. We worked magic in jail: we sang songs, told stories, shared meditations and learned to ground and call on the elements. About fifty of us held an impromptu ritual while waiting in a cell for arraignment and later danced the spiral dance. The guards, the threats, the violence and the concrete could not keep out the love, commitment and joy we shared. The women in jail with me were mostly young, amazingly strong, caring, thoughtful, intelligent and politically aware. There were also older women whose courage and humor were an inspiration to us. I was hungry, sick and in pain a lot of the time but I was never for a moment unhappy to be where I was. I experienced a depth of almost radiant happiness like a pure current in a roiling river that I could tap into whenever my spirit started to flag.

We won. The World Trade Organization will never, now, be able to quietly assume power and consolidate its rule outside public awareness. And a new generation of young activists has been through a life-changing experience. A few uncomfortable days in the company of heroic and beautiful women seems a small price to pay.

> ¤ *Starhawk 1999, excerpted from* An Open Letter to the Pagan Community from Starhawk *after the WTO protests in Seattle, November, 1999*

 ♄♄♄ Jumamosi

♈ ☿ **Saturday**
16

☽△♂	4:23 am	♃ApG	11:07 am	
☉♂☿	6:26 am	☉⚹☽	11:32 am	v/c
☽⚹♃	8:24 am	☉⚹♄	4:50 pm	
☽⚹♅	9:44 am	☽→☿	7:39 pm	
☽⚹☿	10:57 am			

 ☉☉☉ Jumapili

☿ **Sunday**
17

☽□♆	11:10 am
☿△♅	3:08 pm
☽♂♀	4:31 pm

Wild Women
(Saturday Night at the Goddess Conference)

When Jana and Oshia sing

magic begins slow tempo stroking

my spine into snake and the snake-music

begins the go-round, rustles our skirts,

stirs the hair on the back of our necks.

Kiss of Katrina's guitar on bare shoulders

of women dancing: cats of brocade,

green mermaids, silk horses. Lydia's drum

calls on the heartbeat, rhythm's footstep,

as voices ruffle black lace of Crow

Mother, sigh in snowsleeves

of Owls lifting their wings beckoning Moon

cruising nightclouds. Hecate, Venus,

you and I stepping out in the song as it river-

roars through the throats of more singers—skins:

jet/honey/amber/pale alabaster—music rising

in the sweat of each note building

higher and higher scat and symphony

shaping a dancefloor out in the stars/

rainforest/ocean—and we are all flying, wild

women free in their magical bodies—dancing.

□ Peggy Soup 1998

Summer Solstice

Summer Solstice is the high point of the year's outward expansion of growth in Northern countries. We honor our strengths, gather together outdoors and celebrate the beauty of the green world.

One of the herbs associated with Summer Solstice is the Elder tree (*Sambucus spp.*) The healing and magical qualities of the flowers and leaves are at their peak at this time. In some traditions Elder trees are seen as Mother plants that protect and carry the wisdom of the forest areas where they grow. There are strong prohibitions against cutting down Elder trees or harvesting without the plant's permission. Ask the tree for permission to harvest and she will either speak to you or give consent through holding perfectly still. Harvest flowers and add them to pancake batter; make Elderberry wine or syrup from the leaves. The flowers can also be used in protective incense blends and have a strong association with the Fey and with nature spirits.

Summer is an appropriate season to decide where to put our energy and focus. Elder wood amplifies intent and can be used as a wand or an incense to help us direct our will. The ability of the tree to amplify even casual desires can create havoc in our lives unless we have clear intent. Elder is a great teacher and is immensely honored by those who know her.

June
Juni

ℬℬℬ Montag

♉

Monday
18

♉♂♃ 3:12 am
☽□♅ 4:21 pm v/c

Summer Solstice
"Now!" shouts the Solstice Sun.
I'll ride the wave of summer
to Equinox's shore.
▫ Antonia Matthew 1999

♂♂♂ Dienstag

♉
♊

Tuesday
19

☽→♊ 1:42 am
♃△♅ 5:25 am
☽♂♄ 2:52 pm
☽△♆ 4:11 pm
♀⚼♇ 7:14 pm

☿☿☿ Mittwoch

♊

Wednesday
20

☽☍♀ 12:57 am
☽☍♂ 12:44 pm
☽♂☿ 5:09 pm
☽△♅ 7:44 pm
☽♂♃ 8:24 pm v/c

♃♃♃ Donnerstag

♊
♋

Thursday
21

☉→♋ 12:38 am
☽→♋ 4:40 am
☉♂☽ 4:58 am
♂PrG 3:41 pm

Solstice

♋

Sun in Cancer 12:38 am PDT
New Moon in ♋ Cancer 4:58 am PDT
Total Solar Eclipse (4 min., 56 sec.) 5:04 am PDT
Eclipse visible from Africa

♀♀♀ Freitag

♋

Friday
22

☽⚹♀ 7:11 am v/c
♃☍♇ 4:46 pm

All aspects in Pacific Daylight Time; add 3 hours for EDT; add 7 hours for GMT

Year at a Glance for ♋ CANCER (June 21–July 22)

It's a good year for you to redesign your plans for the future. Begin by creating a picture of what a perfect lifestyle might look like even though you may feel a long ways from achieving it. Then, work to eliminate whatever gets in the way of this vision. Think of this process as similar to what a sculptor does in releasing a sculpture from stone. The core impulse is already within you it just needs to be let out by clearing things away.

Stability in work and/or public recognition achieved in the last four years is awe-inspiring, though it is hard to maintain as an enduring lifestyle. In 2000, a friendship opened a promising new door or made a connection for you. By June you are ready to make a move, maybe literally.

Successes in mastering the material world during the last 2–3 years give you a sense of self-reliance. Circumstances, however, often still feel out of your control. Changes happen which you could never have predicted or avoided. There are many shifts deep in your psyche which you may not be able to see clearly for a few years. Learn more about your deep self through psychic or occult therapies. You will experience a profound lift in attitude by June (when Jupiter enters your sign) infusing you with enthusiasm and hope.

If you aren't doing what you are supposed to be doing you may experience health crises. Detoxifying regimes eliminate old residue and clarify your thinking. The tools you use for your own healing now will help you heal others in the future.

© Gretchen Lawlor 2000

Turtle
◻ *Eagle 1999*

--- ♄♄♄   Samstag ---

♋
♌

Saturday
23

☽→♌	5:55 am
☽PrG	10:24 am
☽✶♄	7:08 pm
☽☌♆	7:25 pm

--- ☉☉☉   Sonntag ---

♌

Sunday
24

☽△♀	3:45 am
☽□♀	11:52 am
☽△♂	1:16 pm
☽✶♅	5:15 pm
☽☌♅	10:01 pm

Temple Spinner

I am dreaming back my sisters
Whisper-worn footfalls on the Temple steps
Skywalkers
Storm dwellers
Heavy-breasted cauldron keepers
Songweavers
Snake sisters
Darkmoon dancers

Labyrinth builders
Star bridgers
Fiery-eyed dragon-ryders
Wind seekers
Shape shifters
Corn daughters

Wolf women
Earth stewards
Gentle-handed womb sounders
Dream spinners
Flame keepers
Moon birthers

Come home sisters, come home

© Marie Elena 1999

MOON VII

Moon VII: June 21–July 20

New Moon in ♋ Cancer: June 21; Full Moon in ♑ Capricorn: July 5

Andean Thunderstorm (above)   Magical Passages (below)
© Donna Goodwin 1997

June
Iune

————— ☽☽☽ Pō'akahi —————

♌
♍

Monday
25

♄△Ψ	12:17 am
☽✶♃	12:22 am v/c
♀⊼♂	3:26 am
☽→♍	6:57 am
☉✶☽	2:09 pm
☽□♄	8:48 pm

————— ♂♂♂ Pō'alua —————

♍

Tuesday
26

☽□♀	5:05 am
☽□♂	1:57 pm
☽△♀	5:27 pm
☽□♅	6:28 pm

————— ☿☿☿ Pō'akolu —————

♍
♎

Wednesday
27

☽□♃	3:12 am v/c
☽→♎	9:11 am
☉□☽	8:19 pm
♅sD	10:49 pm
☽△Ψ	11:14 pm
☽△♄	11:58 pm

Waxing Half Moon in ♎ Libra 8:19 pm PDT

————— ♃♃♃ Pō'ahā —————

♎

Thursday
28

☽✶♀	8:04 am
☽✶♂	4:22 pm
☽△♅	10:04 pm

————— ♀♀♀ Pō'alima —————

♎
♏

Friday
29

☽△♅	3:39 am
☽△♃	8:07 am v/c
☽→♏	1:28 pm
☉⊼Ψ	2:00 pm

All aspects in Pacific Daylight Time; add 3 hours for EDT; add 7 hours for GMT

Magic Woman

Something happens in the company of women.
Souls open like the sun, rising between blue mountains.
All we've shared are scattered moments;
Carrot cake, black beans and rice, Liane Foly, Anais Nin,
Strawberries and cream, the richest of green.
Just a few scattered heres and theres, and yet, there's magic.
The world spins on at warp speed,
Above me, below me
Behind me, before me
In spite of me, because of me.
She is there, choosing to be there. Asking for me.
Her energy is intense. She is a driving force.
It's as though a giant, dark red ribbon has been wrapped around me
And she holds the loose end as I spin.
She helps me to unwind, unlock, unleash.
She supports me, encourages me, rocks me, calms me.
She helps create me.
Even as the ribbon strips me naked, shakes me, and opens me to the world,
I am safe. There is magic.
Something happens in the company of women.
Souls open like the sun, rising between blue mountains.

□ *Rebecca Rajswasser 1999*

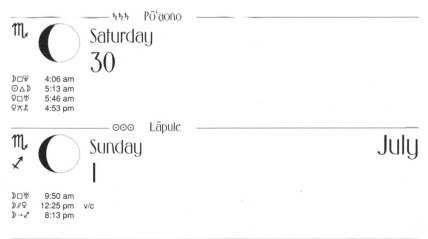

——— ♄♄♄ Pōʻaono ———

♏ Saturday
30

☽□♆ 4:06 am
☉△☽ 5:13 am
♀□♅ 5:46 am
♀⊼♇ 4:53 pm

——— ☉☉☉ Lāpule ———

♏ ♐ Sunday
1

July

☽□♅ 9:50 am
☽☍♀ 12:25 pm v/c
☽→♐ 8:13 pm

July
Julio

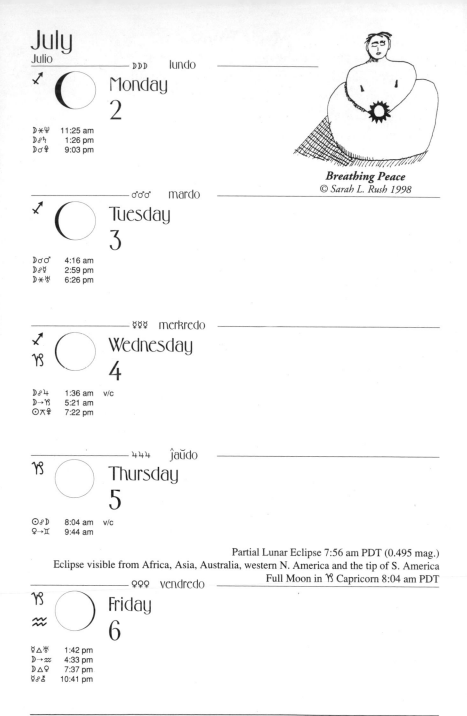

Breathing Peace
© *Sarah L. Rush 1998*

ⅅⅅⅅ   lundo

♐   **Monday**

2

☽⚹♆   11:25 am
☽☍♄   1:26 pm
☽☌♀   9:03 pm

♂♂♂   mardo

♐   **Tuesday**

3

☽☌♂   4:16 am
☽☍☿   2:59 pm
☽⚹♅   6:26 pm

☿☿☿   merkredo

♐
♑   **Wednesday**

4

☽☍♃   1:36 am   v/c
☽→♑   5:21 am
☉⚻♀   7:22 pm

♃♃♃   ĵaŭdo

♑   **Thursday**

5

☉☍☽   8:04 am   v/c
♀→♊   9:44 am

Partial Lunar Eclipse 7:56 am PDT (0.495 mag.)
Eclipse visible from Africa, Asia, Australia, western N. America and the tip of S. America
Full Moon in ♑ Capricorn 8:04 am PDT

♀♀♀   vendredo

♑
♒   **Friday**

6

☿△♅   1:42 pm
☽→♒   4:33 pm
☽△♀   7:37 pm
☿☍♇   10:41 pm

All aspects in Pacific Daylight Time; add 3 hours for EDT; add 7 hours for GMT

Betsy and Emily:
Full Moon Mamas
◻ *Marsea Frace 1999*

Last Trimester

In my body

a flower is full bloom

petals open wide

leaves dripping with rain water

roots overgrown

pushing against the constraints

of the flower pot

moving bellybuttons

out of the way.

◻ *Kara L.C. Jones 1999*

♒ ☽ ♄♄♄   sabato

Saturday
7

☽☌♆   8:34 am
☽△♄   12:05 pm
☽⚹♀   6:50 pm
☉⚻♂   9:10 pm

♒ ☽ ☉☉☉   dimanĉo

Sunday
8

☽⚹♂   12:50 am
☽☌♅   5:22 pm
☽△♅   9:12 pm

July
Julai

□ *Melissa McConnell 1998*

ᗩᗩᗩ **Jumatatu** ──────────

♒ ☽ **Monday**
♓ **9**

☽△♃ 3:28 am v/c
☽ApG 4:21 am
☽→♓ 5:05 am
☽□♀ 2:21 pm

♂♂♂ **Jumanne** ──────────

♓ ☽ **Tuesday**
10

☽□♄ 1:23 am
☽□♀ 7:28 am
☽□♂ 12:51 pm
☉△☽ 7:14 pm

☿☿☿ **Jumatano** ──────────

♓ ☽ **Wednesday**
♈ **11**

☽□♅ 3:17 pm
☽□♃ 5:09 pm v/c
☽→♈ 5:36 pm

♃♃♃ **Alhamisi** ──────────

♈ ☽ **Thursday**
12

☽⚹♀ 8:44 am
☽⚹♆ 9:12 am
♀△♆ 1:49 pm
☽⚹♄ 2:02 pm
♅♂♃ 3:29 pm
♅→♋ 3:47 pm
♃→♋ 5:02 pm
☽△♇ 7:17 pm

♀♀♀ **Ijumaa** ──────────

♈ ☽ **Friday**
13

☽△♂ 12:05 am
☉□☽ 11:45 am
☽⚹♅ 4:52 pm v/c

Waning Half Moon in ♈ Aries 11:45 am PDT

All aspects in Pacific Daylight Time; add 3 hours for EDT; add 7 hours for GMT

Flora

I've always liked the term
"lily-livered." I know it means
cowardly, but this is how
I see it: the liver, sleek
and wine-colored, bursts forth
with lilies, petals drift
and ride the streams of blood.
Think of it: the body
opens into flower, turns orchid-
spleened, jasmine-lunged, breath
tropical, humid with scent.
Poppies bloom between the legs,
morning glories wind
up the spine, each bone filled
with pollen and sweet nectar. The heart
is a rose, of course, plushly
blossomed, and inside the skull,
with each new thought,
a tulip unfurls
in the brain.

Open Heart
© Nicole Di Pierre 1998

◻ *Gayle Brandeis 1997*

♈ ♉♉♉ Jumamosi

♉

Saturday
14

☽→♉   4:13 am
☽✶♃   4:51 am
☽✶♅   8:10 am
☽□♆   6:55 pm

♉ ☉☉☉ Jumapili

Sunday
15

♀♂♄   12:32 am

July
Juli

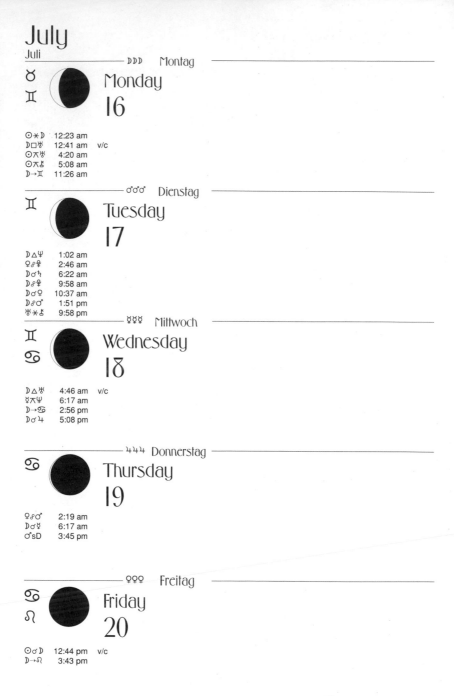

———— ☽☽☽ Montag ————

♉
♊

Monday
16

☉✶☽	12:23 am	
☽□♅	12:41 am	v/c
☉⚹♅	4:20 am	
☉⚹♄	5:08 am	
☽→♊	11:26 am	

———— ♂♂♂ Dienstag ————

♊

Tuesday
17

☽△♆	1:02 am
♀☍♀	2:46 am
☽♂♄	6:22 am
☽☍♀	9:58 am
☽♂♀	10:37 am
☽☍♂	1:51 pm
♅⚹♄	9:58 pm

———— ☿☿☿ Mittwoch ————

♊
♋

Wednesday
18

☽△♅	4:46 am	v/c
☿⚹♆	6:17 am	
☽→♋	2:56 pm	
☽♂♃	5:08 pm	

———— ♃♃♃ Donnerstag ————

♋

Thursday
19

♀☍♂	2:19 am
☽♂♉	6:17 am
♂sD	3:45 pm

———— ♀♀♀ Freitag ————

♋
♌

Friday
20

☉♂☽	12:44 pm	v/c
☽→♌	3:43 pm	

New Moon in ♋ Cancer 12:44 pm PDT

All aspects in Pacific Daylight Time; add 3 hours for EDT; add 7 hours for GMT

Year at a Glance for ♌ LEO (July 22–August 22)

Having struggled persistently and eagerly for years to reach a place of public standing you should now have what you aspired to. In the first half of the year you will continue to enjoy the fruits of your labor. You have a sense of being in the right place. Your peer circle is exciting—you are meeting people who inspire you and introduce you to new worlds.

By mid-year you may begin to feel the limits of your present situation. You like the recognition but find the responsibilities burdensome. Was it worth it? Through spending time alone you are able to gaze dispassionately at the empires, large or small, you have created. You begin an assessment of successes and failures. This is the perfect state to be in.

Beloveds who have already been grumbling about your long hours are going through their own revolution. They long for space to pursue their own dream. Keep the lines of communication open. Relationships are unsettled, unpredictable. If you are not presently involved, opportunities appear from unexpected places. You are being asked to come up with a new spacious model of relating where each of you can experiment with independent passions. If you have children there may be power plays. Something between yourself and your own parent is recycling through your life and may be recycled through your relationship with a child.

Use your creativity as a medium for contemplating the deep issues of this year. You are beginning to invent your future—the clues are already there in your imagination. Next year you will feel more adventurous. For now, reverie restores perspective. © *Gretchen Lawlor 2000*

Strength
© *Chesca Potter 1999*

ħħħ Samstag

♌

Saturday
21

☽☌Ψ	3:52 am	☽PrG	1:56 pm
☿⚹♀	8:02 am	☽△♂	3:49 pm
☽⚹ħ	9:36 am	☽⚹♀	8:43 pm
☽△♀	12:08 pm		

☉☉☉ Sonntag

♌
♍

Sunday
22

☽☌♅	5:34 am	v/c
☉→♌	11:26 am	
☿⚻♂	3:28 pm	
☽→♍	3:29 pm	
☽⚹♃	7:00 pm	

♌

Sun in Leo 11:26 am PDT

Betwixt and Between

Find a quiet place to sit outdoors. Settle in however you like—breathing, chanting, stretching or any kind of mind-body deepening. Make yourself comfortable enough to stay alert and relaxed for an indefinite period of time.

Send your awareness to a place around you that is *betwixt and between.* In other words, find a point of energetic exchange where what exists is neither this nor that but rather in dynamic transaction.

For example, seek out the boundary between rock and river. Where does the river stop flowing into the rock? How porous is stone? How subject to erosion, to temperature change, to the insistent pressure of rushing water? What does the stone yield to the river? Or find the place where leaf becomes sunlight, where root penetrates soil, where your breath meets the air. Explore an edge of contact, experiencing the permeable and mutable qualities of so-called solid matter.

Let this perception lead you deeper into relationship with the numinous, vibrating energy of nature. If you still think the environment is outside you, try holding your breath. Perhaps you will discover that you are not separate from the world nor from the divine. Perhaps you will find **yourself** betwixt and between, neither here nor there, which is to say *in the land of faerie.* May you dwell in timeless time and know that you are blessed.

Return to normal perception slowly and gently. Or don't return at all. It's up to you.

❑ Jessica Montgomery 1999

MOON VIII

Moon VIII: July 20–August 18

New Moon in ♋ Cancer: July 20; Full Moon in ♒ Aquarius: Aug. 3; Sun in ♌ Leo: July 22

Awakening
© *Cynthia Ré Robbins 1990*

July
Iulai

♍

Monday
23

☽□♄	9:48 am
☽□♀	12:00 pm
☽□♂	3:56 pm
☽⚹☿	7:21 pm

♍
♎

Tuesday
24

☽□♀	12:48 am	v/c
☽→♎	4:08 pm	
☉⚹☽	7:51 pm	
☽□♃	8:32 pm	

♎

Wednesday
25

☽△♆	4:40 am
☽△♄	11:36 am
☽⚹♀	1:30 pm
☽⚹♂	5:57 pm

♎
♏

Thursday
26

☽□☿	5:22 am	
☽△♀	7:30 am	
☽△♅	8:10 am	v/c
♀☍♇	1:15 pm	
♀△♅	3:18 pm	
☽→♏	7:17 pm	
☿⚺♇	11:17 pm	

♏

Friday
27

☿⚺♅	12:29 am
☽△♃	12:46 am
☉□☽	3:08 am
☽□♆	8:30 am

Waxing Half Moon in ♏ Scorpio 3:08 am PDT

All aspects in Pacific Daylight Time; add 3 hours for EDT; add 7 hours for GMT

Peeling My Onion

I choose to peel my onion
layer by layer
to see how each translucent skin
almost clones the last one peeled away,
how minute the variations,
how much like the life I've lead
if I peel away the years.

It comforts me that beneath each layer
lies another very nearly exactly the same
so that the core holds no surprises
if I have stayed attentive to the process,
comforts me to know that as I age and change,
I shall be ever who I was and am,
just, year by year, slightly older.

My sacred scriptures are in a bin in my pantry
my mysticism of a very common kind.
When I see folk in their sabbath finery
heading toward their halls of worship
on their holydays, I smile
and listen to what the silence has to say.
Here in the stillness of the moment,
born again pagan that I was born to be,
I'm still peeling my onion.

excerpt ¤ *Veronica M. Murphy 1998*

꜖꜖꜖ Pōʻaono

♏ **Saturday**
28

☽□♅ 1:45 pm
☽△☿ 8:50 pm   v/c

⊙⊙⊙ Lāpule

♏ **Sunday**
♐ **29**

☽→♐ 1:44 am
⊙△☽ 2:34 pm
☽⚹♆ 3:40 pm
♆PrG 8:59 pm

July
Julio

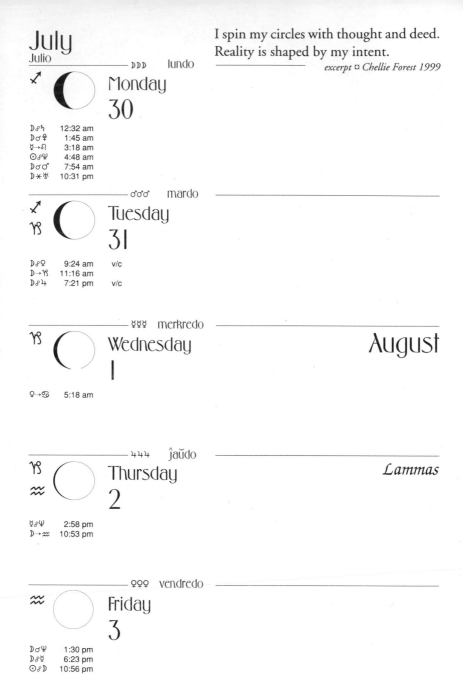

I spin my circles with thought and deed.
Reality is shaped by my intent.

excerpt ¤ Chellie Forest 1999

—))) — lundo —

♐

Monday
30

☽☍♄	12:32 am
☽☌♀	1:45 am
☿→♌	3:18 am
☉☍♇	4:48 am
☽☌♂	7:54 am
☽⚹♅	10:31 pm

— ♂♂♂ — mardo —

♐
♑

Tuesday
31

☽☍♀	9:24 am	v/c
☽→♑	11:16 am	
☽☍♃	7:21 pm	v/c

— ☿☿☿ — merkredo —

♑

Wednesday
1

♀→♋	5:18 am

August

— ♃♃♃ — ĵaŭdo —

♑
♒

Thursday
2

☿☍♆	2:58 pm
☽→♒	10:53 pm

Lammas

— ♀♀♀ — vendredo —

♒

Friday
3

☽☌♆	1:30 pm
☽☍♅	6:23 pm
☉☍☽	10:56 pm

Lunar Lammas
Full Moon in ♒ Aquarius 10:56 pm PDT

All aspects in Pacific Daylight Time; add 3 hours for EDT; add 7 hours for GMT

Cooking
© *Sabrina Vourvoulias 1998*

Lammas

Lammas is a time of harvest and grain festivals in many European cultures. It is also the season for first fruit celebrations as the summer winds down. For all the earth provides, Lammas is a holiday of gratefulness, a time to honor what we are starting to receive.

Magically, Alfalfa (*Medicago sativa*) is an herb that works on many levels. One of the very first plant spells I learned was to place pieces of dried Alfalfa in a jar and to store it in the kitchen to prevent hunger for all who dwelled there. Another version of this spell is to burn Alfalfa ritually and scatter the ashes around your house for general protection as well as protection from hunger.

Alfalfa enriches all who consume it. Alfalfa tea stimulates mother's milk. In the soil it increases fertility and encourages earth worms. As you clean out garden beds and put them to sleep at summer's end, Alfalfa can be powdered or made into a strong tea and sprinkled ritually over the mulch covering the beds. Take the time to remember how much the earth does for us and offer songs and prayers for the earth's continued fertility.

© *Colette Gardiner 2000*

Queens and Kings

Walking barefoot amongst the Queens and Kings of Amaranth and
Quinoa, Sunflower and Hopi corns
floods my body with a rush of energy of awe, and pride,
for I have sown these long rows, weeded them, and watered them
from the Old Acequia off the Rio Hondo,
the last farm before the banks of the Rio Grande.
New Buffalo, with other dedicated sisters and brothers of the Earth.
Growing organic crops for seed makes one more patient
and mindful of each plant's process of turning out the goal—a ripened
ear of corn, a dried shower of cock's comb,
the quinoa about to burst out of tiny dried shell casings,
the bending 8' sunflowers heavy, birds watchful.
Comes the dance of cutting the harvest of stalks
to be loaded onto the truck and taken to the barn to be hung
over bed sheets. Holding the seeds that voluntarily drop;
the dance of thrashing and winnowing on a dry sunny, breezy day—the
capture of each different plant's seeds
into clean mason jars, counted by weight.
Taken to the Sacred Seed room—an old adobe, Earthen floor temple,
cool, dry, dark, a womb where the seeds will sleep
until they're brought out again to sell to seed companies,
or given away, passed on to entrusted local farmers
who will also plant and grow them for seed—our insurance that
at least these strains will continue to thrive the way Creator intended.

□ Claire Johnson 1998

Spawned by a discussion on Costa Rica plant patenting.

Future Seeds
© _Schar Cbear Freeman 1998_

♄♄♄   sabato

♒   Saturday
        4

☽△♄	12:05 am	☉✶♄	2:37 pm	
☽✶♀	12:22 am	☉△♀	4:31 pm	
☽✶♂	8:45 am	☽♂♅	9:52 pm	v/c

☉☉☉   dimanĉo

♒
♓   Sunday
        5

♀✶♄	4:11 am	☉♂♅	2:51 pm
☿△♀	4:27 am	♀♂♃	3:50 pm
♄♂♀	10:03 am	☽△♃	9:58 pm
☽→♓	11:30 am	☽△♀	10:30 pm
☽ApG	2:02 pm		

August
Agosti

───── ☽☽☽ Jumatatu ─────

♓ Monday
6

☽□♀ 1:02 pm
☽□♄ 1:15 pm
☽□♂ 10:39 pm   v/c

Annette, the Messenger
□ *B Holder 1999*

───── ♂♂♂ Jumanne ─────

♓ Tuesday
7

♀⊼♨ 10:19 am
☿△♂ 1:38 pm

───── ☿☿☿ Jumatano ─────

♓
♈ Wednesday
8

☽→♈ 12:05 am
☽□♃ 11:27 am
☽✶♨ 2:20 pm
☽□♀ 5:24 pm

───── ♃♃♃ Alhamisi ─────

♈ Thursday
9

☽△♀ 1:13 am
☽✶♄ 1:52 am
☉△☽ 10:17 am
☽△♂ 11:56 am
☽△☿ 7:54 pm
☽✶♅ 9:53 pm   v/c
☿ApG 10:32 pm

───── ♀♀♀ Ijumaa ─────

♈
♉ Friday
10

☿△♇ 7:46 am
☿☍♅ 7:57 am
☽→♉ 11:23 am
☉△♂ 2:47 pm
☽✶♃ 11:17 pm

─────────────────────────

All aspects in Pacific Daylight Time; add 3 hours for EDT; add 7 hours for GMT

Divine Inheritance

It's 1 a.m. I am making curtains out of a table cloth. I work obsessively. Ignoring an imperfection in the hem, I see a vision of my mother dozing in the living room chair. Even as she sleeps her knitting needles clank together, her crochet hook bobs up and down. In the morning I will have a new sweater. No one will notice that one sleeve is longer than the other or that the stitches are large and irregular. No one will notice that my curtains have holes and are unevenly hung. I know, though, because I am my mother. We are determined, impulsive, not at all precise.

I fulfill another familial impulse, telling almost believable stories to the telephone as I sew. Seems I've inherited my father's obsessions as well. I find myself weaving tales awash with flights of fancy, New York humor, and grandiose ethnic flair. The stories, like the curtains, create themselves. Even in the wee hours, the crochet hook of my combined inheritance bobs up and down creating tapestries of pseudo-history trimmed in uneven hems and antique lace.

What magical synergy! What divine synthesis! I have become my parents.

I decide I must be channeling some ancient, family dybbuk. That is, if the same dybbuk has my father rewriting history and my mother creating heirlooms after midnight. Perhaps I have inherited two? Either way, this is my blessing: the simple and wonderful legacy of my parents making magic in my veins.

□ Rebecca Rajswasser 1999

ካካካ Jumamosi

♉

Saturday

11

☽□♆	1:00 am
♅⚹♇	6:22 am
☽⚹♀	10:02 am

☉☉☉ Jumapili

♉
♊

Sunday

12

☉□☽	12:53 am	
♀⚻♅	2:05 am	
☽□♅	7:03 am	
☽□♉	3:32 pm	v/c
☽→♊	7:59 pm	

Waning Half Moon in ♉ Taurus 12:53 am PD

August
August

☽☽☽ Montag

♊

Monday
13

☽△♆ 8:40 am
☽☍♇ 6:36 pm
☽☌♄ 7:53 pm
☿→♍ 10:04 pm

♂♂♂ Dienstag

♊

Tuesday
14

☽☍♂ 6:38 am
♅PrG 11:06 am
☉⚹☽ 11:11 am
☽△♅ 12:43 pm v/c

☿☿☿ Mittwoch

♊
♋

Wednesday
15

♃⚻♆ 12:43 am
☽→♋ 12:55 am
☽⚹☿ 5:01 am
☉☍♅ 8:25 am
☉△⚷ 10:32 am
☽☌♃ 12:50 pm

♃♃♃ Donnerstag

♋

Thursday
16

☽☌♀ 6:03 am v/c

♀♀♀ Freitag

♋
♌

Friday
17

☽→♌ 2:25 am
☽☍♆ 1:26 pm
☿⚻♆ 3:33 pm
☽△♇ 10:24 pm
☿⚹♃ 11:57 pm

All aspects in Pacific Daylight Time; add 3 hours for EDT; add 7 hours for GMT

© *Norma Rosen 1986*

Igha-Ede Design

The Igha-Ede Design is drawn upon the ground in sifted white chalk by Madame Aigbovia. Although this image utilizes a simple cross design with circles, its iconographical design associations can be quite varied. It can facilitate many things, such as the division of foods in the spiritual and the physical worlds, the transmission of messages between both realms, the sharing of foods among the deities being saluted in a ceremony, the allocation of time in ceremonies, the strengthening of medicinal bath preparation, the detection of physical problems and protection from negative forces by the creation of a non-tangible block or a gate.

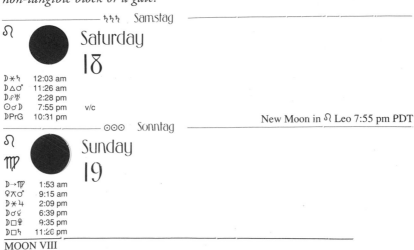

ᚺᚺᚺ Samstag

♌

Saturday
18

☽⚹♄	12:03 am	
☽△♂	11:26 am	
☽☍♅	2:28 pm	
☉♂☽	7:55 pm	v/c
☽PrG	10:31 pm	

○○○ Sonntag

New Moon in ♌ Leo 7:55 pm PDT

♌
♍

Sunday
19

☽→♍	1:53 am
♀⊼♂	9:15 am
☽⚹♃	2:09 pm
☽☌⚷	6:39 pm
☽□♀	9:35 pm
☽□♄	11:26 pm

MOON VIII

butterfly bones

what could
have been
is not

butterflies
that once lived in me
that rose on my breath
fluid and graceful
up the curve of my spine
alighting on hope
at the tip of my breastbone
soaring a wish
as if I
were the sky
endless and blue

flutter out
translucent through
membrane and bone

leaving their mark
a fine etch of silver
grey wings on my skin
like imprints of waves
fleeting impressions
that linger in sand
as they ebb out to sea

these soft powdered bones
of butterfly wings
crumbling to dust
like ash on my skin

MOON IX

Moon IX: August 18–September 17

New Moon in ♌ Leo: Aug. 18; Full Moon in ♓ Pisces: Sep. 2; Sun in ♍ Virgo: Aug. 22

Teach Me to F

© *Mara Friedman*

August
'Aukake

♍

Monday
20

☽□♂	11:48 am
☽⚹♀	1:21 pm v/c
♀⚻♅	4:08 pm
☿□♇	8:23 pm
♀⚻♃	8:52 pm

♍
♎

Tuesday
21

☽→♎	1:19 am
☽△♆	12:16 pm
☿□♄	2:10 pm
☽□♃	2:32 pm
☽⚹♀	9:39 pm
☽△♄	11:47 pm

♎

Wednesday
22

☽⚹♂	1:53 pm
☽△♅	2:16 pm
☉→♍	6:27 pm
☽□♀	6:34 pm v/c

Sun in Virgo 6:27 pm PDT

♍

♎
♏

Thursday
23

☽→♏	2:50 am
♂⚹♅	2:59 am
☉⚹☽	3:27 am
♀sD	9:06 am
☽□♆	2:26 pm
☽△♃	5:36 pm
♂♂♄	9:47 pm

♏

Friday
24

	11:24 am
	6:17 pm

Year at a Glance for ♍ VIRGO (Aug. 22–Sept. 22)

Ferocious beginnings and endings have dominated the past few years for you. If you haven't yet made peace with some daunting core issue, get yourself some help to do so now. The way you handle personal relationships and family obligations may erase old traumas.

Breakdown and decay in your outer life are reflections of a new core-self emerging. Unusual healing modalities, such as visualization or prayer, help you shed layers of old, perhaps ancestral baggage. The reward for this: a richer, more exciting view of the future and your place in it. Don't get caught up in the details this year—stretch, think big.

You are ambitious to let the world see what you have been so carefully crafting in the past few years. You are a spokeswoman for visionary and revolutionary changes. Public acknowledgement for devotion to your sacred work will begin to happen. It is the perfect time to share what you see so naturally with others who do not have your instinctive wise eyes. Your enthusiasm and trust in the quality of your work draws the attention of those who can significantly help your career, especially in the second half of this year.

You may continue to encounter challenges to your ambitions. Rather than seeing them as insurmountable obstacles, view them as opportunities to strengthen your intent. Your opponent becomes a worthy adversary who helps you become more skilled and determined.

Your body is so energetically fine tuned and profoundly sensitive that you need periodic "applications" of nature to soothe yourself. Use music, acupuncture or mind/body medicine to support your psychological and physical well being.

© Gretchen Lawlor 2000

Mer-Crone: A Sea Spirit
© Selina di Girolamo 1998

───── ♄♄♄ Pōʻaono ─────

♏ ♐

Saturday
25

☽△♀	4:16 am v/c
☽→♐	7:59 am
☉□☽	12:55 pm
♆sD	6:01 pm
☽⚹♆	8:23 pm

───── ☉☉☉ Lāpule ─────

Waxing Half Moon in ♐ Sagittarius 12:55 pm PDT

♐

Sunday
26

☽♂♀	7:24 am
☽☍♄	10:21 am
☿⚼♅	7:05 pm
♀→♌	9:12 pm

MOON IX

August
Aŭgusto

─── ☽☽☽ lundo ───

♐
♑
Monday
27

☿□♅	1:56 am	
☽⚹♅	2:15 am	
☽□☿	3:19 am	
☽♂♂	5:50 am	v/c
☽→♑	5:02 pm	

Moon Landscape
□ Florencia Strazza 1999

─── ♂♂♂ mardo ───

♑
Tuesday
28

☉△☽	3:12 am
☿□♂	5:42 am
☽⚼♃	11:33 am

─── ☿☿☿ merkredo ───

♑
Wednesday
29

☉⚼♆	2:36 pm	
☽△♅	11:28 pm	v/c

─── ♃♃♃ ĵaŭdo ───

♑
♒
Thursday
30

☽→♒	4:47 am
☽⚼♀	1:39 pm
☽♂♆	6:05 pm

─── ♀♀♀ vendredo ───

♒
Friday
31

6:11 am
⁚49 am
7 pm

─────────────────

ʼn Pacific Daylight Time; add 3 hours for EDT; add 7 hours for GMT

Moontrade

Lily left in a flooding month but only once I saw the Moon,
a white ghost bur caught in the fur of the midnight city.
Then nothing. Only the nightly count, the empty cup.
Days or weeks I was on the road, on the hill, on my way
till I came round a corner and she'd come clear, risen up
full from the valley to rest on a woolsack of clouds
where she watched the city's scurrying bullion; guinea brass
to her silver coin. And this Moon is questioning me:

how am I spending my time? I'm going too fast, forgetting

Tonight, in one of the hours of her long lidded night
she'll look through the window of my daughter Lily
in Mexico City, pour her silvers over her sleeping,
soothe the cicadas, the clicking Spanish guitars.

Later rain will muffle Moon, and she'll lie unseen
and subversive; so far she's always escaped, in time.
Next month I'll keep better watch. Ask her to come lit
in a white flame dress that spills love to the world's four corners.

I'll call her out with a cry/poem/prayer: *Moon, Moon*
this misty city can't make anything out of your night currency
but I'll do a trade with you. I'll set my cup in the window
of every month, sing you into its circle if you will gift my daughter with
a good dream as she lies sleeping in the City of Magic Possibilities.

excerpt © Rose Flint 1999

─────── ♄♄♄   sabato ───────

≈≈
)(( )   Saturday
1   September

☽♂♅	1:44 am	
♀☍♆	8:55 am	
☽⚹♂	10:36 am	v/c
☽ApG	4·22 pm	
☽→)(	5:32 pm	

─────── ☉☉☉   dimançô ───────

)(( )   Sunday
2

☉⚹♃	8:16 am	
☽△♃	2:16 pm	
☉☍☽	2:43 pm	
☽□♀	6:56 pm	
☽□♄	10:45 pm	

Full Moon in)(Pis

MOON IX

September

───────── ☽☽☽　Jumatatu ──────────────────

♓ ( )　Monday
3

───────── ♂♂♂　Jumanne ──────────────────

♓
♈ ( )　Tuesday
4

☽□♂	1:37 am	v/c
☽→♈	5:58 am	
☽☍♅	5:26 pm	
☽✶♆	6:53 pm	
☉□♀	6:54 pm	

───────── ☿☿☿　Jumatano ──────────────────

♈ ( )　Wednesday
5

☽□♃	3:13 am
☽△♀	4:04 am
☿△♆	5:51 am
☽△♀	7:02 am
☽✶♄	10:57 am

───────── ♃♃♃　Alhamisi ──────────────────

♈
♉ ( )　Thursday
6

☽✶♅	1:40 am	
♀△♀	10:05 am	
☽△♂	3:31 pm	v/c
☽→♉	5:18 pm	
☉□♄	9:11 pm	

───────── ♀♀♀　Ijumaa ──────────────────

♉ ( )　Friday
7

	5:46 am
	2:42 pm
	⌐2 pm
	⌐ pm

───
⌐ in Pacific Daylight Time; add 3 hours for EDT; add 7 hours for GMT

Spirit Work
□ *Shelley Stefan 1999*

♉

———— ☌☌☌ Jumamosi ————

Saturday
♉

♀⚹♄	3:14 am
♂→♑	10:51 am
☽⚼♅	11:30 am v/c
♉□♃	7:30 pm

———— ☉☉☉ Jumapili ————

♉
♊

Sunday
9

☽→♊	2:41 am
☽∠♆	2:32 pm
☿⚹♀	9:40 pm

September

September

♊

───── ☽☽☽ Montag ──────────────────

Monday
10

☽☍♀	2:00 am	
☽△♅	2:28 am	
☽☌♄	5:50 am	
☽⚹♀	10:46 am	
☉☐☽	11:59 am	
☽△♅	6:42 pm	v/c

Waning Half Moon in ♊ Gemini 11:59 am PDT

♊
♋

───── ♂♂♂ Dienstag ──────

Tuesday
11

☽→♋	9:09 am
☽☍♂	11:56 am
☿△♄	3:06 pm

♋

───── ☿☿☿ Mittwoch ──────────────

Wednesday
12

☽☌♃	5:32 am	
☽☐♅	12:32 pm	
☉⚹☽	8:16 pm	v/c

───── ♃♃♃ Donnerstag ─────────

♋
♌

Thursday
13

| ☽→♌ | 12:16 pm |
| ☽☍♆ | 10:36 pm |

───── ♀♀♀ Freitag ─────────────

♌

Friday
14

| 12:06 am |
| 5:05 am |
| 8:57 am |
| ?:27 pm |
| ?2 pm |
| ? pm |

──────────────────────────────────
...ts in Pacific Daylight Time; add 3 hours for EDT; add 7 hours for GMT

She is Blessed

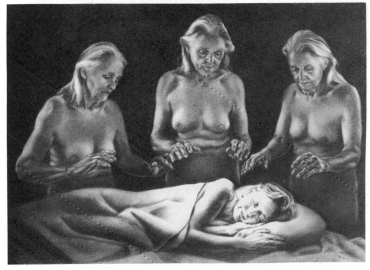

© Megaera 1999

Reiki Prayer

Hands lay along the spine of space.
Hands rest in memory's valley.
Hands lay cover where pain is traced.
Hands lay peace as energies release.
Hands open flow and current shifts.
Hands lay hope when
hands pray Reiki.

▢ Anne Bridgit Foye 1999

♄♄♄ Samstag

♌
♍

Saturday
15
v/c

☽♂♀	1:35 am
♀△♅	4:04 am
☽→♍	12:39 pm
☉□♅	4:24 pm
☽△♂	6:48 pm

☉☉☉ Sonntag

♍

Sunday
16

☽⚹♃	8:05 am
☽□♀	8:42 am
☽PrG	8:52 am
☽□♄	12:08 pm

MOON IX

Transformation

When poisons forced my hair out,

it left patches of my scalp bald, others, furry.

It left me feeling wild, out of control, unbalanced.

I decided to shave my head clean one night—

I needed to feel powerful, stronger than my illness.

I channeled all of my feelings of fear and rage,

my desire to live, into that one act;

challenged anything, even cancer,

to defy or destroy this woman standing before me—

bald head gleaming, my scalp catching light

like some kind of angelic armor.

My new image amazed me—

I was thin, pale, fierce, and Divine—

a Goddess of simplicity.

It was my soft new skull

that taught me not to fear death—

taught me how to fight and how to win.

□ *Jamie Wright 1999*

MOON X

Moon X: September 17-October 16

New Moon in ♍ Virgo: Sep. 17; Full Moon in ♈ Aries: Oct. 2; Sun in ♎ Libra: Sep. 22

Eight of Cups—Rebirth
© *Chesca Potter 1999*

September
Kepakemapa

□ *Ijenna Hupp Andrews 1999*

Creation Magic

New Moon in ♍ Virgo 3:27 am PDT

ᗪᗪᗪ Pōʻakahi

♍
♎ Monday
17

☉☌☽	3:27 am	v/c
☽→♎	12:00 pm	
☿△♅	6:51 pm	
☽□♂	7:58 pm	
☽△♆	9:54 pm	

♂♂♂ Pōʻalua

♎ Tuesday
18

☽□♃	8:02 am
☽✶♀	8:17 am
☽△♄	11:48 am
☽△♅	10:38 pm

☿☿☿ Pōʻakolu

♎
♏ Wednesday
19

☽☌♅	12:40 am	
☽✶♀	9:38 am	v/c
☽→♏	12:27 pm	
☿✶♄	12:34 pm	
♃⊼♀	4:09 pm	
☽□♆	10:48 pm	
☽✶♂	10:50 pm	

♃♃♃ Pōʻahā

♏ Thursday
20

| ☽△♃ | 10:03 am |
| ♀→♍ | 7:09 pm |

♀♀♀ Pōʻalima

♏
♐ Friday
21

	1:04 am	
	2:09 pm	v/c
	02 pm	
	pm	

Year at a Glance for ♎ LIBRA (Sept. 22–Oct. 23)

You complete an intense period of relationship challenges and shed some personal baggage involving intimacy and sex. This has required constant effort and periodic crises as you struggled with these issues. By April, you have learned to stay more consistently true to yourself at the same time relating in a creative and open-minded manner with others.

Libra is steward to the issues of relationship, as each of us are steward to some aspect of life (i.e. Sagittarius—philosophy, Cancer—sanctuary making). You are experiencing, in a very visceral way, a challenge to be more open-minded and more open-hearted in the way you relate intimately. This is your contribution to the transformations required for this new age we are entering. Spiritual values must permeate your intimate encounters as you move beyond limiting possessive forms.

Your capacity for light sociability and casual talk seems to be on hold. For the last few years an eruption of unconscious complexes into your conscious awareness has preoccupied you, perhaps pushed you into depression. A more optimistic view of your own circumstances and of life in general emerges before July 2001, possibly through a journey.

The experiences of the early months of this year will set you on a larger quest to completely restructure your ideals and philosophy of life. Last year you experienced a number of powerful changes as you stepped more deeply and authentically into your life.

Exploration and experimentation with a creative medium: writing, painting, music, theater, etc. has been and continues to be vitally important for you. Find your voice and use it to express the story of your rich internal processes.

© Gretchen Lawlor 2000

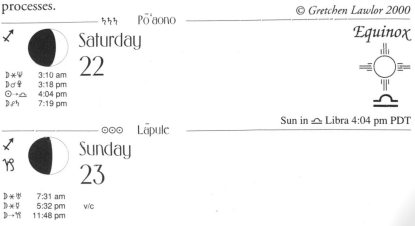

♄♄♄ Pōʻaono

♐

Saturday

22

D⚹Ψ 3:10 am
D☌♀ 3:18 pm
☉→♎ 4:04 pm
D☍♄ 7:19 pm

Equinox

Sun in ♎ Libra 4:04 pm PDT

☉☉☉ Lāpule

♐
♑

Sunday

23

D⚹♅ 7:31 am
D⚹☿ 5:32 pm   v/c
D→♑ 11:48 pm

Kore: At Autumn's Equinox

Kore:

The balance of the year

as night draws even to day.

Core:

The apple halved—

maiden-pale flesh feeds,

blood-red skin protects/attracts,

dark-secreted seeds secure the future.

Kore, you choose the dark,

select to separate

from the Mother's bright ripeness,

plunging your own seeds deep

into mystery-dark winter—

the blood-pulse promise of Spring

carried silent into hue-drained landscape,

we snuggle, nest & burrow,

hibernate & compost,

root & dream our seeds

into the future

as we bite to Winter's core.

◻ Renna Shesso 1999

© *Mara Friedman 1999*

Fall Equinox

At Fall Equinox, in Northern climates, many people celebrate the culmination of the harvest. Our focus turns towards reflection and integrating wisdom. Light and dark balance each other in the same way that dreaming balances outward effort. Crisp nights and the harvest moon lighting the sky reminds us that all things change.

Magically, Peppermint (*Mentha piperita*) invokes our reflective natures. It can help us dream more vividly and to encourage the dreams we do have to be more visionary in nature. To use Peppermint as an incense, place small amounts of the dry leaf on charcoal or burn dry stalks in a small chalice or fireproof bowl throughout the evening to access your intuitive abilities. Peppermint can be a tonic for the mind. It gently stimulates and refreshes mental capacity helping us get in touch with the wisdom of the season. Peppermint is so commonly available that we often overlook its esoteric properties. Try drinking a cup of the tea as you reflect on what you harvested in the previous year and what you need to bring balance.

© *Colette G...*

September
Septembro

♑ — ☽☽☽ lundo
Monday
24

☉□☽ 2:31 am
☽△♀ 8:10 am
☽♂♂ 5:15 pm

Waxing Half Moon in ♑ Capricorn 2:31 am PDT

♑ — ♂♂♂ mardo
Tuesday
25

☽☍♃ 1:56 am
♀⚻♆ 7:32 pm

♑
≈ — ☿☿☿ merkredo
Wednesday
26

☽□♅ 7:38 am   v/c
☽→≈ 11:05 am
♄sR 5:04 pm
☉△☽ 7:14 pm
☽♂♆ 11:24 pm

≈ — ♃♃♃ ĵaŭdo
Thursday
27

☽⚹♀ 1:06 pm
☽△♄ 5:21 pm

≈
♓ — ♀♀♀ vendredo
Friday
28

　 6:15 am
　 9:11 pm
　 10:27 pm   v/c
　 0:31 pm
　 50 pm

pects in Pacific Daylight Time; add 3 hours for EDT; add 7 hours for GMT

© *Carol Wylie 1996*

The principle of magic is not to enslave the universe to our individual will. It is to transform the self to recognize and respond to the limitless opportunities to grow, which are always offered to us.

excerpt © Selina di Girolamo 1999

♄♄♄   sabato

♓

Saturday

29

☽☍♀   10:25 pm

☉☉☉   dimanĉo

♓

Sunday

30

☽⚹♂   12:24 am
☽□♀   1:57 am
☽△♃   4:00 am
☽☌♄   6:02 am   v/c

MOON X

October

Oktoba

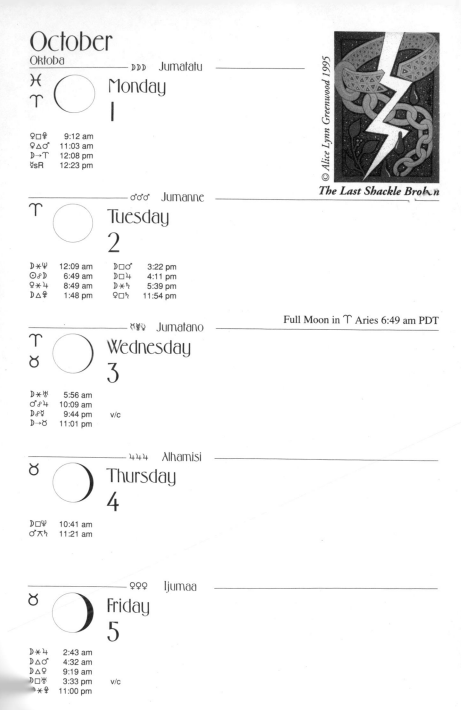

The Last Shackle Broken

ᗪᗪᗪ Jumatatu

♓︎
♈︎

Monday
1

♀□♀	9:12 am
♀△♂	11:03 am
☽→♈︎	12:08 pm
☿sR	12:23 pm

♂♂♂ Jumanne

♈︎

Tuesday
2

☽⚹♆	12:09 am	☽□♂	3:22 pm
☉☌☽	6:49 am	☽□♃	4:11 pm
♀⚹♃	8:49 am	☽⚹♄	5:39 pm
☽△♀	1:48 pm	♀□♄	11:54 pm

Full Moon in ♈︎ Aries 6:49 am PDT

☿☿☿ Jumatano

♈︎
♉︎

Wednesday
3

☽⚹♅	5:56 am	
♂☌♃	10:09 am	
☽☍♅	9:44 pm	v/c
☽→♉︎	11:01 pm	

♃♃♃ Alhamisi

♉︎

Thursday
4

| ☽□♆ | 10:41 am |
| ♂⚹♄ | 11:21 am |

♀♀♀ Ijumaa

♉︎

Friday
5

☽⚹♃	2:43 am	
☽△♂	4:32 am	
☽△♀	9:19 am	
☽□♅	3:33 pm	v/c
☽⚹♀	11:00 pm	

All aspects in Pacific Daylight Time; add 3 hours for EDT; add 7 hours for GMT

Amazon Alive

Dadian, a ruler of the Caucasus, asked to see weapons and clothes that had belonged to the dead female warriors. A messenger brought him their steel helmets and armor, their short skirts and their soft high boots embroidered with stars. Their steel-tipped arrows were gilded. Dadian promised a rich reward for anyone who could bring him such a woman alive.

I dreamed the dream:
      Women everywhere
      smashing free
losing outer shackles: carpools, diaper pins, dustpans, dishpans
                 ladyrazors, pantyhose, stilt heels, eyeliner
                 hardbound bibles by Emily Post
                 (her boned corset? Every hook by Trugrip)
loosing inner chains: "If I don't do it, they won't like me. But if I do?"
      they they they
      reflexes perplexes complexes.
Smashing free everywhere
everywhere a song of Goddess and the tread of
      soft leather boots covered everywhere
      with small bright
          stars.

© Carole Spearin McCauley 1999

ħħħ Jumamosi

♉
♊

Saturday
6

☽→♊   8:12 am
☽△♆   7:27 pm

☉☉☉ Jumapili

♊

Sunday
7

☽☍♀	8:31 am	☉△♄	6:58 pm
☉△☽	11:12 am	☽□♀	11:08 pm
☽♂♄	11:48 am	☽△♅	11:15 pm
☉□♃	1:08 pm		

MOON X

October
Oktober

☽☽☽ Montag

♊
♋

Monday
8

♀⊼♅ 12:25 am
☽△☿ 9:24 am v/c
☽→♋ 3:19 pm

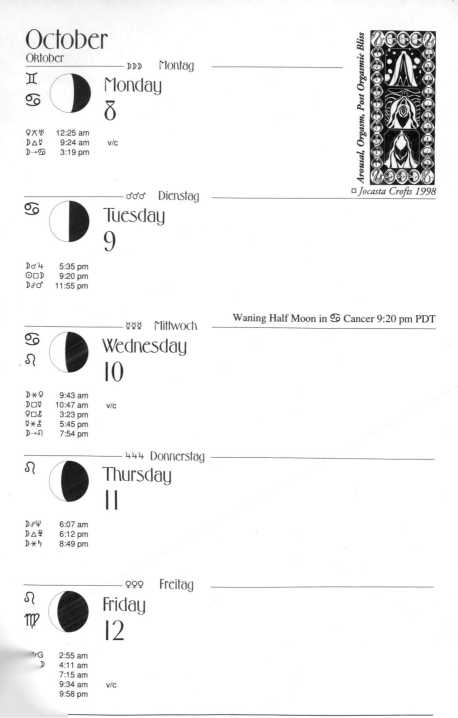

Arousal, Orgasm, Post Orgasmic Bliss
¤ *Jocasta Crofts 1998*

♂♂♂ Dienstag

♋

Tuesday
9

☽☌♃ 5:35 pm
☉□☽ 9:20 pm
☽☍♂ 11:55 pm

Waning Half Moon in ♋ Cancer 9:20 pm PDT

☿☿☿ Mittwoch

♋
♌

Wednesday
10

☽⚹♀ 9:43 am
☽□☿ 10:47 am v/c
♀□⚷ 3:23 pm
☿⚹⚷ 5:45 pm
☽→♌ 7:54 pm

♃♃♃ Donnerstag

♌

Thursday
11

☽☍♆ 6:07 am
☽△♇ 6:12 pm
☽⚹♄ 8:49 pm

♀♀♀ Freitag

♌
♍

Friday
12

rG 2:55 am
☽ 4:11 am
7:15 am
9:34 am v/c
9:58 pm

aspects in Pacific Daylight Time; add 3 hours for EDT; add 7 hours for GMT

Pink Yoni Love-Spell

To magickally replace negative conditioning about our bodies, through self love & consciously identifying with Mother Earth, to support healing work on reproductive system, to nurture the vulva. Perform on new moon, when energies focus inward. Alone or in com-moon-union with other womon. Wear loose clothes. No underwear! Stay warm. Make a pink space using pink cloth, candles, chiffon, dried rose petals, etc. Be imaginative. Declare the space sacred & safe. Take a fruit that looks like a vulva—peach, passionfruit, guava, papaya—are all excellent for yoni magick. Slowly taste fruit. Savor. Squeeze a drop of juice into a bowl of spring-water with rose quartz in it. Visualize your vulva as a ripe, many-layered fruit. Next, place a flower into the bowl. Use a mirror to compare your yoni to this flower. See how you both have petals, (labia) clitoris, (stamen) pollen, (sexual secretions) & a mysterious, dark centre. SEE HOW BEAUTIFUL YOU ARE! Write positive thoughts on pink paper, about how your vulva, fruit & flowers are all expressions of She-sexuality. Many blocks & tears & sad feelings may arise: allow these emotions to flow. Float your positive thoughts on the bowl of water overnight. In morning, bury paper & flower, returning positivity to earth. Plant wildflower seeds to represent your wild nature & to grow as your sexual awareness grows. Pour water from bowl over seeds. Rose quartz is now fully energized with yoni-love & can be used however you want. Blessed Be.

◻ *Felix 1999*

I wrote this after having an operation. I used this spell to heal my damaged self image & to come to terms with the new wound & little blue stitches in my labia.

ħħħ Samstag

♍

Saturday
13

☿△♅	1:45 pm
☿□♂	5:38 pm
☉♂♉	6:43 pm
☽□♀	7:28 pm
☽□ħ	9:49 pm
☽⚹♃	10:26 pm

⊙⊙⊙ Sonntag

♍
♎

Sunday
14

☉△♅	12:36 am	
☉□♂	12:37 am	
☽△♂	8:21 am	
☽PrG	4:11 pm	
☽♂♀	9:52 pm	v/c
☽→♎	10:26 pm	

MOON X

Wild Columbine
(*Aquilegia canadensis*)

Our sex is buried
beneath rotten ferns
in an unmarked grave.
We could call it
the slumbering bear of winter,
solar eclipse in late afternoon,
flower bulb after frost.
We could call it lunar
or lunatic in its plunging orbit.

Yet late at night, while dreaming,
we wrap ourselves in the warmth
of familiar arms; the sharp heat
nubbed low. Would you
come if I took you with me
to the place where the earth
reeks of wild onion,
would you eat with me
the purple seeds of wild columbine
where sweet dirt gives
beneath our weight,

where I will bend
gesturing with both hands
sucking in the damp air
and exhaling the low incantation of flames
until the pile of broken twigs,
promises we couldn't keep,
secrets we tried to speak,
cold silences, weary hope,
unspoken desire,

catches fire.

◻ *Ann Megisikwe Filemyr 1999*

MOON XI

Moon XI: October 16–November 14

New Moon in ♎ Libra: Oct. 16; Full Moon in ♉ Taurus: Oct. 31; Sun in ♏ Scorpio: Oct. 23

Greenwood Lc

© Chesca Potter 1

October

'Okakopa

───── ☽☽☽   Pō'akahi ─────

♎

Monday
15

♀→♎	4:42 am
☽△♆	8:04 am
☽⚹♀	7:51 pm
☽△♄	10:00 pm
☽□♃	10:55 pm

───── ♂♂♂   Pō'alua ─────

♎
♏

Tuesday
16

☽♂♉	3:32 am	
☽△♅	8:19 am	
☽□♂	10:58 am	
☉♂☽	12:23 pm	v/c
☽→♏	11:03 pm	

───── ☿☿☿   Pō'akolu ─────

New Moon in ♎ Libra 12:23 pm PDT

♏

Wednesday
17

☽□♆	8:57 am
♆sD	6:49 pm
☉⚹⚷	9:13 pm

───── ♃♃♃   Pō'ahā ─────

♏

Thursday
18

☽△♃	12:33 am	
☽□♅	10:11 am	
☽⚹♂	3:30 pm	v/c

───── ♀♀♀   Pō'alima ─────

♏
♐

Friday
19

☽→♐	1:47 am
☿□♃	4:48 am
☽⚹♀	11:05 am
☽⚹♆	12:20 pm

───────────────────────────

All aspects in Pacific Daylight Time; add 3 hours for EDT; add 7 hours for GMT

Beauty

◻ *Donna Reid 1999*

Prosperity Moon Spell

Years ago someone told me about this spell for receiving money; I do not know where it comes from.

Place a silver dish containing water in the light of a waxing moon so that the moon is reflected in it.

Dip your hands in the water,
and as they dry naturally—palms faced up toward the heavens—
imagine money & prosperity coming into your life.

Once your hands are completely dry,
give a prayer of gratitude
and know that you will receive income from an unexpected source
before the moon waxes again in her next cycle.

◻ *Annalisa Cunningham 1999*

♄♄♄ Pōʻaono

♐

Saturday
20

♀△♆	12:36 am
☽σ♀	1:37 am
☽♂♄	3:31 am
☽⚹♅	4:08 am
☽⚹♅	3:21 pm

☉☉☉ Lāpule

♐
♑

Sunday
21

♅△♄	3:45 am	
☉⚹☽	4:42 am	v/c
☽→♑	8:11 am	

October
Oktobro

There is Magic
when I choose to see you
as Spirit having a human experience.
excerpt ¤ Claire Johnson 1999

☽☽☽ lundo

♑

Monday 22

☽□♀	12:16 am
☽□☿	11:21 am
☽☍♃	1:52 pm
☿sD	5:23 pm

♂♂♂ mardo

♑ ♒

Tuesday 23

☉→♏	1:26 am	
☽☌♂	1:11 pm	v/c
☽→♒	6:26 pm	
☿△♄	7:33 pm	
☉□☽	7:58 pm	

♏

Sun in Scorpio 1:26 am PDT
Waxing Half Moon in ♒ Aquarius 7:58 pm PDT

☿☿☿ merkredo

♒

Wednesday 24

☽☌♆	6:26 am
☽△♀	6:16 pm
☽✶♇	9:39 pm
☽△♄	11:03 pm
☽△☿	11:53 pm

♃♃♃ ĵaŭdo

♒

Thursday 25

☽☌♅	12:32 pm	v/c

♀♀♀ vendredo

♒ ♓

Friday 26

♀✶♇	3:19 am
☽→♓	6:56 am
☽ApG	1:18 pm
☉△☽	2:03 pm
△♄	2:24 pm
♃	5:54 pm

All aspects in Pacific Daylight Time; add 3 hours for EDT; add 7 hours for GMT

Year at a Glance for ♏ SCORPIO (Oct. 23–Nov. 21)

About 2¹/₂ years ago you began to be more involved in the world after a long process of inward growth. Concentrating your awareness on close companions you redefined your relationship needs and clarified your contractual agreements. Either deepen or move on before July.

You are beginning to take on more of a public persona and will need to balance time with intimates with time to develop your own resources. This is part of a larger cycle of learning to hold true to your deep self in the company of others. In about four years you will begin to peak in an area of expertise. What you do this year to stabilize your personal affairs prepares you for maximum impact then.

From July through the end of the year, travel or a course in metaphysics will be inspirational and sheds light on the profound changes you have experienced in the last year.

Your imagination is particularly active and powerful and can be used to influence your future positively through meditation and fantasy. Your subconscious erupts into your reality through dream images, reliving childhood memories or past life issues. Inexplicable longings may precipitate a move. Otherwise, consider alterations to the home configuration for the emergence of new facets of yourself.

Someone close to you will challenge what you do with your assets and resources. This precipitates a crisis having to do with control issues. You are being asked to clarify inner values, in the process of which, financial problems may disappear. You benefit from joint financial investments through April but need to have very clear legal agreements.

© *Gretchen Lawlor 2000*

Stramonium Trance
□ *Tracy Litterick 1996*

♄♄♄ sabato

♓ ☽ Saturday
27

♂→♒ 10:19 am
☽□♀ 10:30 am
☽□♄ 11:29 am
☽△♃   2:31 pm   v/c
♀□♃   6:36 pm

☉☉☉ dimanĉo

♓ ☽ Sunday
♈ **28**

☽→♈   6:15 pm
☽⚹♂   8:14 pm

Daylight Savings Time ends 2:00 am PDT

October
Oktoba

♈ 🌙 **Monday**
29

☉□♆	1:31 am
☽⚹♆	6:11 am
☽△♀	9:17 pm
☽⚹♄	9:50 pm

Ancestor Mothers
© Megaera 1992

— ♂♂♂ Jumanne —

♈ 🌕 **Tuesday**
30

☽□♃	1:06 am	
☽☍♀	7:17 am	
☽☍☿	7:19 am	
☿☌♀	11:06 am	
☽⚹♅	11:17 am	v/c
♅sD	2:55 pm	

— ☿☿☿ Jumatano —

♈
♉ 🌕 **Wednesday**
31

Samhain/Hallowmas

☽→♉	4:48 am	
☽□♂	10:06 am	
☽□♆	4:20 pm	
☉☍☽	9:41 pm	
♀△♅	10:59 pm	

Full Moon in ♉ Taurus 9:41 pm PST

— ♃♃♃ Alhamisi —

♉ 🌕 **Thursday**
1

November

☿△♅	1:04 am	
☽⚹♃	10:33 am	
☽□♅	8:20 pm	v/c
♄☍♀	10:08 pm	

— ♀♀♀ Ijumaa —

♉
♊ 🌖 **Friday**
2

♃sR	7:35 am	
☽→♊	1:12 pm	
☽△♂	9:28 pm	
☿☌♀	11:22 pm	

All aspects in Pacific Standard Time; add 3 hours for EST; add 8 hours for GMT

Samhain

Samhain is the time of year's ending and the witches' new year. This is a particularly good season to do divination work of any kind and to communicate with the ancestors because the veil between the worlds is so thin. For those who work close to the earth it can be a chance to focus on something other than the garden.

Thyme (*Thymus vulgaris*) is one herb that can be used as a magical offering to those who have passed over. As an incense it can help us communicate with those on the other side of the veil. Throw one pinch of Thyme onto the fire with each name you call for those who have died in the preceding year. It can also be burned continuously as you call out the names of the honored dead, those who made significant contributions to social change or who were prominent members of their community. Honoring those who have paved the way for us with their efforts can be powerful. They often have much to tell us.

Burial at Mountainlight

There is no sound
THUD
like the sound of fresh dirt
THUD
on the top of a coffin.
There is no grave
like this grave
not for thousands of years.

Woman-dug
Woman-embellished.

They painted all day
paleolithic white walls
amber burnish
black earth designs.

Beauty right there in the pit.
Art on the smooth skinned belly
of the Mother
open to receive her daughter.
Her daughter, Silver.

We build our own houses
grow our own food
Why would we not bury our own dead?

The sacred task is smooth
tricky but smooth
ropes, timbers, women
lowering
wooden casket
down into
deep cradle,
lined with women's love
resplendent with lesbian artistry
ancient magic reborn into this century
this Circle
of Spirit-Revolution.

excerpt © Bethroot Gwynn 1999

Silver's Grave
© *Sequoia 1999*
Grave dug by Southern Oregon wimmin; grave art by Sequoia with help from Amara.

――――――― ꜣꜣꜣ Jumamosi ―――――――

♊

Saturday
3

☽△♆ 12:23 am
☽♂♄ 2:21 pm
☽♋♀ 2:39 pm

――――――― ☉☉☉ Jumapili ―――――――

♊
♋

Sunday
4

☽△♅ 3:25 am
☽△♀ 11:18 am
☽△☿ 11:45 am   v/c
☽→♋ 7:44 pm

November

ЖЖЖ Montag

♋

Monday
5

☿⚹♄	12:43 am
♂☌♆	4:44 am
♀⚹♄	7:30 am
☉☌♄	2:50 pm
☉△☽	8:16 pm
☽☌♃	11:32 pm

♂♂♂ Dienstag

♋

Tuesday
6

| ☽□♀ | 9:41 pm | |
| ☽□☿ | 11:10 pm | v/c |

☿☿☿ Mittwoch

♋
♌

Wednesday
7

☽→♌	12:34 am
☽☍♆	11:08 am
☿→♏	11:53 am
☽☍♂	1:58 pm
☉△♃	4:01 pm
☽⚹♄	11:41 pm

♃♃♃ Donnerstag

♌

Thursday
8

☽△♀	12:43 am	
☉□☽	4:21 am	
♀→♏	5:28 am	
☽☍♅	12:30 pm	v/c

♀♀♀ Freitag

Waning Half Moon in ♌ Leo 4:21 am PST

♌
♍

Friday
9

☽→♍	3:49 am
☽⚹♀	5:58 am
♁☿	8:39 am

All aspects in Pacific Standard Time; add 3 hours for EST; add 8 hours for GMT

The Scandinavian Goddess Freya, a member of the earliest pantheon of Goddesses and gods called the Vanir, controlled and taught a form of magic called *seidhr*. It consisted of the reading of lots or runes, the casting of spells and a kind of trance which allowed one to see the future. In this way, fate could be predicted and sometimes even controlled. Even after the coming of a new pantheon called the Aesir, ruled by the god Odin, the use of the runes for divination, prediction and magic remained the domain of the Goddess and Her priestesses. These traveling wise women, often known as volvas, moved from village to village offering readings of the runes, throughout the entire period of Scandinavian history prior to Christianity.

© *Susan Gray 1999, excerpted from*
A Woman's Guide to the Runes
(Barnes & Noble)

Shaman Woman/
Goddess on Spiritboat—
petroglyphs at Nämforsen
© *Monica Sjöö 1995*

ᚺᚺᚺ   Samstag

♍ Saturday
10

☽□♄   2:05 am
☽□♀   3:27 am
☽⚹♃   5:55 am
☉⚹☽   10:40 am   v/c

⊙⊙⊙   Sonntag

♍ Sunday
♎ 11

☽→♎   5:53 am
☽PrG   9:27 am
♅□♆   10:59 am
☽△♆   4:06 pm
☽△♂   11:54 pm

Old Woman Speaks

Tell me
>   what do you know
>   of the depth of your sea

have you swam shore to shore
>   and returned breathless to the sand

have you climbed mountains
>   made music, created fire

have you done something dangerous
>   from which you might not return

have you stood naked in front of a mirror
>   and said, "Hmmm, I do look good."
>   and then danced around to get a better look

have you pressed your lips against those of another
>   and lost track of where you ended
>   and they began

have you loved
>   known loss, let go, held on
>   surrendered to something

have you been scared
>   lost, confused, truly sad

have you felt joy at your very core
>   and laughed like a crazy woman

have you told stories
>   heard stories, made stories, shared stories

have you come
>   face to face with a wild thing
>   and listened deeply to what the earth has to say

have you walked
>   in the path of another
>   or slept under an open sky

do you know what I am saying
>   have you lived
>   tell me.

◻ *Tami Kent 1999*

MOON XII

Moon XII: November 14–December 14

New Moon in ♏ Scorpio: Nov. 14; Full Moon in ♊ Gemini: Nov. 30; Sun in ♐ Sagittarius: Nov. 21

Priestess
© Carol Wylie 1998

November
Nowemapa

─── ⅮⅮⅮ Pō'akahi ───

♎︎

Monday
12

☽△♄	3:40 am
☽⚹♀	5:23 am
☽□♃	7:37 am
☽△♅	4:42 pm v/c
☉□♅	11:32 pm

each moon
blessed terra cotta rivers emerge
singing down thighs

daughters everywhere
anchor into her
and squat low mud-red tears
salted with potential life
return home to feed mama
    holly taya shere 1999

─── ♂♂♂ Pō'alua ───

♎︎
♏︎

Tuesday
13

♀□♆	4:02 am
☽→♏︎	7:44 am
☽□♆	6:09 pm
☽♂♀	7:29 pm

─── ☿☿☿ Pō'akolu ───

♏︎

Wednesday
14

☽♂♅	1:01 am
☽□♂	4:40 am
☽△♃	9:48 am
☽□♅	7:18 pm
♂△♄	10:00 pm
☉♂☽	10:40 pm v/c

Lunar Samhain
New Moon in ♏︎ Scorpio 10:40 pm PST

─── ♃♃♃ Pō'ahā ───

♏︎
♐︎

Thursday
15

☽→♐︎	10:51 am
☿⚻♄	4:18 pm
☽⚹♆	9:46 pm

─── ♀♀♀ Pō'alima ───

♐︎

Friday
16

☿□♂	8:33 am
☽☍♄	9:27 am
☽⚹♂	11:39 am
☽♂♀	12:09 pm
♂⚹♀	9:26 pm

─────────────────────────

All aspects in Pacific Standard Time; add 3 hours for EST; add 8 hours for GMT

Grandma's Remedy

"Soak your feet in a bowl of moonlight," my grandma used to say,
"The moon will soothe what ails you in an effervescent way."

¤ Rhea Giffin 1998

──────── ♄♄♄　Pōʻaono ────────

♐
♑
🌑
Saturday
17

☽∗♅　12.14 am　v/c
♉△♃　4:57 am
☽→♑　4:40 pm

──────── ☉☉☉　Lāpule ────────

♑
🌑
Sunday
18

♂⊼♃　4:32 am
♀⊼♄　8:13 am
☽∗♀　5:21 pm
☽☍♃　9:18 pm

November

Novembro

Monday
19

☽ ✶ ♉   3:24 am
☉ ✶ ☽   9:57 pm   v/c

♑
♒

Tuesday
20

☽ → ♒   1:55 am
♀ △ ♃   7:31 am
☽ ☌ ♆   2:22 pm
☿ □ ♅   7:51 pm

♒

Wednesday
21

☽ △ ♄   2:36 am
☽ ✶ ♀   6:41 am
☽ □ ♀   10:50 am
☽ ☌ ♂   1:01 pm
☽ ☌ ♅   7:57 pm
☉ → ♐   10:00 pm
☽ □ ☿   11:37 pm   v/c

Sun in Sagittarius 10:00 pm PST

♒
♓

Thursday
22

☽ → ♓   1:52 pm
☉ □ ☽   3:21 pm

Waxing Half Moon in ♓ Pisces 3:21 pm PST

♓

Friday
23

☽ Ap G   7:49 am
♀ □ ♂   8:43 am
☽ □ ♄   2:41 pm
☽ □ ♀   7:24 pm
☽ △ ♃   8:03 pm

All aspects in Pacific Standard Time; add 3 hours for EST; add 8 hours for GMT

Year at a Glance for ♐ SAGITTARIUS (Nov. 21–Dec. 21)

During this year, you come to the end of a 15-year cycle of personal exploration and inward growth. You begin to receive invitations to share your experiences and insights, finally.

A unique style of expression is still emerging. Experiment with different media. Be open to inspirations from your dreams. Give yourself the gift of idle hours. Develop your insights through poetry or music as images and imagination most potently convey your remarkable awareness.

Someone will enter your life this year, perhaps during a journey. They possess a profoundly different orientation to life and make an impression upon you. Make the most of this connection—take a chance, especially April–June (though be more careful if it involves investing money).

This is a year for action in relationships: if you are single this is a good year for partnership, if you are involved, it is time to reconsider and renegotiate the commitment. A general impatience to get on with life versus a need to clarify existing commitments creates tension. You are learning to stay true to yourself while in the company of others. Be very clear about the agreements you make with others and then live up to them.

There has been considerable crisis in your life since 1993. You are only beginning to see the enormity of the personal transformation you have been experiencing. Through this you are becoming more potent, more significant. This will require you to develop control over just how you project your personality to others—you are just as capable of being a negative force as a positive one. Commit to a physical/spiritual exercise program such as yoga or martial arts. © *Gretchen Lawlor 2000*

Study for Artemis
© *Durga Bernhard 1999*

♓ ☽ ──── ♄♄♄ sabato ────

Saturday
24

☽△♀ 6:32 am
☽△♅ 9:29 pm v/c

♓ ☽ ──── ☉☉☉ dimanĉo ────
♈

Sunday
25

☽→♈ 2:21 am
♀□♅ 2:50 am
☉△☽ 9:21 am
☽✶♆ 3:07 pm

November

Novemba

♈

Monday
26

☽✶♄	2:17 am
☽△♀	7:27 am
☽□♃	7:32 am
☿→♐	10:23 am
♂☌♅	11:07 am
♃⚹♀	4:16 pm
☽✶♅	8:11 pm
☽✶♂	8:43 pm v/c

♂♂♂ Jumanne

♈
♉

Tuesday
27

☽→♉	1:06 pm

☿☿☿ Jumatano

♉

Wednesday
28

☽□♆	1:24 am
☉✶♆	7:35 am
☽✶♃	4:35 pm

♃♃♃ Alhamisi

♉
♊

Thursday
29

☽□♅	5:05 am
☽□♂	8:50 am
☽☍♀	3:21 pm v/c
☽→♊	9:04 pm

♀♀♀ Ijumaa

♊

Friday
30

☽☍♉	8:14 am
☽△♆	8:52 am
☉☍☽	12:49 pm
☿✶♆	1:40 pm
☽☌♄	6:08 pm
☽☍♀	11:50 pm

Full Moon in ♊ Gemini 12:49 pm PST

All aspects in Pacific Standard Time; add 3 hours for EST; add 8 hours for GMT

Twenty Blessings

May grass grow short at your feet.
May Venus shine through your window.
May cats wind themselves around your legs.
May you hear bitterns boom in the reeds.
May your friends write you letters.
May you walk through waves on the shore.
May dogs roll their eyes at you.
May the Moon's magic re-create you.
May you sit with stones at your back.
May butterflies fly in your garden.
May you hear the sound of geese at sunset.
May you always sing in harmony.
May foxgloves grow tall around you.
May you heal the world with your touch.
May you remember the flight of the Golden Plover.
May you be filled with joy at sunrise.
May your crops be plentiful.
May you walk in the cool of the day.
May daisies decorate your room.
May all shadows be made by bright sunshine.
May silence give you peace.

© *Sue Richards 1999*

♄♄♄ Jumamosi

♊ ◯ Saturday
1

December

☽△♅ 11:17 am
☽△♂ 5:48 pm   v/c

☉☉☉ Jumapili

♊ ☽ Sunday
♋ 2

☽→♋ 2:30 am
♀→♐ 3:11 am

December
Dezember

☽☽☽ Montag

♋

Monday
3

☽☌♃	3:04 am	v/c
♄PrG	3:30 am	
☉☍♄	6:13 am	
☿☍♄	4:47 pm	

♂♂♂ Dienstag

♋ ♌

Tuesday
4

☽→♌	6:15 am	
☽△♀	11:16 am	
☉☌☿	1:36 pm	
☽☍♆	5:33 pm	
☿ApG	11:08 pm	

☿☿☿ Mittwoch

♌

Wednesday
5

☽⚹♄	1:33 am	
☉△☽	5:10 am	
☽△☿	5:52 am	
☿⚻♃	6:51 am	
☽△♇	7:51 am	
☉⚻♃	3:26 pm	
☽☍♅	6:44 pm	

♃♃♃ Donnerstag

♌ ♍

Thursday
6

☿☌♇	12:12 am	
☽☍♂	6:20 am	v/c
☽→♍	9:11 am	
☽PrG	2:35 pm	
☽□♀	7:06 pm	
☉☌♇	7:53 pm	

♀♀♀ Freitag

♍

Friday
7

☽□♄	4:03 am	
☽⚹♃	8:23 am	
☽□♇	10:45 am	
♀⚹♆	10:59 am	
☉□☽	11:52 am	
☽□☿	2:57 pm	v/c
♇ApG	3:06 pm	

Waning Half Moon in ♍ Virgo 11:52 am PST

All aspects in Pacific Standard Time; add 3 hours for EST; add 8 hours for GMT

Greetings from Wales

Each morning i emerge again, taking note of how my shadow drapes itself across the chair, along the ground and softly dances beside me—its gliding steps tucked surely, firmly against my own clumsy one.

Shadows are my Teachers. Suggesting, pointing, they whisper, never attempting to explain. Shadows are manifestations of possibility seeded; imagination's evidence—growing and stretching and shrinking as they travel over the surfaces of form. In their hesitancy to describe, their unwillingness to concretize, they are perhaps a more accurate indication of things in existence then the objects themselves . . .

excerpt © sproutingcrow 1999

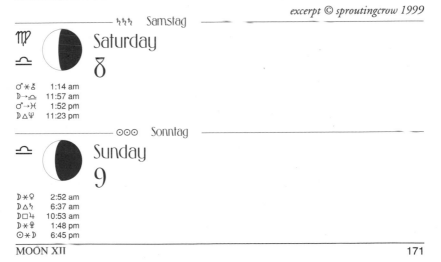

———————— ♄♄♄ Samstag ————————
♍ ☍ Saturday
8

♂✶⚷	1:14 am
☽→♎	11:57 am
♂→♓	1:52 pm
☽△♆	11:23 pm

———————— ☉☉☉ Sonntag ————————
♎ Sunday
9

☽✶♀	2:52 am
☽△♄	6:37 am
☽□♃	10:53 am
☽✶♀	1:48 pm
☉✶☽	6:45 pm

Spell for Earth Healing

This working is designed for those who wish to enhance their connection with Mother Earth in ways both spiritual and practical. You'll need:

Clarity of intention

Moon: New to Full

Day: Sunday (growth, healing) or other day as appropriate

Candle: Brown (stability, home), Blue (if water is involved) or White (cleansing, protection)

Awl (or pointy tool)

Oil: One with a Sun (or other appropriate) vibration (or the goods to make some)

Rather than concentrating on what's wrong, this working focuses on building practical energy around positive change. Lay out your supplies so you are facing the East, place of dawn and new beginnings. Sit calmly, envisioning what a healed world will look like. When that image is clear, carve a few key words or phrases into your candle: *Clean Water, Thriving Songbirds* or *Peace,* for example. Anoint the candle with oil, still holding in mind your clear visions of positive change for Planet Earth. Light the candle.

As the candle burns, write out your intentions. **What will you do to help bring about positive change?** When you formulate a clear aim that you choose to express as a promise, "For the next three months, I will . . . " write out your intention. Breathe on it (Air), pass it quickly through the candle flame (Fire), sign it with a thumb print in a drop of wax (Water) and press the paper to the ground with both hands (Earth) to help it take root. Place this paper under the candle holder until the candle is burned away, then post it in your home and act in accord.

◻ *Renna Shesso 1998, excerpted from* Candle Magick II: Beginnings, Blessings & Healings, *Fire Brand/Ink 1998*

MOON XIII

Moon XIII: December 14–January 13

New Moon in ♐ Sagittarius: Dec. 14; Full Moon in ♋ Cancer: Dec.30; Sun in ♑ Capricorn: Dec. 21

Shekhinah
© *Sandra Stanton 1999*

ecember

kēmapa

☽☽☽ Pōʻakahi

♎ ♏

Monday 10

☽✶☿ 12:19 am
☽△♅ 12:43 am v/c
☿✶♅ 3:56 am
☽→♏ 3:09 pm
☽△♂ 5:52 pm
♀☍♄ 6:32 pm

♂♂♂ Pōʻalua

♏

Tuesday 11

☽□♆ 2:53 am
☽△♃ 2:05 pm
⚷→♑ 3:04 pm

☿☿☿ Pōʻakolu

♏ ♐

Wednesday 12

☽□♅ 4:48 am v/c
♀⚻♃ 1:49 pm
☽→♐ 7:30 pm

♃♃♃ Pōʻahā

♐

Thursday 13

☽□♂ 1:18 am
☽✶♆ 7:43 am
☉✶♅ 7:49 am
☽☍♄ 2:29 pm
☽☌♀ 10:02 pm
☽☌♇ 11:02 pm

♀♀♀ Pōʻalima

♐

Friday 14

♀☌♇ 8:51 am
☽✶♅ 10:37 am
☉☌☽ 12:47 pm

New Moon in ♐ Sagittarius 12:47 pm PST
Annular Solar Eclipse (3 min., 53 sec.) 12:53 pm PST
Eclipse visible from North and Central America and northern South America

All aspects in Pacific Standard Time; add 3 hours for EST; add 8 hours for GMT

August 11, 1999: Solar Eclipse in Europe
During the solar eclipse the little holes between the leaves of a tree serve as projectors of the sun. As a result of this natural process, underneath the tree all these little "moons" were visble on the sidewalk as solar eclipse magic.

© Marja de Vries 1999

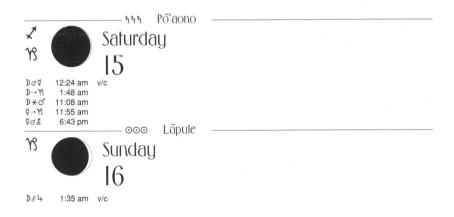

————————————————— ♄♄♄ Pōʻaono —————————————————

♐
♑

Saturday
15

☽♂☿	12:24 am	v/c
☽→♑	1:48 am	
☽⚹♂	11:08 am	
☿→♑	11:55 am	
☿♂♄	6:43 pm	

————————————————— ☉☉☉ Lāpule —————————————————

♑

Sunday
16

| ☽☍♃ | 1:35 am | v/c |

Prayer for Remembering
the Blackbird

And sometimes all I can do
is skate over my own surface
　　　—reflections frozen in ice

And sometimes my bones are runes
scattered in ocean's merciless tide
　　　—and I am deciphered by water

Three Ravens
© Lisa de St. Croix 1999

　　　　　Sometimes
I fly so fast through the midnight forest
that my hair writes fine silver prayer flags
in the snatching hawthorns
　　　and I am naked. So naked.

And there are times when all I see is grey
and I have no memory of pearl or oyster. Then
　　　only the mist will speak to me.

Sometimes there is no running in me
　　　there is no singing in me
　　　there is no loving in me
　　　and I am less than a leaf
　　　less than a leaf's winter lace
　　　so close am I to frost's roaring
　　　and sucking, frost's cold mouth opening.

And in these times, I must lie so.
Let Time enfold me　　into the journey.

　　　Only　　　　let me trust then
to Blackbird　　　　waking the Sun.
　　　　　　　　© Rose Flint 1999

© *Mara Friedman 1995*

Winter Solstice

At Winter Solstice we keep vigil as the night waxes to its peak, creating the shortest day and the longest night in the Northern Hemisphere. We steep in the darkness, assess our blessings and prepare to greet the light. Many cultures focus on celebrations involving candles and lights. Some of the traditions we associate with modern times are actually much older. For example stars and evergreens were both considered symbols for the immortality of the soul. One ancient plaque depicts the Goddess seated with her child at breast, a tree behind her and a star shining in the sky above. This season is an excellent time for tree magic. Traditionally, trees are honored with gifts of cakes and libations of cider poured on the ground around the tree. Evergreens in particular are seen as magical since they remain green when all else appears dead. We are reminded that spring will come and life will return. During the solstice season, we can bring holly or evergreen boughs into the home. Evergreens freshen the air in tightly sealed winter houses. Outside, hang seed heads for birds from tree branches. Trees provide us with so much they deserve all the magical support we can give them. This is a good season to offer prayers for the continued health of all trees worldwide and the ecosystems they support. © *Colette Gardiner 2000*

December

Decembro ——— ꭑꭑꭑ lundo ———

Monday
17

☽→♒ 10:43 am

——— ♂♂♂ mardo ———

Tuesday
18

☽☌♆ 12:23 am
☽△♄ 6:49 am
☽⚹♀ 5:17 pm

——— ☿☿☿ merkredo ———

Wednesday
19

☽⚹♀ 5:05 am
☽☌♅ 5:58 am
♀⚹♅ 1:41 pm
☉⚹☽ 6:41 pm v/c
☽→♓ 10:09 pm

——— ♃♃♃ ĵaŭdo ———

Thursday
20

☽⚹♅ 2:28 pm
☽☌♂ 3:58 pm
☽□♄ 6:30 pm
☽△♃ 10:35 pm

——— ♀♀♀ vendredo ———

Friday
21

Solstice

☽ApG 5:02 am
☽□♀ 5:46 am
☿⚹♂ 9:47 am
☉→♑ 11:21 am
☿⚼♄ 7:23 pm

Sun in Capricorn 11:21 am PST

All aspects in Pacific Standard Time; add 3 hours for EST; add 8 hours for GMT

Year at a Glance for ♑ CAPRICORN (Dec. 21–Jan. 20)

Early in the year your strong need for respect may be thwarted. Though you work hard, unforseen circumstances undermine your efforts. It's time to rely on and believe in your personal experience rather than depending upon external judgements. Develop efficient skills and routines behind the scenes as you prepare for a debut onto a more public stage within the next two years.

Why the difficulties and lack of recognition? Your values are changing towards the appreciation of inner, spiritual dimensions and gifts. Your efforts are most successful when devoted to projects with common benefit. Apprentice yourself to a cause or consider starting a co-op. By doing so, you attract support or opportunities from others in the second half of the year.

Many Capricorns have uncovered an artistic gift in the last 18 months. Do not let this go. This gift is a critical medium to help you reveal and celebrate your natural wisdom and deep sensuality. If you have ever threatened to get down to the business of turning your creative imagination into reality, the first half of this year is an ideal time.

For the past few years, responsibilities regarding love and/or children have been in center view. Your efforts to stabilize these situations should be paying off. Beloveds blossom. In the first half of the year you may need to be in the wings for them, cooling your heels. By June, you begin to step into the light yourself. By mid-year, you may decide to turn a love contact into a more formal tie. You've laid rich loving foundations from which both of you will grow.

© *Gretchen Lawlor 2000*

The Speaker of the Forest
© *Sylvia Huerta 1998*

Waxing Half Moon in ♈ Aries 12:56 pm PST

───── ♄♄♄ sabato ─────

♓
♈

Saturday
22

☽□♀	12:44 am	v/c
♂□♄	5:35 am	
☽→♈	10:45 am	
☉□☽	12:56 pm	
☉♂⚷	3:25 pm	
⚷☍♃	10:59 pm	

───── ☉☉☉ dimanĉo ─────

♈

Sunday
23

☽⚹♆	1:08 am
☽⚹♄	6:37 am
☽□♃	10:21 am
☽□♅	12:13 pm
☽△♀	6:15 pm

December
Desemba

♈
♉

Monday
24

☽✶♅	6:51 am
♂△♃	11:54 am
☽△♀	7:21 pm v/c
☽→♉	10:12 pm

♉

Tuesday
25

☉△☽	5:36 am
☽□♆	12:08 pm
☽✶♃	8:10 pm
☽✶♂	10:30 pm
♀→♑	11:25 pm

♉

Wednesday
26

☽△♉	6:51 am
☽□♅	4:22 pm v/c

♉
♊

Thursday
27

☽→♊	6:39 am
♀♂♅	7:46 am
☽△♆	7:52 pm
☽♂♄	11:54 pm

♊

Friday
28

☽□♂	8:36 am
☽♂♀	11:10 am
☽△♅	10:24 pm v/c

All aspects in Pacific Standard Time; add 3 hours for EST; add 8 hours for GMT

Sacred Visitors
© Schar Cbear Friedman 1998

♄♄♄ Jumamosi

♊
♋

Saturday
29

☽→♋ 11:40 am
⚷ApG 3:12 pm
☽☍♀ 7:58 pm

☉☉☉ Jumapili

♋

Sunday
30

☉☍☽ 2:40 am
☽♂♃ 6:09 am
♂□♀ 10:50 am
☽△♂ 3:01 pm
☉⊼♄ 4:31 pm
♃PrG 5:00 pm

Appulse Lunar Eclipse 2:30 am PST
Eclipse visible from the Americas, Asia and Australi
Full Moon in ♋ Cancer 2:40 am PS

MOON XIII

December
Dezember

☽☽☽ Montag

♋ ♌

Monday 31

☽☍☿ 5:43 am v/c
☽→♌ 2:09 pm
☉☍♃ 9:53 pm

♂♂♂ Dienstag

January 2002

♌

Tuesday 1

☽☍♆ 2:29 am
☽⚹♄ 5:29 am
☽△♀ 4:40 pm
☽PrG 11:09 pm

☿☿☿ Mittwoch

♌ ♍

Wednesday 2

☽☍♅ 3:16 am v/c
♀⚻♄ 7:17 am
☽→♍ 3:34 pm

♃♃♃ Donnerstag

♍

Thursday 3

♀☍♃ 4:22 am
☽□♄ 6:41 am
☽⚹♃ 8:34 am
☽△♀ 9:01 am
☉△☽ 1:36 pm
☿→♒ 1:38 pm
☽□♀ 6:15 pm
☽☍♂ 11:30 pm v/c

♀♀♀ Freitag

♍ ♎

Friday 4

☽→♎ 5:23 pm
☽△☿ 8:35 pm

Ritual of Release

This ritual was gifted to me in a dream. Willing or not, each shedding of old skin leaves us in greater freedom. The entire living universe does receive us; unconditionally, daily, with infinite love and compassion.

Pass smudge and feather, blessing ourselves with sweet smoke as we speak our names aloud, adding: *I come to the circle to lighten my load.* Ring a bell before passing the smudge pot widdershins.

Call into the center those whose strength and courage inspire us. Call the spirits of each direction, name their transformative aspects: In the East, wind scours and cleanses; in the South, fire catalyzes and purifies; in the West, water douses and renews; in the North, earth generates and consumes.

Hold the rim in a simple spoken chant: *The air receives you, the fire receives you, the water receives you, the earth receives you.* Repeat as we come to the center altar one at a time. Pour all we wish to release into a handful of salt, then sprinkle it into a large bowl of water—just so easily does the universe dissolve one thing into another. When all are complete, ring the bell three times for silence.

Carry the bowl of burdens to running water with the bell as the only accompaniment. Raise energy with a singing chant. At the crest, howl, yell and clap hands as salt water is poured into moving water and our burdens, like tears, disappear into the creative flow.

Dismiss with prayers for the freedom of all beings. Blessed be.

□ *Jessica Montgomery 1999*

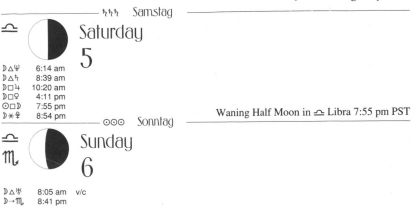

ħħħ Samstag

♎︎

Saturday
5

☽△♆ 6:14 am
☽△ħ 8:39 am
☽□♃ 10:20 am
☽□♀ 4:11 pm
☉□☽ 7:55 pm
☽⚹♀ 8:54 pm

Waning Half Moon in ♎︎ Libra 7:55 pm PST

☉☉☉ Sonntag

♎︎
♏︎

Sunday
6

☽△♅ 8:05 am v/c
☽→♏︎ 8:41 pm

January
'Ianuali

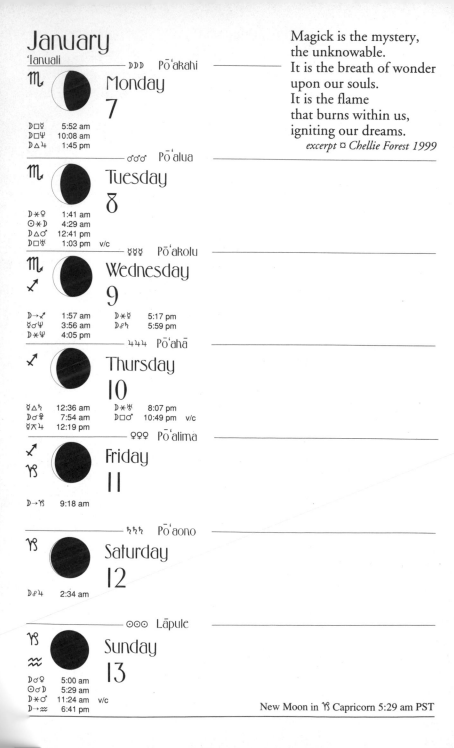

——— ☽☽☽ Pōʻakahi ———

♏ **Monday**
7

☽□☿ 5:52 am
☽□♆ 10:08 am
☽△♃ 1:45 pm

——— ♂♂♂ Pōʻalua ———

♏ **Tuesday**
8

☽⚹♀ 1:41 am
☉⚹☽ 4:29 am
☽△♂ 12:41 pm
☽□♅ 1:03 pm v/c

——— ☿☿☿ Pōʻakolu ———

♏
♐ **Wednesday**
9

☽→♐ 1:57 am   ☽⚹☿ 5:17 pm
☿☌♆ 3:56 am   ☽☍♄ 5:59 pm
☽⚹♆ 4:05 pm

——— ♃♃♃ Pōʻahā ———

♐ **Thursday**
10

☿△♄ 12:36 am   ☽⚹♅ 8:07 pm
☽☌♀ 7:54 am   ☽□♂ 10:49 pm v/c
☿⚼♃ 12:19 pm

——— ♀♀♀ Pōʻalima ———

♐
♑ **Friday**
11

☽→♑ 9:18 am

——— ♄♄♄ Pōʻaono ———

♑ **Saturday**
12

☽☍♃ 2:34 am

——— ☉☉☉ Lāpule ———

♑
♒ **Sunday**
13

☽☌♀ 5:00 am
☉☌☽ 5:29 am
☽⚹♂ 11:24 am v/c
☽→♒ 6:41 pm

Magick is the mystery,
the unknowable.
It is the breath of wonder
upon our souls.
It is the flame
that burns within us,
igniting our dreams.

excerpt ¤ Chellie Forest 1999

New Moon in ♑ Capricorn 5:29 am PST

Dewi II

¤ *Gyps Curmi 19*

HOW TO BECOME A WE'MOON CONTRIBUTOR

We'Moon is an exploration of a world created in Her image. We welcome artwork by, for and about womyn. Our focus on womyn is an affirmation of the range and richness of a world where womyn are whole unto themselves. Many earth-based cultures traditionally have womyn-only spaces and times, which, through deepening the female experience, are seen to enhance womyn's contributions to the whole of society. **We'Moon** invites all womyn who love and honor womyn to join us in this spirit, and we offer what we create from such a space for the benefit of all beings.

Currently creating WE'MOON '02: PRIESTESSING THE PLANET
Now accepting contributions for WE'MOON '03

If you are interested in being a **We'Moon** contributor contact us—send a business-sized SASE (self-addressed stamped #10 envelope) or an SAE and 2 international postal coupons. By July 2001, we will send you a Call for Contributions (which includes information about the theme and how to submit your art and writing) and a Release Form to return with your work. *Please do not send in any work without first receiving a Call for Contributions...thanks.*

HOW TO ORDER *WE'MOON* AND MOTHER TONGUE INK PRODUCTS

Call or write to request our catalog or order direct—we take credit cards.
- **We'Moon '01** (w/ lay-flat binding: $14.95 or w/ spiral binding: $15.95)
- **We'Moon '01 Unbound** (w/ no binding for customized use: $14.95)
- **We'Moon on the Wall '01** (12" x 12", color wall calendar, 32pp: $12.95)
Any edition $3.00 ea. surface s/h. Free s/h for orders of 3+ to same address.
- **Lunar Power Packet '99** and **Lunar Power Packet '00**: $10 ea. Each Lunar Power Packet (LPP) includes a mix of 13 beautiful, full-color, 4"x 6" postcards of 8 original art pieces that have been published in either We'Moon '99 or We'Moon '00 and a LUNAR POWER bumpersticker, woman-made, black on white, 2" x 10". LPP s/h : $1.50 ea.
- New! **LPP '01** includes 13 greeting cards w/ envelopes (instead of postcards): $13
- Inquire about additional charges for 1st class or air mail. When ordering by mail please include the following: a check or money order in U.S. funds made out to Mother Tongue Ink *and* a note listing your name, address, phone number, and product and quantity ordered.

Mother Tongue Ink write: P.O. Box 1395-A Estacada, OR 97023 or call: 503-630-7848 or toll free 877-693-6666 (877-0 WE-MOON) or email: wemoon@teleport.com

DEDICATION: WOMEN'S MAGIC OVERCOMES!

The fence around the US military occupation of Greenham Commons (UK) finally came down! . . . twenty years after the first women, mothers and children, marched from Wales across England to set up camp around the ten miles of fence surrounding the base. Since 1981, thousands of women from around the world came to protest, bear witness to and take action against the military maneuveurs of the Cruise Missile housed there. Greenham was home for many women who lived there days, months, even years at a time, in impossible conditions: outside in the rain, facing eviction daily, cooking meals over wood fires, sleeping in makeshift "benders." They monitored the activities inside the gates and notified a network of concerned citizens when the Cruise missile was about to come out. They were continually arrested and "zapped" with radioactive currents, all the while keeping their spirits up with creative acts of magical power, cutting holes in the fence and pulling off incredible stunts inside the base and outside the gates, keeping the pressure up and the spotlight on the illegal US military nuclear presence in Greenham Commons. Thank you, Greenham women, for your courageous ongoing magic; we celebrate your success . . . and invite contributions for next year's **We'Moon** by and about others "Priestessing the Planet."

ACKNOWELEDGEMENTS

We are growing and expanding and life is very full here at Mother Tongue Ink and We'Moon Land. I am grateful to both entities for their mutual support. I feel blessed to be part of a successful enterprise that is so well-loved and doing such good work.

Thanks to the immediate Mother Tongue Ink crew: Amy, Tarie and Musawa—it has been a great year of harmonious and productive flow. Gratitude to the Creatrix Crones: to Musawa for your perspective, patience and wisdom and to Bethroot for your passion, thoroughness and ongoing finesse. Melodie, Lori and Wyndy, thanks for your work during production. Appreciation to all womyn who diligently sat in weaving circles sharing responses to art and writing; and to weaving circle hosts: Full Circle Temple, Interstate Firehouse Cultural Center, Katya, Fly Away Home and We'Moon Land. Gratitude to Gisela and Rosemary who tirelessly spin the web for the German edition.   □ *Beth Freewomon, We'Moonager.*

Announcing: We'Moon Ancestors

In honor of we'moon crossing over, we wish to name and honor contibutors to **We'Moon** and we'moon culture who have gone between the worlds of life and death recently and welcome them to the ranks of our ancestors! Please send us notice of new we'moon ancestors from year to year.

Rebecca Livingston AKA Pinki/Tanith (Mar. 24, 1962–Jan. 5, 1996): Pinki, named for her bright pink hair, was one of the founders of Greenham Women's Peace Camp in 1981 where she lived and performed acts of guerilla theatre/magic for four years. From her punk rock roots in London during the seventies, she grew into a powerful feminist political-spiritual activist in the '80's and '90's. She went on to study Sumerian Goddess culture, and then, international law, being awarded a posthumous degree from the School of Oriental and African Studies. Long live the divine inspiration of Pinki Tanith!

Karen Anna (May 13, 1943–Feb. 3, 2000) was an artist, social lesbian activist, a mentor, a photographer and a caring woman of uncompromising honesty and a generous, mothering spirit who helped many women and gay youth. Karen died consciously and peacefully at her hand-built home on up-country Maui land, surrounded by her lover, friends, and flowers and plants that she grew. She died at the age of 56 after a 12-year struggle with cancer. Her art appears in **We'Moon '99**.

Cover Notes

Front cover art *Priestess 9* **by Ulla Anobile.** I created the Priestess mask series to honor the way the earthly and the sacred have always intertwined in woman's lives. In *Priestess 9*, two woman stir a magic cauldron in the moonlight, thus transforming their visions into nourishment through an awareness of the deeper meaning behind their ordinary, repetitive movement.

Back cover art *Corn Spirit* **by Diane Rigoli.** This painting evolved from my experience of growing corn and other plants in my own garden. May we all know a profound connection to the spirit of plants and defend their right to grow unadulterated by the manipu- ions of genetic engineering.

© Copyrights ¤ and Contacting Contributors

Copyrights of individual works in **We'Moon '01** belong to each contributor. Please honor the copyrights: © means <u>do not reproduce without the express permission of the artist or author</u>. Some we'moon prefer to free the copyright on their work. ¤ means <u>this work may be passed on among women who wish to reprint it "in the spirit of We'Moon", with credit given (to them and **We'Moon**) and a copy sent to the author/artist</u>. Contributors can be contacted directly when their addresses are given in the bylines, or by sending us a letter with an envelope with sufficient postage plus $1 handling fee for each contributor to be contacted.

Contributor Bylines and Index*

Beth Freewomon (Estacada, OR): Been underwater but surfacing. *Open*ing in '00 indeed! Ever since ♀♂♄ . . . intense *opportunities*—learning to *open* and accept. Receive the fruits, remember the keys, retain the blessings. Three's a charm. *Magic* in '01: the void and the One *come* together. Practice makes perfect. *Opie*.   pp. 9, 23

Bethroot Gwynn (Fly Away Home, OR) has been living on wimmin's land for 25 years, growing food, art, ritual. She loves working with the **We'Moon** art and writing! FFI about work exchange visits or spiritual gatherings on the land, send SASE to Fly Away Home, PO Box 593, Myrtle Creek, OR 97457.   pp. 27, 158

Boand (Los Angeles, CA) potter, painter, peace/spirit/deep country ♀, currently painting and meditating deeply in the desert.   p. 50

Candida Sea Blyth (South Devon, England) loves living on the edge of Dartmoor, South West Britain. She makes her own paint from soil, celebrating and honouring her love of the land and nature. She also shares this through teaching.   p. 91

Carol Wylie (Saskatchewan, Canada): I am an artist in the lovely prairies of Western Canada. Having reached my 40's, I am now discovering a wonderful sisterhood of womyn. We have such power in unity and such joy.   pp. 145, 163

Carole Spearin McCauley (Greenwich, CT) longtime laborer in the Women's movement in N.Y. area. Medical/science writer, editor and novelist; author of much short work and 12 books, including *Pregnancy After 35* (Dutton; Pocket Books) and the *Pauli Golden Amateur-Sleuth Mystery Series* (Women's Press, England).   p. 147

Carolyn Hillyer (Dartmoor, Devon, England) is an artist, composer, musician and writer. She paints large bold images of the pre-Celtic foremothers of the ancient moorland where she lives. She performs, exhibits and holds workshops. Contact her at Postbridge, Dartmoor, Devon PL20 6TJ U.K. or seventhwave.music@virgin.net.   p.59

Cassendre Xavier (Philadelphia, PA) is a Haitian-American multi-media artivist and events promoter. She has never had a cavity. Snail-mail: PO Box 30204, Philadelphia, PA 19103 (215) 574-2129. E-mail: cx321@hotmail.com. Website: http://cassendrexavier.homestead.com.   p. 70

Chellie Forest (Herts, England) is a witch, writer and goddess sculptress. Her goal is to learn and to teach and to travel ever onward. She works in dedication to her soul sisters and to the mother of us all.   pp. 120, 184

Chesca Potter (Oxford, England): I am an author and artist who loves the landscape and who is dedicated to seeking and honoring the Goddess within it.   pp. 115, 139, 151

Claire Johnson (Sitka, AK): I intend to be an Anchor for/of joy on Earth—I am ceremonial leader of Woman's Way Long Dance, caretaker of White Bear Sweat Lodge, artist (beadwork, hoop drums), healer.   pp. 122, 154

Colette Gardiner (Eugene, OR) is an herbalist and a plant lover. She has spent 20 years working with the green world and offers walks, classes, consults, lay and professional apprenticeships. She enjoys spending time in the garden with her ne assistants.   pp. 49, 67, 85, 103, 121, 143, 157, 177

Colleen Redman (Floyd, VA) is a member of "Woman of the 7th Veil," poetry and improv movement troupe. She is co-editor and regular contributor to *A Muse Letter* in Floyd. Still seeking the properties and influence of each alphabet letter sound. Please co-respond: 151 Ridge Haven, Floyd, VA 24091.   p. 95

Cynthia Ré Robbins (Lyons, Co): My art has been my magickal means of transformation and manifestation. I have painted my way through recovery and healing to find peace and strength, aiming for playfulness and joy! WWW.art4spirit.com.   pp. 44, 45, 117

Danielle Diamond (New York, NY) photographer, writer, yogini, seeking the light within and in all beings of all worlds, lives from the heart with the breath guiding her on the journey into the Divine Feminine radiating La Luna.   p. 69

Diana Tigerlily (Marion, IL): I am a witch and a writer, pleasantly humbled by life's intricate design and paying extra attention these days to spider webs.   p. 65

Diane Goldsmith (Nelson, BC, Canada) lover of dawn and twilight, chocolate and lattés. Writer of stories and poems. Keeper of journals.   p. 128

Diane Rigoli (Santa Fe, NM) weaves together the visible and invisible worlds with her art. She works as an artist, illustrator and graphic designer. Contact her at: PO Box 724, Santa Fe, NM 87504 or rigoliarts@earthlink.net.   back cover

Donna Goodwin (Santa Fe, NM): I am a native New Mexican artist. Currently, much of my art is inspired by a recent trip to Machu Picchu and the Sacred Valley of Peru. The radiance and magic I experienced there is beyond anything I can express.   p. 107

Donna Reid (Tahoe City, CA) owner of "A Day In Your Life" Photography in Tahoe City, CA. Photographer of over 10 years with a degree in Photojournalism. Web site: tahoeguide.com/go/hotpics. Specializes in black & white photography capturing life as it unfolds.   p. 153

Durga Bernhard (Red Hook, NY) is a painter, printmaker, illustrator for more than 15 children's books, teacher of West African dance/drum, and mother of two children. Her images of spirit and earth have long been inspired by ancient and tribal cultures from all over the world. 320 River Rd. Red Hook, NY 12571. p. 167

Eagle Hawk (Tesuque, NM) has been living on land in ♀'s community for fifteen years. I love to photograph wimmin children animals & the beautiful earth herself. The turtle photo was taken with an underwater camera.   p. 105

Emily K. Grieves (San Francisco, CA) is a painter, poet, and healer living in San Francisco. She received a BFA degree in art from the University of Montana. Currently, she has a home-based practice in energetic healing, shamanism, and intuitive acupressure.   p. 87

Felix (Dublin, Ireland) keeper-of-circles with limitless imagination, boundless enthusiasm, and a witch-streak the size of the milky way, come dance with me in the stars my sistahs . . . felixbadanimal@hotmail.com.   p. 149

Florencia Strazza (Miami Beach, FL): Being pregnant awakened my connection with the moon and women power—this needed to be translated to the visual language of form & color with the intention of expressing the music of feminine world.

Gayle Brandeis (Riverside, CA) is a writer and dancer living in Riverside, CA with her partner and their two children. Her book *FRUITFLESH: Luscious Lessons for Women Writers,* is forthcoming from Harper San Francisco.   p. 113

Germaine Knight (Bournemouth, England): I am on the path of self-healing, using the power of the written word to ease and express my journey. Learning to live by intuition, especially in my mothering. Mother Earth and my family continually inspire me.   p. 8

Gretchen Lawlor (Seattle/Whidbey Island, WA) is an astrologess and naturo-pathic practitioner who does astrological consults in person, by mail and by phone. (360) 221-4341; light@whidbey.com; PO Box 753, Langley, WA 98260. See my quarterly predictions on We'Moon website, also my work at http://glawlor.hypermart.net or starIQ.com.   pp. 12–13, Moons II–XIII

Gyps Curmi (The Channon, NSW, Australia): As someone who ticks most of the boxes of the socially inscribed object, I seek to find the places where we as womyn come together in our shared experiences and our connection to this land whilst acknowledging and validating difference.   pp. 3, 32, 185

Harriet L. Hunter (Woodstock, NY) is currently working on a new Tarot deck based on images she channels or dreams. The process is truly a magical journey which brings great joy.   p. 99

Heather Rowntree (Santa Fe, NM) a choice-centered astrologer who has been counseling with astrology for 20 years.   pp. 15–20

holly taya shere (philadelphia, pa): i live love laugh & learn each day & night, each waxing & waning & all the in betweens as fully as i can. look for me dancing yoga naked on a brasilian beach or just kickin' it, nowhere in particular, with family. p. 164

Ildiko Cziglenyi (Trinidad, CA) a young water colorist/dancer/coconut carver living among the redwoods in Humbolt Co. Through her art she shares the beauty & purity of life through her images of the Goddess within ourselves & in nature. For info. on cards & prints contact her: PO Box 1141, Trinidad, CA 95570, 1-888-235-4132.   pp. 92, 93

J. Davis Wilson (Eugene, OR): I am an eco-poet in various states of evolution. I am melding my reality to include loving pre-lingual people, ancient forests, urban gardens & daily practices of freedom. More poetry! j.davis@efn.org   p. 98

J. Lilith Taylor (Trinidad, CA): Living and loving in the Redwood Forest, learning to weave the Magick thru my art, transforming the earth, protecting and healing for Her purpose.   p. 63

Jacqueline Elizabeth Letalien (Arcata, CA) is a poet who lives in the North Coast wilderness among the redwoods with her partner Dora and the cats Keety and Lynna.   pp. 42, 57

Jamie Wright (Northport, NY) is a woman emerging, birthing herself into joy fter her battle with cancer. She is twenty-four years young, burning brightly with e light of gratitude & celebrating. She gives thanks for her family, her friends, the sweetness of love, ever present.   pp. 89, 138

Janine Canan (Sonoma, CA) is a psychiatrist who integrates psychology and spirituality with medicine. She is the author of many books of poetry. She lives with Devi, a Samoyed and practices bhakti yoga. She is working on a new collection called *Elegy in the Lotus*. *In the Palace of Creation: Selected Works by Janine Canan 1969–1999* is forthcoming.   p. 39

Jen Shifflet (Seattle, WA) is a painter, silversmith and muralist. She lives in the Pacific Northwest where she teaches art to children and seniors with mental & physical disabilities. She is co-founder of a rural group that creates community based mural projects.   p. 86

Jessica Montgomery (Portland, OR) is a ceremonialist and dabbler in a wide range of creative expressions, including dance, tile painting, fiber arts, writing, accessorizing and vegan cookie baking. She is author of the *Breitenbush Ritual Book*, and leads pilgrimages for womyn to sacred sites in England.   pp. 80, 116, 183

Jjenna Hupp Andrews (Mt. Pleasant, MI): I am an artist dancing a spiral path through this and other realities, enjoying the company of Archetypal energies; absorbing into my Life their love and energy and channeling what they have to teach through my art . . .   p. 140

Jocasta Crofts (Bristol, England): I teach Iyengar Yoga, have a ramshackle garden, love to dance and perform on air-borne ropes. I am very physical. I am awakening and healing my sexuality thanks to Tantra. My Mum died 2 years ago, I miss her.   p. 148

Kara L.C. Jones (Seattle, WA) has been published in *American Tanka* and *Poets West Literary Journal*; online at *New Works Review* and *Gaia*. CJ Ink published her book, *Che-wa*. She and NightHawk run Kota Press in memory of their son. www.kotapress.com   p. 111

Kara Mathiason (Enumclaw, WA): I am a Mother, supported by my loving partner. I ride the intense wave of life with a magical three year old boy child. Together we love, play, dance, paint, write and LIVE!   p. 53

Karen Vogel (Occidental, CA): I am a sculptor, scholar and co-creator of the *Motherpeace Tarot* deck. I also teach a unique blend of Motherpeace Tarot, with coyote sacred clown energy and the wisdom found through direct experience in nature. For a schedule of my work or to get a tarot reading contact me at: kvogel@svn.net or (707) 874-3309.   p. 27

Katheryn Trenshaw (Devon, England) is a painter, sculptor, workshop leader, mom & midwife of women remembering wholeness. She is American living in the land of Magical Stone Circles that inspire her. Her first book, *Breaking the Silence*, is due out in 2000. PO Box 3, Totnes, Devon, TQ9 5WJ, UK, merrymeet@lineone.net.   pp. 64, 94

Kim Antieau (Stevenson, WA): I create to connect. I have two novels published: *The Jigsaw Woman* and *The Gaia Websters*. I also have a comic strip, *Vic & Jane*, about a feminist and her dog. E-mail: kantieau@hotmail.com.   p. 46

Lauren Sydney Wales (Mason, OH) is a dreamer, poet, unschooler and novice potter. She sometimes believes herself a modern sibyl inspired by a divine source. Other times, she just isn't sure where all the words come from.   p. 66

Lilian de Mello (Kapaa, HI): Nowadays especially interested in b&w, infrared, image & emulsion transfers, photo collages to develope "Soul Healing Imagery" for myself and all women. Looking for emotions & the goddess aspect of women and nature. Multi-layered images searching for feelings and soul. E-mail: ldmphoto@gte.net.
pp. 57, 157

Linda Zurich (Ottsville, PA) is a writer, a lifelong seeker and delighted sojourner along the path upon Gaia. Loving life, in joy and gratitude, opening her heart to share peace.
p. 34

Lisa de St. Croix (Romah, NM): Painting in a ritualistic way, I weave together layers of my prophetic dreams, the many forms of the Goddess, and the magical place where I live between the Zuni and Navaho reservations in New Mexico. p. 176

Loes Raymakers (Amsterdam, The Netherlands) shamanic artist and teacher of shamanic techniques, painter, poet, drummer and toolmaker. Reiki master and traveller.
p. 79

Lori Nicolosi (Hainesport, NJ): mudslut-earthgirl, magic bowl maker, I cast pregnant bellies and make belly bowls. I sculpt with clay, grow organic gardens and weave lots of other stuff into this life. Let's share, write me, PO Box 763, Hainesport, NJ 08036.
p. 37

Lucy Kemp (Warwickshire, England): I am working hard, learning fast and sharing whatever I can. I would love to start an artists network, sending art through the post or the Web. Myzzola@yahoo.com.
p. 15

Lynn Dewart (San Diego, CA): I left the corporate world to follow my muse, artist/teacher now leading a simpler, mindful, meaning-full life of integrity. I am fascinated with detail and symbology, truth and depth of the inner world, play and integration and Tarot.
pp. 20, 55

Mara Friedman (Lorane, OR) lives and creates in the nourishing green womb of the Pacific Northwest. Her paintings honor the beautiful spirit of the Sacred Feminine. For a catalog of cards and prints, write her at PO Box 23, Lorane, OR 97451 or mara@newmoonvisions.com.
pp. 74, 129, 143, 177

Marguerite Bartley (Ballydehob, Co. Cork, Ireland): Writing, art, discovering new things and understandings are how I spend my days. I design and sell handcrafted cards. Family and friends are deep in my heart but my deepest contentment is in my living alone. It's a creative need.
pp. 61, 96, 97

Mari Susan Selby (Santa Fe, NM) is a poet of the Earth, a Dakini of strong laughter, and an astrologer of individual and planetary evolution. (505) 992-8072. p. 24

Marie Elena (Oakland, CA) is a teacher, writer, and ceremonialist of the Sacred Healing Arts. She is the owner and founder of Moonflower Creations, resources and services for balanced living. Marie Elena's personal commitment is to honor the beauty and sacredness of daily life.
p. 106

Marie Perret (Seryeac, France): I am an english born psychotherapist & artist living & working in S. W. France. Over a period of fourteen years I experienced a series of "inner journeys" through painting and meditation. I give slide show/ lks about healing art.
p. 51

Marja de Vries (Oldenzaal, The Netherlands): As a fabric artist I make wall-hangings; using meditation I see the images depicting the essence of someone's personal symbols. For more information, write or call me: Lindestraat 30, 7572 TV Oldenzaal, The Netherlands; phone (0451) 53393. pp. 82, 175

Marsea Frace (Williams, OR) celebrates life by living everywhere. Currently creekside in S. Oregon. Performing political theatre with "Sticks-n-Stones" about issues such as Big Mtn. Often seen dancing with a camera in her hand. E-mail: Marsea@hotbot.com. p. 111

May Trillium (Portland, OR): I love to have my armpits nibbled and to eat candy. I adore having my arms scratched. I'm still a vegetarian and an artist. pp. 2, 18, 54

Megaera (Daylesford, Victoria, Australia): I live with my wonderdog Maeve in a big, beautiful garden. I make woman-loving art, tutor young girls, and feel very blessed. Cards and prints available from PO Box 263, Daylesford, Victoria, 3460 Australia. pp. 137, 156

Meghan Lewis (Ann Arbor, MI) Ph.D. is an ecofeminist researcher of contemporary Goddess iconography, an art therapist and mid-wife in training. Her paintings are as maps in her explorations along the magical path. Meghasus@aol.com PO Box 8227, Ann Arbor, MI 48107. p. 62

Melissa Harris (West Hurley, NY): I'm an artist & originator of Creatrix-A Company celebrating women's love of life, love, beauty, nature & magic. Contact me at (914) 340-9632 or Creatrix@ulster.net or see my web site www.melissaharris.com/creatrix. pp. 81, 85

Melissa McConnell (Bellingham, WA): Born on Winter Solstice eighteen years ago, I am inspired and blessed by: music, healing, Burke, my voice, Great Goddess, rhythm, breath, words, art, friendship, family, organic food, hugs, earth, sunsets, moon, dance, chi kung, madrona trees, and sacred love. p. 112

Michelle Waters (Santa Cruz, CA): Painter, eco-activist, lover of all creatures. My art is inspired by my love for the Earth, and my prayer for her healing. I welcome connection and collaboration! Flyingcat@hotbot.com or www.sasquatch.com/~michelle. p. 76

Miranda (London, England): I am a pre-Saturn return Leo Singer/songwriter and choreographer. Dancing the many rhythms of life. p. 40

Monica Sjöö (Bristol, Avon, England) is a Swedish-born artist and writer. She is co-author of *The Great Cosmic Mother* and sole author of *New Age and Armageddon*. Based in Britain for many years, she is involved in Goddess Earth Mysteries and is rediscovering ancient Sweden. pp. 49, 161

Musawa (NM/OR): As we go to press, I am a refugee from the wildfire that is burning Los Alamos (twenty miles from ARF wimmin's land); seeking healing sanctuary where it is safe to breathe, especially for my dog, Solstice, who has a tumor pressing on her lungs. Living in the moment. pp. 6, 9, 21, 23, 26, 27

Nancy Bennett (Victoria, BC, Canada) practising witch, member of 13th hou Founder of The H.A.G.S (Honorable Aging Goddess Society) Lover of Rich Mother of Natasha and Amanda and freelance writer of many subjects.

Nell Stone Wagenaar (Portland, OR) is a recent transport from Michigan settling into a new life in Oregon with her partner and 5-year-old daughter. She is working at Portland's Neighborhood Mediation Center but is looking for a writing/editing job. p. 26

Nicole DiPierre (Flagstaff, AZ): Art is a foundation for me—teaching me to see things in a different light from which I've been taught. When my mind is quiet— I feel in touch with the things that really matter. p. 113

Norma Rosen (Longbeach, CA) mother, artist, sales rep, designer, writer, teacher, healer, ex-wife of a chief priestess and traditional doctor from Benin City, Nigeria. p. 127

Pam Fox (Georgetown, TX): I'm a dyke who lives with my critter pals in the woods of Central Texas. pp. 37, 47

Peggy Soup (Kansas City, MO): Learning, loving & living from rainbows through Global Peace into Zion. Free the word. Peace. p. 103

Penny Sisto (Floyds Knobs, IN) is an internationally known fabric artist. Her work can be seen at Thirteen Moons Gallery, Santa Fe. Sisto was born in the outer Island off the north coast of Scotland. Spent 3 1/2 yrs with the Masai Tribe. Raised 7 kids. p. 77

Phyllis J. Hanniver (Sacramento, CA): I am a poet on a spiritual journey learning about Spirit of love. I love cats (especially Poquita, Jack & Spike), my partner Gwendelynn, nature & playing with Legos! I'm a writer, artist & photographer. p. 83

Rebecca Rajswasser (Brooklyn, NY): In the midst of late 20's angst, I have declared a life change. I live in a city of stories. Look for my work at www.justwritten.com. Please sing, dance, shout your stories to the trees and to the heavens. pp. 109, 125

Renna Shesso (Denver, CO) is the author of *Candle Magic: Simple Workings, Bright Invitings* and *Rune Reader*, creates art, ritual & fire brand/ink candles, teaches wicca & shamanic journeying. Good friends, her sister and various mountain hot springs help fuel her spirits. pp. 142, 172

Rhea Giffin (Coeur d'Alene, ID): My art fills me with passion for exploring the symbolic and metaphoric potential of bowls. Something so primitive and familiar, their stories are endless. Reach me at Storybowl Land, POB 1151, Coeur d'Alene, ID 83816, USA. p. 165

Rose Flint (Bath, England) is a poet, artist and art therapist. She is a Priestess of Avalon and the resident poet at the Goddess Conference held in Glastonbury every Lammas. pp. 102, 133, 176

Roxi (Enderby, B.C., Canada) lives a quiet life in the "Smoky Mountains" of B.C., Canada with her sweet man Tony and son Bram. She loves small town life, good friends, living in nature, music and "walking with love." A year in Grenada painting was a gift from her late son Shea. p. 61

Sabrina Vourvoulias (Earlville, NY) was born in Thailand, grew up in Guatemala, d now resides in Hamilton, New York. Her writing and/or illustrations have eared in *SageWoman, Tides, Graham House Review, The Sarah Lawrence w*, and local newspapers. p. 121

Sandra Pastorius (Santa Cruz, CA): I published the *Lunar Muse-a Monthly Moon Guide* for ten years. I continue to offer spiritual guidance as an astrologer, ceremonialist and mentor. POB 2344, Santa Cruz, CA 95063.   p. 24

Sandra Stanton (Farmington, ME) is a painter whose work is dedicated to the many faces of the goddess, Her creatures & our Beautiful Mother Earth. Her work can be seen at www.goddessmyths.com. Prints available at 180 Main Street, Suite 336, Farmington, ME 04938.   pp. 35, 67, 173

Sarah L. Rush M.S.(Ojai, CA) connects with nature daily and paints, draws, and teaches what she learns. Contact Rush's Arts, PMB 252, 323 E. Matilija St. #110, Ojai, CA 93023 for catalog, Language of Trees workshop schedule & additional information.   p. 110

Sara-Lou Klein (Denver, CO) is an artist, feminist, witch striving for serenity in a violent world. With the help of her mate; Russell, her cat; Floey, Friends, Family, and especially the Goddess; she attempts to Just BEe and Get Through.   p. 89

Schar Cbear Freeman (Kaua'i, HI) is an artist and poet of American Native and Spanish heritages, living, writing and painting her dreams on the Garden Island Kaua'i, Hawai'i. Website: www.womenfolk.com/poetsite/cbear.   pp. 123, 181

Selina Di Giralmo (Chilterns, Bucks, England) is an artist and a poet. Priestess to the dark goddess, mother of sons, witch. Reclaiming endarkenment and celebrating womb-scape in the Chiltern Hills with rich mud, wise blood and wild ritual. Contact selinawitch@talk21.com.   pp. 131, 145

Selka D. Kind (ON, Canada)   p. 84

Sequoia (Grants Pass, OR): Nature loving emerging gentle soul.   pp. 43, 159

Shelley Stefan (Portland, OR): Art is fresh air to my spirit and warmth to my heart. With a life full of passion and beautiful challenges, I feel so blessed to have become a Sensitive One to the pulse of creativity . . . Thank You Goddess. Thank You Spirits.   p. 135

Shoshana Rothaizer (Flushing, NY): New Yorker who connects with Mother Nature's rhythms in both city and country. Her photos were published in *The Lesbian Polyamory Reader*, including the cover. For a brochure of her postcards, send a SASE to: 147-44 69th Rd., Flushing, NY 11367.   p. 171

sproutingcrow AKA Jessica Bryl (Crozet, VA): Currently i tuck myself in Virginia hills & bend my back toward the sun, turning brown with sweat & earth, tending so much bounty that grows here. i change, i turn, i watch, i witness.   p. 171

Starhawk (San Francisco, CA): peace activist and one of the foremost voices of eco-feminism. Her lectures and workshops draw on her 25 years of research and experience in the Goddess movement. She is the author of many books, has consulted on several films and is currently co-writing a workbook for Reclaiming Traditional Magic.   p. 101

Sudie Rakusin (Hillsborough, NC) is an artist and an ecofeminist. Her love and concern for the Earth and Her creatures influences all her choices and permeate her work. She lives in the woods with her dog companion and her ever expanding gardens.   p

Sue Richards (Edgbaston, England): I look for the extraordinary in the ordinary. My Celtic roots draw me to the sea and mountains of West Wales, where I find my calm. Working in an organic garden feeds my body and spirit.   p. 169

Susan Gray (Reseda, CA) has taught feminist Wicca for 20 years. She now works mostly at writing, and at establishing a community in cyberspace for creative women who work alone, called Breakroom.net. Her book *The Woman's Book of Runes*, is available, with runes, from Barnes and Noble.   p. 161

Susan Herport Methvin (Anniston, AL)**:** I am a poet and teacher working toward complete restoration of the feminine and learning to respect and love my own body. I am a breast cancer and marrow transplant survivor, mother, grandmother and partner.   p. 92

Susan Levitt (San Francisco, CA) is an astrologer, tarot reader, and feng shui consultant in the Bay Area. She is the author of *Taoist Feng Shui* and *Taoist Astrology* and maintains a web site at www.taofengshui.com.   pp. 22, 23, 25

Suzy Coffee (Manton, CA): Gardener, writer and Registered Nurse, learning and practicing alternative Earth centered healing. Poetry is "good medicine" for the angst of feminist and political protest, which I write on a local level.   p. 51

Sylvia M. Huerta (Boulder, CO): I am an artist who speaks through drawing, painting, photography and music. I am a survivor. I dance to house music in the mountains until the sun sets. lamariplsa62@hotmail.com.   p. 179

Tamara Thiebaux (Wolfville, NS, Canada)   p. 71

Tami Kent (Portland, OR) is a poet with a desire to express the depth of wisdom & sensuality present in women and mother earth.   p. 162

Tarmes (Kea'au, Hawai'I): I'm lucky to live on the big Island of Hawai'i, where I print, paint, tattoo and play with the turtles. Catalog of prints, cards, etc. available at PO Box 2062, Kea'ua, Hawai'i 96749.   p. 25

Trace Ashleigh (Santa Cruz, CA) is a published poet, exhibited photographer, art model, performance artist, professional musician, drumming instructor ,production company director—a true renaissance woman living her creative inspiration.   p. 31

Tracy Litterick (S. Yorks, England): I am inspired by wild women, witches, the magic of homeopathy and the beautiful moors surrounding my city. I'm exploring the inner world on my healing journey through my images of animal spirit, dreams, and ancient women's cultures.   pp. 6, 155

Ulla Anobile (Los Angeles, CA) her papier mache masks and sculpture have been exhibited nationally in museums and galleries. Born In Finland, she now lives in Los Angeles, CA.   front cover

Veronica M. Murphy (Toledo, OH): Performing poet, lawyer and teacher with 56 years of experience in dancing on my limitations and an ever increasing capacity for joy.   p. 119

Vicki Noble (Freedom, CA) feminist healer and teacher, author of *Motherpeace: A Way to the Goddess* and *Shakti Woman: Feeling Our Fire, Healing Our World* has recently completed *The Double Goddess: Women Sharing Power*. She directs the Motherpeace Institute in Freedom, California.   p. 27

ASTEROIDS

The asteroids, a belt of planetary bodies orbiting in the solar system mostly between Mars and Jupiter, were discovered in the early 1800's. Since the sighting of new planets in the solar system corresponds to the activation of new centers of consciousness in the human psyche, the discovery of these planetary bodies, carrying the names of hundreds of goddesses, points to an awakening of a feminine-defined principle.

Because traditional astrology uses a ten-planet system (and only two of these symbols, the Moon and Venus, represent feminine archetypes), astrology by default has not had a set of symbols by which to describe other avenues of feminine expression. It has tried to fit all other women's experiences into masculine-defined archetypes.

The asteroids signify new archetypal symbols in the astrological language and they specifically address the current psychological and social issues that are arising in today's world due to the activation of the feminine principle. Synchronistic with the publication of the asteroid goddess ephemeris, the forefront of the women's movement emerged into society. At this time new aspects of feminine expression began to enter into human consciousness. Women became imbued with the possibilities of feminine creativity and intelligence that expanded and transcended the traditional roles of wife and mother (Venus and the Moon). This also marked a time of the rediscovery of women's ancient history, the growth of women's culture and sexuality independent of men, and the rebirth of the Goddess in women's spirituality.

On the following page the mandala of asteriod goddesses can help us to better understand the meaning of Ceres, Pallas, Juno and Vesta (the first four asteroids discovered). The large circle in the mandala represents the Moon, which is the foundation of the feminine principle and contains potential expressions of the feminine nature. Behind the Moon resides the Sun. The union of these two energies gives rise to what mystics define as "oneness." In the center of the mandala resides Venus, the core essence of the feminine nature in her activated form, who embodies the well-spring of feminine creative, magnetic, sexual, reproductive vital life force. Venus is surrounded by Ceres, Pallas, Vesta and Juno who represent the primary relationships of a woman's life, that of mother, daughter, sister and partner, respectively. Each asteroid utilizes the creative sexual energy c Venus at the center of the circle in her own unique way, as s expresses various functions and activities of the feminine principle. They are placed at the four cardinal directions of the mandala. In the horoscope this fourfold division is designated by the four angles: the Ascendent and Descendent, which define the line of the horizon, and the Midheaven and Nadir, which mark the meridian line.

Ceres, as the Great Mother and Goddess of agriculture, gives birth to the world of physical form; she births children and provides food for their survival. As the Nadir (IC) she represents a point of foundation, roots, and family.

Pallas Athene, as the daughter and the Goddess of Wisdom, generates mental and artistic creations from her mind. At the Midheaven (MC), where visible and socially useful accomplishments are realized, she represents the principle of creative intelligence.

Vesta, as the Sister, is the Temple Priestess and is a virgin in the original sense of being whole and complete in oneself. As the Ascendant (ASC.), Vesta corresponds to the Self. She signifies the principle of spiritual focus and devotion to following one's calling.

Juno, as the Goddess of Marriage, fosters and sustains union with a partner. Placed at the Descendant (DESC.), the point of one-to-one relationships, Juno symbolizes the principle of relatedness and commitment to the other.

© *Demetra George 1996 excerpted and reprinted from* Asteroid Goddesses Natal Report *(a software program published by Astrolabe)*

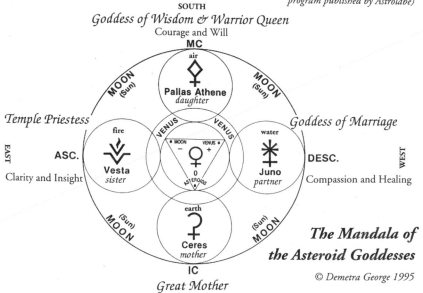

SOUTH
Goddess of Wisdom & Warrior Queen
Courage and Will

MC
air

Pallas Athene
daughter

MOON (Sun)   MOON (Sun)

Temple Priestess   *Goddess of Marriage*

fire   VENUS   VENUS   water

EAST   ASC.   MOON   VENUS   DESC.   WEST
Clarity and Insight   **Vesta** *sister*   0 ASTEROIDS   **Juno** *partner*   Compassion and Healing

earth

MOON (Sun)   (Sun) MOON

Ceres *mother*

The Mandala of the Asteroid Goddesses

IC
Great Mother
Silence and Strenth
NORTH

© *Demetra George 1995*

2001 ASTEROID EPHEMERIS

2001	Ceres 1	Pallas 2	Juno 3	Vesta 4
JAN 1	16♐27.6	22♏36.6	06♈07.8	26♒21.4
11	20 30.1	26 26.6	10 40.2	00♓57.9
21	24 26.7	00♐05.2	15 25.5	05 38.1
31	28 16.1	03 30.0	20 22.3	10 21.3
FEB 10	01♑56.7	06 38.2	25 29.0	15 06.3
20	05 27.1	09 26.7	00♉44.3	19 52.5
MAR 2	08 45.4	11 51.2	06 07.7	24 38.9
*12	11 49.4	13 47.4	11 37.6	29 24.9
22	14 37.0	15 10.2	17 13.5	04♈09.8
APR 1	17 05.3	15 54.2	22 54.5	08 53.2
11	19 11.3	15R54.4	28 39.8	13 34.2
21	20 51.9	15 07.6	04♊28.7	18 12.5
MAY 1	22 03.2	13 33.2	10 20.6	22 47.5
11	22 42.0	11 17.0	16 14.3	27 18.4
21	22R45.7	08 30.4	22 09.7	01♉44.8
31	22 12.7	05 31.4	28 05.8	06 05.9
JUN 10	21 04.4	02 40.7	04♋01.7	10 20.8
20	19 25.2	00 16.2	09 56.7	14 28.9
30	17 23.6	28♏30.8	15 50.0	18 28.9
JUL 10	15 12.5	27 30.2	21 40.7	22 19.6
20	13 04.8	27D14.7	27 28.0	25 59.5
30	11 14.0	27 41.5	03♌10.6	29 26.6
AUG 9	09 50.4	28 45.5	08 47.7	02♊38.8
19	08 59.9	00♐21.6	14 18.2	05 33.5
29	08D45.3	02 24.9	19 40.7	08 07.1
SEP 8	09 06.1	04 50.8	24 53.8	10 16.1
18	09 59.8	07 35.4	29 56.0	11 56.0
28	11 23.4	10 35.7	04♍45.4	13 01.7
OCT 8	13 13.2	13 48.7	09 19.8	13 28.8
18	15 25.9	17 12.2	13 36.6	13R13.3
28	18 05.5	20 44.4	17 33.3	12 33.3
NOV 7	20 47.4	24 22.8	21 25.7	10 31.8
17	23 50.7	28 06.6	24 10.1	08 18.6
27	27 06.1	01♐54.3	26 41.2	05 42.2
DEC 7	00♒31.4	05 44.4	28 33.9	03 07.4
17	04 05.1	09 36.1	00♎03.0	00 50.6
27	07 45.5	13 28.0	01 03.0	29♉06.9
JAN 6	11♒31.3	17♐19.0	01♎32.2	28♉05.0

2001	Sappho 80	Amor 1221	Pandora 55	Icarus 1566
JAN 1	05♈41.1	29♓R28.6	26♓15.2	07♑32.4
11	11 35.2	27 35.0	00♈06.6	12 59.9
21	17 33.6	26 52.0	04 00.2	18 06.2
31	23 35.3	27D18.8	08 11.5	22 55.3
FEB 10	29 38.5	28 49.2	12 32.2	27 29.5
20	05♉42.7	01♈15.2	17 00.4	01♒50.6
MAR 2	11 46.6	04 30.4	21 34.6	05 59.7
12	17 49.4	08 28.6	26 13.4	09 57.0
22	23 50.4	13 04.8	00♉55.5	13 42.8
APR 1	29 49.1	18 16.1	05 40.1	17 16.5
11	05♊44.8	23 59.7	10 26.0	20 37.0
21	11 37.1	00♉14.1	15 12.6	23 43.0
MAY 1	17 25.7	06 58.3	19 59.3	26 32.0
11	23 09.9	14 11.6	24 45.1	29 00.6
21	28 49.7	21 53.5	29 29.6	01♓04.4
31	04♋24.7	00♌03.9	04♊12.2	02 36.3
JUN 10	09 54.4	08 41.6	08 52.3	03 09.8
20	15 18.8	17 45.8	13 29.3	03R22.0
30	20 37.5	27 14.6	18 02.6	02 01.8
JUL 10	25 49.9	07♍04.8	22 31.5	28♒59.9
20	00♌55.9	17 12.3	26 55.4	23 44.2
30	05 54.8	27 31.7	01♋13.3	15 50.6
AUG 9	10 45.8	07♎55.5	05 24.2	05 35.3
19	15 28.6	18 16.2	09 27.1	24♑21.3
29	20 01.8	28 26.2	13 20.5	14 10.4
SEP 8	24 24.4	08♏31.9	17 02.9	06 20.4
18	28 35.1	17 48.3	20 32.4	00 59.8
28	02♍31.9	26 52.4	23 46.5	27♐40.2
OCT 8	06 12.6	05♐29.5	26 42.5	25 41.7
18	09 06.9	13 40.0	29 17.4	24 23.6
28	12 35.0	21 25.4	01♌27.0	22 56.1
NOV 7	15 17.7	28 47.3	03 07.5	19 51.8
17	17 13.2	05♑48.0	04 14.4	11 57.1
27	18 41.6	12 29.7	04 43.4	27♏16.1
DEC 7	19 29.3	18 54.2	04R31.8	04♐D46.9
17	19R31.5	25 03.5	03 38.6	16♐20.3
27	18 45.5	00♒59.2	02 07.0	25 34.2
JAN 6	17♍12.8	06♒42.2	00♌05.5	03♑14.9

2001	Psyche 16	Eros 433	Lilith 1181	Toro 1685
JAN 1	09♌39.1	01♓35.4	26♈39.0	20♐05.1
11	08 39.3	07 45.1	25♈36.1	25 50.2
21	08D18.9	14 08.3	23 51.9	01♑43.8
31	08 38.3	20 45.1	21 38.0	07 47.3
FEB 10	09 34.6	27 35.0	19 11.6	14 02.5
20	11 23.4	04♈38.0	16 52.0	20 32.0
MAR 2	13 00.3	11 54.3	14 56.2	27 18.5
12	15 20.9	19 23.7	13 36.4	04♒25.7
22	18 01.2	27 06.0	12 57.9	11 58.0
APR 1	20 57.7	05♉01.9	13D01.3	20 00.4
11	24 07.3	13 09.0	12 43.8	28 38.3
21	27 27.7	21 28.7	15 00.6	07♓58.2
MAY 1	00♍56.8	29 59.8	16 47.7	18 05.0
11	04 32.2	08♊41.1	18 58.3	29 01.9
21	08 13.0	17 31.5	21 30.1	10♈48.8
31	11 59.3	26 29.8	24 19.0	23 19.9
JUN 10	15 47.6	05♋34.1	27 21.7	06♉21.7
20	19 38.0	14 42.7	00♉35.7	19 40.4
30	23 29.7	23 53.8	03 59.2	02♊58.7
JUL 10	27 21.7	03♌05.3	07 30.1	16 01.9
20	01♎13.5	12 15.5	11 07.0	28 39.1
30	05 04.4	21 22.4	14 48.8	10♋41.8
AUG 9	08 53.4	00♍24.0	18 34.3	22 04.5
19	12 40.1	09 19.1	22 22.6	02♌45.2
29	16 23.4	18 06.0	26 12.9	12 44.0
SEP 8	20 02.6	26 43.5	00♊04.3	22 03.0
18	23 36.6	05♎10.9	03 56.2	00♍45.8
28	27 04.2	13 27.5	07 47.8	08 55.6
OCT 8	00♏24.1	21 32.6	11 38.2	16 35.6
18	03 34.9	29 26.4	15 26.7	23 49.1
28	06 34.5	07♏08.8	19 12.5	00♎38.4
NOV 7	09 21.0	14 39.9	22 54.5	07 05.6
17	11 51.9	22 00.1	26 31.8	13 12.4
27	14 04.3	29 09.6	00♋03.0	18 59.6
DEC 7	15 55.1	06♐08.9	03 26.8	24 27.6
17	17 21.0	12 58.4	06 41.7	29 49.1
27	18 18.2	19 38.4	09 45.8	04♏25.8
JAN 6	18♏43.9	26♐09.2	12♋37.2	08♏53.9

2001	Diana 78	Hidalgo 944	Urania 30	Chiron 2060
JAN 1	12♒22.6	06♈48.9	00♏44.0	22♐32.1
11	15 49.4	08 29.0	03 07.2	23 37.9
21	19 21.2	10 07.5	06 03.2	24 40.2
31	22 56.8	11 43.0	09 26.2	25 37.7
FEB 10	26 34.9	13 14.0	13 11.1	26 29.6
20	00♓14.5	14 38.8	17 13.5	27 14.8
MAR 2	03 54.9	15 56.0	21 30.2	27 52.5
12	07 34.7	17 03.7	25 58.0	28 21.8
22	11 13.4	18 00.5	00♐34.5	28 42.2
APR 1	14 49.9	18 44.6	05 17.9	28 53.3
11	18 23.1	19 14.5	10 06.8	28♐R55.5
21	21 52.1	19 28.8	14 50.0	28 47.4
MAY 1	25 15.8	19R26.3	19 54.4	28 31.0
11	28 32.9	19 06.3	24 51.6	28 06.8
21	01♈42.0	18 28.8	29 49.9	27 35.9
31	04 41.5	17 34.5	04♑48.7	26 59.9
JUN 10	07 29.3	16 25.4	09 47.4	26 20.6
20	10 03.5	15 04.2	14 45.5	25 40.0
30	12 21.0	13 34.9	19 42.6	25 00.1
JUL 10	14 19.0	12 02.3	24 38.3	24 23.0
20	15 54.0	10 31.4	29 32.2	23 50.5
30	17 01.7	09 07.3	04♒24.0	23 24.0
AUG 9	17 38.5	07 54.2	09 13.1	23 04.9
19	17R40.3	06 55.6	13 59.3	22 54.0
29	17 04.5	06 14.0	18 42.0	22♐D51.8
SEP 8	15 51.1	05 50.5	23 21.2	23 08.5
18	14 03.9	05D45.4	27 54.4	23 14.3
28	11 51.1	05 58.5	02♓17.2	23 38.5
OCT 8	09 26.6	06 28.8	06 44.7	24 10.8
18	07 05.7	07 14.9	10 59.3	24 50.4
28	05 05.1	08 15.5	15 04.9	25 06.6
NOV 7	03 32.9	09 28.8	19 00.1	26 28.4
17	02 40.0	10 53.3	22 43.0	27 25.0
27	02D44.0	12 27.2	26 11.2	28 25.2
DEC 7	03 20.9	14 09.0	29 22.2	29 28.6
17	04 36.7	15 57.1	02♈12.6	00♑32.6
27	06 27.5	17 49.9	04 38.6	01 37.5
JAN 6	08♈48.7	19♈45.9	06♈36.0	02♑41.8

Giving the positions of asteroids every
ten days in LONGITUDE at 00:00 GMT

Noon Planetary Ephemeris: GMT* — January 2001

Day	Sid.Time	☉	0 hr ☽	Noon ☽	True ☊	☿	♀	♂	♃	♄	♅	♆	♇
1 M	18 44 49	11♑ 8 32	18♓41 48	24♓46 1	15♋31.0	15♑ 4.9	27♒31.1	5♏13.8	2♊ 9.0	24♉34.2	18♒40.5	5♒20.7	13♐47.1
2 Tu	18 48 45	12 9 42	0♈53 50	7♈ 5 50	15R31.2	16 42.6	28 37.1	5 48.8	2R 4.4	24R31.7	18 43.4	5 22.8	13 49.2
3 W	18 52 42	13 10 51	13 22 34	19 44 32	15 31.2	18 20.5	29 42.9	6 23.8	1 59.9	24 29.3	18 46.4	5 25.0	13 51.3
4 Th	18 56 38	14 12 0	26 12 15	2♉46 8	15 31.1	19 58.8	0♓48.5	6 58.7	1 55.6	24 27.0	18 49.4	5 27.1	13 53.4
5 F	19 0 35	15 13 9	9♉26 33	16 13 45	15D31.0	21 37.4	1 53.7	7 33.6	1 51.6	24 24.8	18 52.4	5 29.3	13 55.4
6 Sa	19 4 32	16 14 17	23 7 52	0♊ 8 55	15 31.0	23 16.2	2 58.7	8 8.4	1 47.7	24 22.7	18 55.4	5 31.4	13 57.5
7 Su	19 8 28	17 15 25	7♊16 43	14 30 59	15 31.2	24 55.3	4 3.4	8 43.2	1 44.0	24 20.7	18 58.5	5 33.6	13 59.5
8 M	19 12 25	18 16 33	21 51 10	29 16 35	15 31.4	26 34.7	5 7.8	9 17.9	1 40.4	24 18.9	19 1.6	5 35.8	14 1.5
9 Tu	19 16 21	19 17 41	6♋46 24	14♋19 34	15R31.5	28 14.3	6 11.9	9 52.6	1 37.1	24 17.1	19 4.7	5 38.0	14 3.5
10 W	19 20 18	20 18 48	21 55 0	29 31 28	15 31.4	29 54.0	7 15.6	10 27.2	1 34.0	24 15.4	19 7.9	5 40.2	14 5.5
11 Th	19 24 14	21 19 55	7♌ 7 44	14♌42 35	15 31.0	1♒33.8	8 19.1	11 1.7	1 31.1	24 13.9	19 11.0	5 42.4	14 7.5
12 F	19 28 11	22 21 2	22 14 51	29 43 30	15 30.3	3 13.6	9 22.2	11 36.2	1 28.3	24 12.4	19 14.2	5 44.7	14 9.4
13 Sa	19 32 7	23 22 8	7♍ 7 35	14♍26 22	15 29.4	4 53.4	10 24.9	12 10.6	1 25.8	24 11.1	19 17.4	5 46.9	14 11.3
14 Su	19 36 4	24 23 14	21 39 16	28 45 53	15 28.5	6 33.0	11 27.3	12 44.9	1 23.5	24 9.8	19 20.6	5 49.1	14 13.2
15 M	19 40 1	25 24 21	5♎46 0	12♎39 32	15 27.8	8 12.2	12 29.3	13 19.2	1 21.3	24 8.7	19 23.9	5 51.4	14 15.1
16 Tu	19 43 57	26 25 27	19 26 33	26 7 16	15D27.5	9 51.0	13 30.9	13 53.4	1 19.4	24 7.7	19 27.1	5 53.6	14 17.0
17 W	19 47 54	27 26 32	2♏41 56	9♏10 56	15 27.8	11 29.1	14 32.1	14 27.6	1 17.7	24 6.8	19 30.4	5 55.9	14 18.8
18 Th	19 51 50	28 27 38	15 34 39	21 53 34	15 28.6	13 6.3	15 32.9	15 1.7	1 16.1	24 6.0	19 33.7	5 58.1	14 20.6
19 F	19 55 47	29 28 43	28 8 7	4♐18 46	15 29.8	14 42.3	16 33.3	15 35.7	1 14.8	24 5.3	19 37.0	6 0.4	14 22.4
20 Sa	19 59 43	0♒29 48	10♐26 1	16 30 16	15 31.2	16 16.9	17 33.3	16 9.7	1 13.7	24 4.7	19 40.3	6 2.7	14 24.2
21 Su	20 3 40	1 30 53	22 31 59	28 31 33	15 32.5	17 49.6	18 32.8	16 43.5	1 12.8	24 4.3	19 43.7	6 5.0	14 25.9
22 M	20 7 36	2 31 57	4♑29 22	10♑25 47	15R33.2	19 20.0	19 31.8	17 17.3	1 12.1	24 3.9	19 47.0	6 7.2	14 27.6
23 Tu	20 11 33	3 33 0	16 21 6	22 15 39	15 33.2	20 47.7	20 30.3	17 51.0	1 11.6	24 3.7	19 50.4	6 9.5	14 29.3
24 W	20 15 30	4 34 3	28 9 43	4♒ 3 33	15 32.1	22 12.1	21 28.4	18 24.7	1 11.3	24 3.6	19 53.8	6 11.8	14 31.0
25 Th	20 19 26	5 35 4	9♒57 26	15 51 34	15 29.9	23 32.6	22 25.9	18 58.2	1D11.3	24D 3.6	19 57.2	6 14.1	14 32.7
26 F	20 23 23	6 36 5	21 46 14	27 41 41	15 26.8	24 48.6	23 22.8	19 31.7	1 11.4	24 3.7	20 0.6	6 16.4	14 34.3
27 Sa	20 27 19	7 37 5	3♓38 9	9♓35 56	15 23.0	25 59.3	24 19.2	20 5.0	1 11.7	24 3.9	20 4.0	6 18.6	14 35.9
28 Su	20 31 16	8 38 4	15 35 17	21 36 33	15 19.0	27 3.9	25 15.0	20 38.3	1 12.3	24 4.3	20 7.4	6 20.9	14 37.4
29 M	20 35 12	9 39 2	27 40 3	3♈46 8	15 15.1	28 1.7	26 10.2	21 11.5	1 13.0	24 4.7	20 10.9	6 23.2	14 39.0
30 Tu	20 39 9	10 39 58	9♈55 11	16 7 37	15 12.0	28 51.8	27 4.7	21 44.6	1 14.0	24 5.3	20 14.3	6 25.5	14 40.5
31 W	20 43 5	11 40 54	22 23 50	28 44 17	15 10.0	29 33.3	27 58.6	22 17.6	1 15.1	24 6.0	20 17.7	6 27.7	14 42.0

Longitude — February 2001

Day	Sid.Time	☉	0 hr ☽	Noon ☽	True ☊	☿	♀	♂	♃	♄	♅	♆	♇
1 Th	20 47 2	12♒41 48	5♉ 9 23	11♉39 34	15♋ 9.3	0♓ 5.6	28♓51.8	22♏50.5	1♊16.5	24♉ 6.8	20♒21.2	6♒30.0	14♐43.4
2 F	20 50 59	13 42 40	18 15 14	24 56 45	15D 9.7	0 28.0	29 44.3	23 23.4	1 18.1	24 7.7	20 24.7	6 32.3	14 44.9
3 Sa	20 54 55	14 43 32	1♊44 25	8♊38 27	15 11.1	0 39.8	0♈36.0	23 56.1	1 19.8	24 8.7	20 28.1	6 34.5	14 46.3
4 Su	20 58 52	15 44 22	15 38 58	22 45 58	15 12.6	0R40.7	1 27.0	24 28.7	1 21.8	24 9.8	20 31.6	6 36.8	14 47.7
5 M	21 2 48	16 45 10	29 59 16	7♋18 33	15 13.8	0 30.5	2 17.1	25 1.3	1 24.0	24 11.1	20 35.1	6 39.1	14 49.0
6 Tu	21 6 45	17 45 57	14♋43 18	22 12 47	15R13.8	0 9.4	3 6.4	25 33.7	1 26.4	24 12.4	20 38.6	6 41.3	14 50.3
7 W	21 10 41	18 46 43	29 46 8	7♌22 17	15 12.3	29♒37.7	3 54.9	26 6.0	1 28.9	24 13.9	20 42.0	6 43.5	14 51.6
8 Th	21 14 38	19 47 28	15♌ 0 1	22 38 3	15 9.0	28 56.1	4 42.4	26 38.3	1 31.7	24 15.4	20 45.5	6 45.8	14 52.9
9 F	21 18 34	20 48 11	0♍15 4	7♍49 45	15 4.2	28 5.7	5 29.0	27 10.4	1 34.6	24 17.1	20 49.0	6 48.0	14 54.1
10 Sa	21 22 31	21 48 52	15 20 50	22 47 14	14 58.6	27 7.9	6 14.6	27 42.4	1 37.8	24 18.9	20 52.5	6 50.2	14 55.3
11 Su	21 26 28	22 49 33	0♎ 7 59	7♎22 19	14 52.8	26 4.4	6 59.2	28 14.3	1 41.1	24 20.8	20 55.9	6 52.4	14 56.5
12 M	21 30 24	23 50 13	14 29 42	21 29 48	14 47.8	24 56.8	7 42.7	28 46.1	1 44.6	24 22.8	20 59.4	6 54.6	14 57.6
13 Tu	21 34 21	24 50 51	28 22 28	5♏ 7 46	14 44.2	23 47.2	8 25.2	29 17.8	1 48.3	24 24.9	21 2.9	6 56.8	14 58.7
14 W	21 38 17	25 51 28	11♏45 53	18 17 11	14 42.4	22 37.4	9 6.5	29 49.4	1 52.2	24 27.2	21 6.4	6 59.0	14 59.8
15 Th	21 42 14	26 52 4	24 42 6	1♐ 1 9	14D42.1	21 29.2	9 46.7	0♐20.8	1 56.3	24 29.5	21 9.8	7 1.2	15 0.8
16 F	21 46 10	27 52 40	7♐14 56	13 24 2	14 43.1	20 24.2	10 25.6	0 52.1	2 0.5	24 31.9	21 13.3	7 3.4	15 1.8
17 Sa	21 50 7	28 53 13	19 29 6	25 30 46	14 44.7	19 23.8	11 3.3	1 23.3	2 5.0	24 34.5	21 16.8	7 5.5	15 2.8
18 Su	21 54 3	29 53 46	1♑29 37	7♑26 16	14 45.9	18 29.0	11 39.7	1 54.4	2 9.6	24 37.1	21 20.2	7 7.7	15 3.8
19 M	21 58 0	0♓54 17	13 21 17	19 15 11	14R46.1	17 40.8	12 14.7	2 25.3	2 14.4	24 39.9	21 23.7	7 9.8	15 4.7
20 Tu	22 1 57	1 54 47	25 8 27	1♒ 1 33	14 44.4	16 59.6	12 48.3	2 56.1	2 19.4	24 42.7	21 27.1	7 11.9	15 5.6
21 W	22 5 53	2 55 15	6♒54 52	12 48 46	14 40.6	16 25.8	13 20.4	3 26.7	2 24.6	24 45.7	21 30.6	7 14.0	15 6.4
22 Th	22 9 50	3 55 42	18 43 32	24 39 29	14 34.3	15 59.5	13 51.0	3 57.2	2 29.9	24 48.7	21 34.0	7 16.1	15 7.2
23 F	22 13 46	4 56 7	0♓36 49	6♓35 45	14 26.0	15 40.7	14 20.0	4 27.6	2 35.4	24 51.9	21 37.4	7 18.2	15 8.0
24 Sa	22 17 43	5 56 30	12 36 28	18 39 6	14 16.1	15 29.2	14 47.4	4 57.7	2 41.1	24 55.1	21 40.8	7 20.3	15 8.8
25 Su	22 21 39	6 56 52	24 43 48	0♈50 43	14 5.7	15D24.7	15 13.0	5 27.8	2 46.9	24 58.5	21 44.2	7 22.3	15 9.5
26 M	22 25 36	7 57 12	6♈59 58	13 11 43	13 55.5	15 27.0	15 36.9	5 57.7	2 52.9	25 1.9	21 47.6	7 24.4	15 10.2
27 Tu	22 29 32	8 57 30	19 26 6	25 43 20	13 46.7	15 35.6	15 58.9	6 27.4	2 59.1	25 5.5	21 51.0	7 26.4	15 10.8
28 W	22 33 29	9 57 46	2♉ 3 36	8♉27 8	13 40.0	15 50.3	16 19.0	6 56.9	3 5.4	25 9.1	21 54.3	7 28.4	15 11.4

Ephemeris reprinted with permission from Astro Communications Services, Inc.

Each planet's retrograde period is shaded gray.

*Giving the positions of planets daily at noon, in LONGITUDE Greenwich Mean Time

NOON EPHEMERIS: GMT* — MARCH 2001

Day	Sid.Time	☉	0 hr ☽	Noon ☽	True ☊	☿	♀	♂	♃	♄	♅	♆	♇
1 Th	22 37 26	10♓58 0	14♉54 11	21♉25 2	13♋35.7	16♒10.6	16♈37.1	7♐26.3	3♊11.9	25♉12.9	21♒57.7	7♒30.4	15♐12.0
2 F	22 41 22	11 58 12	27 59 58	4♊39 18	13R 33.8	16 36.2	16 53.2	7 55.5	3 18.6	25 16.7	22 1.0	7 32.3	15 12.6
3 Sa	22 45 19	12 58 22	11♊23 16	18 12 10	13D 33.7	17 6.7	17 7.2	8 24.6	3 25.4	25 20.6	22 4.3	7 34.3	15 13.1
4 Su	22 49 15	13 58 30	25 6 12	2♋ 5 31	13 34.3	17 41.8	17 19.0	8 53.4	3 32.4	25 24.6	22 7.6	7 36.2	15 13.6
5 M	22 53 12	14 58 36	9♋10 9	16 20 3	13R 34.6	18 21.1	17 28.6	9 22.1	3 39.5	25 28.7	22 10.9	7 38.1	15 14.0
6 Tu	22 57 8	15 58 40	23 35 1	0♌54 41	13 33.4	19 4.3	17 35.9	9 50.6	3 46.8	25 32.9	22 14.1	7 40.0	15 14.4
7 W	23 1 5	16 58 41	8♌18 30	15 45 47	13 29.9	19 51.3	17 40.8	10 19.0	3 54.2	25 37.2	22 17.4	7 41.9	15 14.8
8 Th	23 5 1	17 58 41	23 15 37	0♍47 0	13 23.7	20 41.7	17 43.4	10 47.1	4 1.7	25 41.6	22 20.6	7 43.8	15 15.1
9 F	23 8 58	18 58 38	8♍18 46	15 49 43	13 15.1	21 35.3	17R 43.5	11 15.0	4 9.4	25 46.1	22 23.8	7 45.6	15 15.4
10 Sa	23 12 55	19 58 33	23 18 37	0♎44 16	13 4.9	22 31.9	17 41.2	11 42.8	4 17.3	25 50.6	22 27.0	7 47.4	15 15.7
11 Su	23 16 51	20 58 27	8♎ 5 34	15 21 33	12 54.3	23 31.3	17 36.3	12 10.3	4 25.3	25 55.2	22 30.2	7 49.2	15 16.0
12 M	23 20 48	21 58 19	22 31 27	29 34 39	12 44.5	24 33.3	17 29.0	12 37.6	4 33.4	25 60.0	22 33.3	7 51.0	15 16.2
13 Tu	23 24 44	22 58 9	6♏30 47	13♏19 39	12 36.6	25 37.9	17 19.1	13 4.7	4 41.7	26 4.7	22 36.4	7 52.7	15 16.3
14 W	23 28 41	23 57 57	20 1 16	26 35 49	12 31.0	26 44.7	17 6.8	13 31.6	4 50.0	26 9.6	22 39.5	7 54.5	15 16.5
15 Th	23 32 37	24 57 44	3♐ 3 37	9♐25 7	12 28.0	27 53.8	16 52.0	13 58.3	4 58.6	26 14.6	22 42.6	7 56.2	15 16.6
16 F	23 36 34	25 57 29	15 40 50	21 51 23	12D 26.9	29 5.0	16 34.7	14 24.8	5 7.2	26 19.6	22 45.7	7 57.8	15 16.6
17 Sa	23 40 30	26 57 12	27 57 25	3♑59 38	12 26.9	0♓18.2	16 15.1	14 51.0	5 16.0	26 24.7	22 48.7	7 59.5	15 16.7
18 Su	23 44 27	27 56 54	9♑58 42	15 55 20	12R 27.0	1 33.3	15 53.2	15 16.9	5 24.9	26 29.9	22 51.7	8 1.1	15R 16.7
19 M	23 48 23	28 56 34	21 50 13	27 43 59	12 26.0	2 50.2	15 29.0	15 42.7	5 34.0	26 35.2	22 54.7	8 2.8	15 16.7
20 Tu	23 52 20	29 56 12	3♒37 15	9♒30 37	12 23.0	4 8.9	15 2.7	16 8.1	5 43.2	26 40.5	22 57.7	8 4.3	15 16.6
21 W	23 56 17	0♈55 48	15 24 37	21 19 43	12 17.3	5 29.3	14 34.5	16 33.3	5 52.4	26 46.0	23 0.6	8 5.9	15 16.5
22 Th	0 0 13	1 55 23	27 16 22	3♓14 55	12 8.8	6 51.4	14 4.3	16 58.2	6 1.9	26 51.4	23 3.5	8 7.4	15 16.4
23 F	0 4 10	2 54 55	9♓15 41	15 18 55	11 57.6	8 15.0	13 32.5	17 22.9	6 11.4	26 57.0	23 6.4	8 9.0	15 16.2
24 Sa	0 8 6	3 54 26	21 24 48	27 33 28	11 44.5	9 40.2	12 59.2	17 47.2	6 21.0	27 2.6	23 9.2	8 10.4	15 16.0
25 Su	0 12 3	4 53 54	3♈45 1	9♈59 29	11 30.5	11 6.9	12 24.6	18 11.3	6 30.8	27 8.3	23 12.0	8 11.9	15 15.8
26 M	0 15 59	5 53 20	16 16 53	22 37 11	11 16.9	12 35.2	11 48.9	18 35.1	6 40.6	27 14.1	23 14.8	8 13.3	15 15.5
27 Tu	0 19 56	6 52 45	29 0 22	5♉26 23	11 4.9	14 4.9	11 12.3	18 58.6	6 50.6	27 19.9	23 17.6	8 14.7	15 15.2
28 W	0 23 52	7 52 7	11♉55 12	18 26 50	10 55.4	15 36.0	10 35.0	19 21.7	7 0.7	27 25.8	23 20.3	8 16.1	15 14.9
29 Th	0 27 49	8 51 27	25 1 15	1♊38 31	10 48.8	17 8.6	9 57.4	19 44.6	7 10.9	27 31.8	23 23.0	8 17.5	15 14.5
30 F	0 31 46	9 50 45	8♊18 42	15 1 52	10 45.1	18 42.7	9 19.6	20 7.1	7 21.2	27 37.8	23 25.7	8 18.8	15 14.1
31 Sa	0 35 42	10 50 0	21 48 8	28 37 38	10 43.8	20 18.1	8 41.9	20 29.3	7 31.6	27 43.9	23 28.3	8 20.1	15 13.7

LONGITUDE — APRIL 2001

Day	Sid.Time	☉	0 hr ☽	Noon ☽	True ☊	☿	♀	♂	♃	♄	♅	♆	♇
1 Su	0 39 39	11♈49 14	5♋30 30	12♋26 48	10♋43.6	21♓55.0	8♈ 4.5	20♐51.2	7♊42.1	27♉50.1	23♒30.9	8♒21.4	15♐13.2
2 M	0 43 35	12 48 24	19 26 39	26 30 1	10R 43.3	23 33.3	7R 27.8	21 12.7	7 52.7	27 56.3	23 33.4	8 22.6	15R 12.7
3 Tu	0 47 32	13 47 33	3♌36 52	10♌47 0	10 41.6	25 13.0	6 51.9	21 33.9	8 3.4	28 2.6	23 36.0	8 23.8	15 12.2
4 W	0 51 28	14 46 39	18 0 9	25 15 55	10 37.5	26 54.1	6 17.1	21 54.7	8 14.2	28 8.9	23 38.5	8 25.0	15 11.6
5 Th	0 55 25	15 45 43	2♍33 44	9♍52 57	10 30.7	28 36.7	5 43.5	22 15.1	8 25.1	28 15.3	23 40.9	8 26.1	15 11.1
6 F	0 59 21	16 44 44	17 12 47	24 32 21	10 21.2	0♈20.7	5 11.4	22 35.2	8 36.1	28 21.7	23 43.3	8 27.3	15 10.4
7 Sa	1 3 18	17 43 43	1♎50 44	9♎ 6 57	10 10.0	2 6.2	4 41.0	22 54.9	8 47.2	28 28.2	23 45.7	8 28.3	15 9.8
8 Su	1 7 15	18 42 41	16 20 6	23 29 19	9 58.2	3 53.2	4 12.5	23 14.2	8 58.3	28 34.8	23 48.1	8 29.4	15 9.1
9 M	1 11 11	19 41 36	0♏33 50	7♏33 0	9 47.1	5 41.6	3 45.9	23 33.2	9 9.6	28 41.4	23 50.4	8 30.4	15 8.4
10 Tu	1 15 8	20 40 29	14 26 20	21 13 31	9 37.8	7 31.5	3 21.5	23 51.7	9 20.9	28 48.0	23 52.6	8 31.4	15 7.7
11 W	1 19 4	21 39 21	27 54 24	4♐28 58	9 31.0	9 22.9	2 59.3	24 9.8	9 32.3	28 54.7	23 54.9	8 32.4	15 6.9
12 Th	1 23 1	22 38 11	10♐57 21	17 19 51	9 26.8	11 15.9	2 39.4	24 27.4	9 43.8	29 1.5	23 57.1	8 33.4	15 6.1
13 F	1 26 57	23 36 59	23 36 50	29 48 47	9 25.0	13 10.3	2 21.8	24 44.6	9 55.4	29 8.2	23 59.2	8 34.3	15 5.3
14 Sa	1 30 54	24 35 45	5♑56 16	11♑59 52	9D 24.7	15 6.2	2 6.7	25 1.4	10 7.1	29 15.1	24 1.4	8 35.1	15 4.5
15 Su	1 34 50	25 34 30	18 0 15	23 58 6	9R 24.9	17 3.6	1 54.0	25 17.7	10 18.8	29 22.0	24 3.4	8 36.0	15 3.6
16 M	1 38 47	26 33 13	29 54 4	5♒48 53	9 24.5	19 2.5	1 43.8	25 33.6	10 30.6	29 28.9	24 5.5	8 36.8	15 2.7
17 Tu	1 42 44	27 31 54	11♒43 12	17 37 40	9 22.6	21 2.8	1 36.1	25 48.9	10 42.5	29 35.9	24 7.5	8 37.6	15 1.8
18 W	1 46 40	28 30 34	23 32 56	29 29 34	9 18.5	23 4.5	1 30.8	26 3.7	10 54.4	29 42.9	24 9.4	8 38.3	15 0.8
19 Th	1 50 37	29 29 12	5♓28 6	11♓29 3	9 11.8	25 7.5	1 28.0	26 18.1	11 6.5	29 49.9	24 11.3	8 39.1	14 59.8
20 F	1 54 33	0♉27 48	17 32 49	23 39 47	9 2.7	27 11.8	1D 27.5	26 31.9	11 18.6	29 57.0	24 13.2	8 39.7	14 58.8
21 Sa	1 58 30	1 26 22	29 50 13	6♈ 4 20	8 51.8	29 17.2	1 29.4	26 45.2	11 30.7	0♊ 4.2	24 15.0	8 40.4	14 57.8
22 Su	2 2 26	2 24 54	12♈22 17	18 44 7	8 40.0	1♉23.6	1 33.6	26 57.9	11 43.0	0 11.3	24 16.8	8 41.0	14 56.7
23 M	2 6 23	3 23 25	25 9 49	1♉39 19	8 28.5	3 30.8	1 40.1	27 10.1	11 55.3	0 18.5	24 18.6	8 41.6	14 55.7
24 Tu	2 10 19	4 21 54	8♉12 29	14 49 7	8 18.3	5 38.8	1 48.8	27 21.7	12 7.6	0 25.8	24 20.3	8 42.2	14 54.6
25 W	2 14 16	5 20 21	21 29 1	28 11 56	8 10.3	7 47.2	1 59.6	27 32.7	12 20.1	0 33.1	24 21.9	8 42.7	14 53.4
26 Th	2 18 12	6 18 46	4♊57 39	11♊45 55	8 4.9	9 55.9	2 12.5	27 43.2	12 32.6	0 40.4	24 23.5	8 43.2	14 52.3
27 F	2 22 9	7 17 9	18 36 30	25 29 15	8 2.2	12 4.5	2 27.5	27 53.0	12 45.1	0 47.7	24 25.1	8 43.7	14 51.1
28 Sa	2 26 6	8 15 30	2♋23 57	9♋20 30	8D 1.5	14 12.9	2 44.4	28 2.3	12 57.7	0 55.1	24 26.6	8 44.1	14 49.9
29 Su	2 30 2	9 13 49	16 18 45	23 18 38	8 2.0	16 20.7	3 3.2	28 10.9	13 10.4	1 2.5	24 28.1	8 44.5	14 48.7
30 M	2 33 59	10 12 6	0♌20 3	7♌22 55	8R 2.6	18 27.6	3 23.8	28 18.9	13 23.1	1 9.9	24 29.5	8 44.8	14 47.5

*Giving the positions of planets daily at noon, in LONGITUDE Greenwich Mean Time

NOON EPHEMERIS: GMT*

MAY 2001

Day	Sid.Time	☉	0 hr ☽	Noon ☽	True ☊	☿	♀	♂	♃	♄	♅	♆	♇
1 Tu	2 37 55	11♉10 21	14♌27 5	21♌32 26	8♋ 2.2	20♉33.3	3♈46.2	28♐26.2	13♊35.9	1♊17.4	24♒30.9	8♒45.2	14♐46.2
2 W	2 41 52	12 8 33	28 38 45	5♍45 48	7R 59.9	22 37.5	4 10.3	28 33.0	13 48.7	1 24.8	24 32.2	8 45.5	14R 44.9
3 Th	2 45 48	13 6 44	12♍53 14	20 0 42	7 55.4	24 40.0	4 36.1	28 39.0	14 1.5	1 32.3	24 33.5	8 45.7	14 43.6
4 F	2 49 45	14 4 53	27 7 43	4♎13 49	7 48.9	26 40.3	5 3.5	28 44.4	14 14.5	1 39.9	24 34.8	8 45.9	14 42.3
5 Sa	2 53 41	15 2 59	11♎18 25	18 20 58	7 40.9	28 38.4	5 32.4	28 49.2	14 27.4	1 47.4	24 36.0	8 46.1	14 41.0
6 Su	2 57 38	16 1 4	25 20 53	2♏17 38	7 32.4	0♊33.9	6 2.8	28 53.2	14 40.4	1 55.0	24 37.1	8 46.3	14 39.6
7 M	3 1 35	16 59 8	9♏10 41	15 59 35	7 24.3	2 26.6	6 34.7	28 56.6	14 53.5	2 2.6	24 38.2	8 46.4	14 38.3
8 Tu	3 5 31	17 57 9	22 44 0	29 23 37	7 17.6	4 16.4	7 7.9	28 59.3	15 6.6	2 10.2	24 39.3	8 46.5	14 36.9
9 W	3 9 28	18 55 9	5♐58 18	12♐27 58	7 12.8	6 3.2	7 42.4	29 1.2	15 19.7	2 17.8	24 40.3	8 46.6	14 35.5
10 Th	3 13 24	19 53 8	18 52 39	25 12 30	7 10.1	7 46.7	8 18.3	29 2.4	15 32.9	2 25.4	24 41.2	8 46.6	14 34.1
11 F	3 17 21	20 51 5	1♑27 46	7♑38 45	7D 9.3	9 26.8	8 55.3	29R 2.9	15 46.1	2 33.1	24 42.2	8R 46.6	14 32.6
12 Sa	3 21 17	21 49 1	13 45 53	19 49 35	7 10.0	11 3.6	9 33.6	29 2.7	15 59.4	2 40.8	24 43.0	8 46.6	14 31.2
13 Su	3 25 14	22 46 56	25 50 24	1♒48 54	7 11.4	12 36.8	10 13.0	29 1.7	16 12.7	2 48.5	24 43.8	8 46.5	14 29.7
14 M	3 29 10	23 44 49	7♒45 39	13 41 18	7 12.7	14 6.5	10 53.4	28 60.0	16 26.0	2 56.2	24 44.6	8 46.4	14 28.3
15 Tu	3 33 7	24 42 41	19 36 29	25 31 50	7R 13.2	15 32.5	11 34.9	28 57.4	16 39.4	3 3.9	24 45.3	8 46.3	14 26.8
16 W	3 37 4	25 40 32	1♓27 59	7♓25 33	7 12.4	16 54.8	12 17.5	28 54.2	16 52.8	3 11.6	24 46.0	8 46.2	14 25.3
17 Th	3 41 0	26 38 21	13 25 10	19 27 23	7 9.9	18 13.4	13 0.9	28 50.1	17 6.2	3 19.3	24 46.6	8 46.0	14 23.8
18 F	3 44 57	27 36 10	25 32 43	1♈41 40	7 5.7	19 28.1	13 45.3	28 45.3	17 19.7	3 27.1	24 47.2	8 45.7	14 22.2
19 Sa	3 48 53	28 33 57	7♈54 39	14 12 0	7 0.3	20 39.0	14 30.6	28 39.8	17 33.2	3 34.8	24 47.7	8 45.5	14 20.7
20 Su	3 52 50	29 31 43	20 34 0	27 0 49	6 54.2	21 46.0	15 16.8	28 33.4	17 46.7	3 42.6	24 48.2	8 45.2	14 19.1
21 M	3 56 46	0♊29 28	3♉32 32	10♉ 9 9	6 48.0	22 49.0	16 3.7	28 26.3	18 0.2	3 50.3	24 48.6	8 44.9	14 17.6
22 Tu	4 0 43	1 27 11	16 50 34	23 36 36	6 42.6	23 48.0	16 51.5	28 18.5	18 13.8	3 58.1	24 49.0	8 44.5	14 16.0
23 W	4 4 39	2 24 54	0♊26 56	7♊21 14	6 38.5	24 42.9	17 40.0	28 9.9	18 27.4	4 5.9	24 49.3	8 44.1	14 14.5
24 Th	4 8 36	3 22 35	14 19 5	21 20 0	6 36.0	25 33.6	18 29.2	28 0.5	18 41.0	4 13.7	24 49.6	8 43.7	14 12.9
25 F	4 12 33	4 20 15	28 23 32	5♋29 8	6D 35.1	26 20.1	19 19.1	27 50.5	18 54.7	4 21.4	24 49.8	8 43.3	14 11.3
26 Sa	4 16 29	5 17 54	12♋36 20	19 44 38	6 35.6	27 2.3	20 9.7	27 39.7	19 8.4	4 29.2	24 50.0	8 42.8	14 9.7
27 Su	4 20 26	6 15 31	26 53 35	4♌ 2 46	6 36.9	27 40.0	21 0.9	27 28.2	19 22.1	4 37.0	24 50.1	8 42.3	14 8.1
28 M	4 24 22	7 13 6	11♌11 47	18 20 17	6 38.3	28 13.3	21 52.7	27 16.1	19 35.8	4 44.8	24 50.2	8 41.7	14 6.5
29 Tu	4 28 19	8 10 41	25 27 59	2♍34 34	6R 39.2	28 42.1	22 45.1	27 3.3	19 49.5	4 52.5	24R 50.3	8 41.2	14 4.9
30 W	4 32 15	9 8 13	9♍39 49	16 43 28	6 39.1	29 6.3	23 38.1	26 49.8	20 3.2	5 0.3	24 50.2	8 40.6	14 3.3
31 Th	4 36 12	10 5 44	23 45 18	0♎45 7	6 37.8	29 25.9	24 31.7	26 35.8	20 17.0	5 8.1	24 50.2	8 39.9	14 1.7

LONGITUDE

JUNE 2001

Day	Sid.Time	☉	0 hr ☽	Noon ☽	True ☊	☿	♀	♂	♃	♄	♅	♆	♇
1 F	4 40 9	11♊ 3 14	7♎42 41	14♎37 48	6♋35.4	29♊40.8	25♈25.8	26♐21.2	20♊30.7	5♊15.8	24♒50.1	8♒39.3	14♐ 0.1
2 Sa	4 44 5	12 0 43	21 30 15	28 19 50	6R 32.2	29 51.0	26 20.4	26R 6.0	20 44.5	5 23.5	24R 49.9	8R 38.6	13R 58.5
3 Su	4 48 2	12 58 10	5♏ 6 22	11♏49 38	6 28.7	29 56.7	27 15.5	25 50.2	20 58.3	5 31.3	24 49.7	8 37.9	13 56.8
4 M	4 51 58	13 55 37	18 29 30	25 5 47	6 25.4	29R 57.7	28 11.1	25 34.0	21 12.1	5 39.0	24 49.4	8 37.1	13 55.2
5 Tu	4 55 55	14 53 2	1♐38 24	8♐ 7 16	6 22.8	29 54.2	29 7.2	25 17.3	21 25.9	5 46.7	24 49.1	8 36.4	13 53.6
6 W	4 59 51	15 50 27	14 32 21	20 53 39	6 21.1	29 46.3	0♉ 3.7	25 0.1	21 39.7	5 54.4	24 48.8	8 35.6	13 52.0
7 Th	5 3 48	16 47 50	27 11 15	3♑25 15	6D 20.4	29 34.3	1 0.7	24 42.5	21 53.6	6 2.1	24 48.4	8 34.7	13 50.4
8 F	5 7 44	17 45 13	9♑35 50	15 43 14	6 20.6	29 18.2	1 58.1	24 24.6	22 7.4	6 9.8	24 47.9	8 33.9	13 48.8
9 Sa	5 11 41	18 42 35	21 47 42	27 49 35	6 21.5	28 58.4	2 55.9	24 6.3	22 21.2	6 17.5	24 47.4	8 33.0	13 47.2
10 Su	5 15 38	19 39 57	3♒49 14	9♒47 6	6 22.9	28 35.2	3 54.1	23 47.7	22 35.1	6 25.1	24 46.9	8 32.1	13 45.6
11 M	5 19 34	20 37 18	15 43 37	21 39 17	6 24.3	28 9.1	4 52.7	23 28.8	22 48.9	6 32.7	24 46.3	8 31.2	13 43.9
12 Tu	5 23 31	21 34 38	27 34 37	3♓30 11	6 25.4	27 40.3	5 51.7	23 9.7	23 2.8	6 40.3	24 45.7	8 30.2	13 42.3
13 W	5 27 27	22 31 58	9♓26 32	15 24 15	6 26.1	27 9.4	6 51.0	22 50.4	23 16.6	6 47.9	24 45.0	8 29.2	13 40.8
14 Th	5 31 24	23 29 17	21 23 56	27 26 8	6R 26.2	26 36.9	7 50.7	22 31.0	23 30.5	6 55.5	24 44.2	8 28.2	13 39.2
15 F	5 35 20	24 26 36	3♈31 27	9♈40 25	6 25.7	26 3.4	8 50.7	22 11.5	23 44.3	7 3.1	24 43.5	8 27.2	13 37.6
16 Sa	5 39 17	25 23 55	15 53 34	22 11 20	6 24.8	25 29.4	9 51.0	21 52.0	23 58.1	7 10.6	24 42.6	8 26.1	13 36.0
17 Su	5 43 13	26 21 13	28 34 11	5♉ 2 25	6 23.6	24 55.5	10 51.7	21 32.4	24 12.0	7 18.1	24 41.8	8 25.0	13 34.4
18 M	5 47 10	27 18 31	11♉36 19	18 16 2	6 22.4	24 22.4	11 52.6	21 12.9	24 25.8	7 25.6	24 40.9	8 23.9	13 32.9
19 Tu	5 51 7	28 15 49	25 1 38	1♊53 2	6 21.4	23 50.4	12 53.9	20 53.5	24 39.7	7 33.1	24 39.9	8 22.8	13 31.3
20 W	5 55 3	29 13 6	8♊50 3	15 52 23	6 20.7	23 20.3	13 55.4	20 34.2	24 53.5	7 40.5	24 38.9	8 21.7	13 29.8
21 Th	5 59 0	0♋10 23	22 59 34	0♋11 3	6D 20.4	22 52.5	14 57.2	20 15.2	25 7.3	7 47.9	24 37.9	8 20.5	13 28.2
22 F	6 2 56	1 7 40	7♋26 12	14 44 15	6 20.4	22 27.4	15 59.3	19 56.3	25 21.1	7 55.3	24 36.8	8 19.3	13 26.7
23 Sa	6 6 53	2 4 56	22 4 24	29 25 51	6 20.7	22 5.6	17 1.6	19 37.8	25 34.9	8 2.7	24 35.7	8 18.1	13 25.2
24 Su	6 10 49	3 2 12	6♌47 43	14♌ 9 13	6 21.0	21 47.4	18 4.2	19 19.6	25 48.7	8 10.0	24 34.5	8 16.9	13 23.7
25 M	6 14 46	3 59 27	21 29 33	28 48 1	6 21.3	21 33.1	19 7.0	19 1.8	26 2.4	8 17.3	24 33.3	8 15.6	13 22.2
26 Tu	6 18 42	4 56 42	6♍ 4 0	13♍16 57	6 21.4	21 22.9	20 10.1	18 44.4	26 16.2	8 24.5	24 32.0	8 14.3	13 20.7
27 W	6 22 39	5 53 55	20 26 27	27 32 8	6 21.5	21 17.2	21 13.3	18 27.5	26 29.9	8 31.7	24 30.7	8 13.0	13 19.2
28 Th	6 26 36	6 51 9	4♎33 47	11♎31 13	6 21.5	21D 16.1	22 16.8	18 11.1	26 43.6	8 38.9	24 29.4	8 11.7	13 17.8
29 F	6 30 32	7 48 21	18 24 23	25 13 15	6 21.5	21 19.7	23 20.5	17 55.3	26 57.3	8 46.1	24 28.0	8 10.4	13 16.4
30 Sa	6 34 29	8 45 34	1♏57 51	8♏38 17	6 21.7	21 28.1	24 24.5	17 40.0	27 11.0	8 53.2	24 26.6	8 9.0	13 14.9

*Giving the positions of planets daily at noon, in LONGITUDE Greenwich Mean Time

Noon Ephemeris: GMT* July 2001

Day	Sid.Time	☉	0 hr ☽	Noon ☽	True ☊	☿	♀	♂	♃	♄	♅	♆	♇
1 Su	6 38 25	9♋42 46	15♏14 39	21♏47 6	6♋22.0	21♊41.4	25♉28.6	17♐25.3	27♊24.7	9♊ 0.3	24♒25.2	8♒ 7.6	13♐13.5
2 M	6 42 22	10 39 57	28 15 46	4♐40 50	6 22.4	21 59.6	26 32.9	17R 11.2	27 38.3	9 7.3	24R 23.7	8R 6.3	13R 12.1
3 Tu	6 46 18	11 37 9	11♐ 2 27	17 20 48	6 22.8	22 22.8	27 37.5	16 57.8	27 51.9	9 14.3	24 22.2	8 4.9	13 10.8
4 W	6 50 15	12 34 20	23 36 3	29 48 23	6 23.0	22 50.9	28 42.2	16 45.1	28 5.5	9 21.3	24 20.6	8 3.4	13 9.4
5 Th	6 54 11	13 31 32	5♑57 59	12♑ 5 1	6R 23.0	23 23.9	29 47.1	16 33.0	28 19.1	9 28.2	24 19.0	8 2.0	13 8.1
6 F	6 58 8	14 28 43	18 9 43	24 12 17	6 22.7	24 1.8	0♊52.2	16 21.7	28 32.6	9 35.1	24 17.4	8 0.6	13 6.7
7 Sa	7 2 5	15 25 54	0♒12 56	6♒11 55	6 21.9	24 44.5	1 57.5	16 11.2	28 46.2	9 41.9	24 15.7	7 59.1	13 5.4
8 Su	7 6 1	16 23 6	12 9 30	18 5 59	6 20.7	25 32.0	3 3.0	16 1.4	28 59.6	9 48.7	24 14.0	7 57.6	13 4.2
9 M	7 9 58	17 20 17	24 1 42	29 57 0	6 19.2	26 24.3	4 8.7	15 52.3	29 13.1	9 55.4	24 12.3	7 56.1	13 2.9
10 Tu	7 13 54	18 17 29	5♓52 15	11♓47 53	6 17.6	27 21.2	5 14.5	15 44.1	29 26.5	10 2.1	24 10.5	7 54.6	13 1.6
11 W	7 17 51	19 14 42	17 44 19	23 42 3	6 16.1	28 22.7	6 20.5	15 36.6	29 39.9	10 8.8	24 8.7	7 53.1	13 0.4
12 Th	7 21 47	20 11 55	29 41 33	5♈43 21	6 15.0	29 28.8	7 26.7	15 29.9	29 53.3	10 15.4	24 6.9	7 51.6	12 59.2
13 F	7 25 44	21 9 8	11♈47 58	17 55 58	6D 14.5	0♋39.4	8 33.0	15 24.1	0♋ 6.6	10 21.9	24 5.0	7 50.1	12 58.0
14 Sa	7 29 40	22 6 22	24 7 51	0♉24 10	6 14.6	1 54.4	9 39.4	15 19.1	0 19.9	10 28.4	24 3.1	7 48.5	12 56.9
15 Su	[illegible] 37	23 3 36	6♉45 25	13 12 5	6 15.4	3 13.7	10 46.1	15 14.9	0 33.2	10 34.9	24 1.2	7 47.0	12 55.7
16 M	7 37 34	24 0 51	19 44 35	26 23 15	6 16.6	4 37.4	11 52.9	15 11.5	0 46.4	10 41.3	23 59.3	7 45.4	12 54.6
17 Tu	7 41 30	24 [illegible] 7	3♊ 8 21	10♊ 0 1	6 17.9	6 5.2	12 59.8	15 9.0	0 59.6	10 47.6	23 57.3	7 43.8	12 53.5
18 W	7 45 27	25 55 24	[illegible] 58 17	24 3 1	6 18.9	7 37.1	14 6.9	15 7.4	1 12.8	10 53.9	23 55.3	7 42.2	12 52.4
19 Th	7 49 23	26 52 41	1♋[illegible]	8♋30 34	6R 19.2	9 12.9	15 14.1	15D 6.6	1 25.9	11 0.2	23 53.3	7 40.7	12 51.4
20 F	7 53 20	27 49 58	15 52 17	[illegible] 18 18	6 18.5	10 52.6	16 21.4	15 6.6	1 38.9	11 6.3	23 51.2	7 39.1	12 50.4
21 Sa	7 57 16	28 47 17	0♌47 40	8♌19 20	6 16.8	12 35.9	17 28.9	15 7.5	1 52.0	11 12.4	23 49.1	7 37.5	12 49.4
22 Su	8 1 13	29 44 35	15 52 9	23 24 57	6 [illegible]	14 22.6	18 36.5	15 9.3	2 4.9	11 18.5	23 47.0	7 35.9	12 48.4
23 M	8 5 9	0♌41 54	0♍56 35	8♍25 56	6 11.0	[illegible] 12.6	19 44.2	15 11.8	2 17.9	11 24.5	23 44.9	7 34.2	12 47.4
24 Tu	8 9 6	1 39 13	15 52 0	23 13 53	6 7.9	18 [illegible]	20 52.1	15 15.3	2 30.8	11 30.4	23 42.8	7 32.6	12 46.5
25 W	8 13 3	2 36 33	0♎30 53	7♎42 27	6 5.3	20 1.1	22 0.0	15 19.5	2 43.6	11 36.3	23 40.6	7 31.0	12 45.6
26 Th	8 16 59	3 33 53	14 48 12	21 47 55	6 3.6	21 59.1	23 8.1	15 24.6	2 56.4	11 42.1	23 38.4	7 29.4	12 44.8
27 F	8 20 56	4 31 13	28 41 32	5♏29 8	6D 3.1	23 59.3	24 16.3	15 [illegible]	3 9.1	11 47.8	23 36.2	7 27.7	12 43.9
28 Sa	8 24 52	5 28 34	12♏10 52	18 47 1	6 3.7	26 1.1	25 24.7	15 37.2	3 21.8	11 53.5	23 34.0	7 26.1	12 43.1
29 Su	8 28 49	6 25 55	25 17 54	1♐43 54	6 5.1	28 4.4	26 33.1	15 44.7	3 34.4	11 59.1	23 31.7	7 24.5	12 42.3
30 M	8 32 45	7 23 17	8♐ 5 24	14 22 50	6 6.7	0♌ 8.8	27 41.6	15 53.0	3 47.0	12 4.0	23 29.5	7 22.9	12 41.6
31 Tu	8 36 42	8 20 40	20 36 37	26 47 8	6 8.0	2 13.9	28 50.3	16 2.0	3 59.5	12 10.1	23 27.2	7 21.2	12 40.8

Longitude August 2001

Day	Sid.Time	☉	0 hr ☽	Noon ☽	True ☊	☿	♀	♂	♃	♄	♅	♆	♇
1 W	8 40 38	9♌[illegible]	2♑[illegible] 46	8♑59 55	6♋ 8.3	4♌19.4	29♊59.1	16♐11.8	4♋11.9	12♊15.5	23♒24.9	7♒19.6	12♐40.1
2 Th	8 44 35	10 15 [illegible]	15 [illegible] 53	21 4 0	6R 7.2	6 25.1	1♋ 8.0	16 22.4	4 24.3	12 20.9	23R 22.6	7R 18.0	12R 39.4
3 F	8 48 32	11 12 52	27 [illegible]	3♒ [illegible] 51	6 4.5	8 30.6	2 17.0	16 33.6	4 36.7	12 26.1	23 20.3	7 16.3	12 38.8
4 Sa	8 52 28	12 10 17	8♒59 5	[illegible] 31	6 0.0	10 35.8	3 26.1	16 45.6	4 48.9	12 31.3	23 18.0	7 14.7	12 38.2
5 Su	8 56 25	13 7 44	20 51 23	26 46 54	5 54.2	12 40.3	4 35.3	16 58.3	5 1.1	12 36.4	23 15.6	7 13.1	12 37.6
6 M	9 0 21	14 5 11	2♓42 19	8♓37 52	5 47.4	14 44.1	5 44.6	17 11.7	5 13.3	12 41.4	23 13.3	7 11.5	12 37.0
7 Tu	9 4 18	15 2 39	14 33 47	20 30 22	5 40.3	16 47.0	6 54.1	17 25.8	5 25.4	12 46.4	23 10.9	7 9.9	12 36.5
8 W	9 8 14	16 0 9	26 27 54	2♈26 43	5 33.6	18 46.2	8 3.6	17 40.5	5 37.4	12 51.3	23 8.6	7 8.3	12 36.0
9 Th	9 12 11	16 57 40	8♈27 10	14 29 39	5 28.0	20 49.4	9 13.3	17 [illegible]	5 49.3	12 56.1	23 6.2	7 6.7	12 35.5
10 F	9 16 7	17 55 12	20 34 34	26 42 23	5 24.0	22 48.8	10 23.0	18 12.0	6 1.2	13 0.8	23 3.8	7 5.1	12 35.1
11 Sa	9 20 4	18 52 46	2♉53 34	9♉ 8 36	5 21.8	24 46.8	11 32.9	18 28.7	6 13.0	13 5.5	23 1.4	7 3.5	12 34.7
12 Su	9 24 1	19 50 21	15 28 0	21 52 16	5D 21.3	26 43.5	12 42.8	18 46.0	6 24.7	13 10.1	22 59.0	7 1.9	12 34.3
13 M	9 27 57	20 47 58	28 21 52	4♊57 17	5 22.1	28 38.8	13 52.9	19 3.9	6 36.4	13 14.5	22 56.6	7 0.3	12 34.0
14 Tu	9 31 54	21 45 36	11♊38 55	18 27 4	5 23.3	0♍32.7	15 3.0	19 22.4	6 48.0	13 19.0	22 54.2	6 58.7	12 33.7
15 W	9 35 50	22 43 16	25 22 0	2♋23 47	5R 24.1	2 25.1	16 13.3	19 41.6	6 59.5	13 23.3	22 51.9	6 57.2	12 33.4
16 Th	9 39 47	23 40 57	9♋32 24	16 47 36	5 23.6	4 16.1	17 23.6	20 1.3	7 10.9	13 27.5	22 49.5	6 55.6	12 33.1
17 F	9 43 43	24 38 39	24 8 56	1♌35 48	5 21.2	6 5.6	18 34.1	20 21.6	7 22.3	13 31.7	22 47.1	6 54.1	12 32.9
18 Sa	9 47 40	25 36 24	9♌ 7 20	16 42 29	5 16.6	7 53.7	19 44.6	20 42.5	7 33.5	13 35.7	22 44.7	6 52.6	12 32.7
19 Su	9 51 36	26 34 9	24 20 3	1♍58 44	5 10.2	9 40.4	20 55.2	21 3.9	7 44.7	13 39.7	22 42.3	6 51.1	12 32.6
20 M	9 55 33	27 31 56	9♍37 7	17 13 49	5 2.5	11 25.6	22 5.9	21 25.9	7 55.8	13 43.6	22 39.9	6 49.5	12 32.5
21 Tu	9 59 30	28 29 43	24 47 32	2♎17 2	4 54.7	13 9.5	23 16.7	21 48.4	8 6.8	13 47.4	22 37.5	6 48.1	12 32.4
22 W	10 3 26	29 27 32	9♎41 18	16 59 31	4 47.6	14 51.9	24 27.5	22 11.4	8 17.7	13 51.1	22 35.1	6 46.6	12 32.3
23 Th	10 7 23	0♍25 23	24 11 3	1♏15 31	4 42.3	16 33.0	25 38.5	22 34.9	8 28.6	13 54.7	22 32.8	6 45.1	12D 32.3
24 F	10 11 19	1 23 14	8♏12 44	15 2 44	4 39.0	18 12.7	26 49.5	22 59.0	8 39.3	13 58.2	22 30.4	6 43.7	12 32.3
25 Sa	10 15 16	2 21 7	21 45 41	28 21 53	4D 37.7	19 51.0	28 0.6	23 23.5	8 50.0	14 1.7	22 28.1	6 42.2	12 32.4
26 Su	10 19 12	3 19 1	4♐51 45	11♐15 48	4 37.9	21 28.0	29 11.8	23 48.6	9 0.5	14 5.0	22 25.7	6 40.8	12 32.4
27 M	10 23 9	4 16 56	17 34 34	23 48 37	4 38.7	23 3.6	0♌23.1	24 14.1	9 11.0	14 8.2	22 23.4	6 39.4	12 32.6
28 Tu	10 27 5	5 14 53	29 58 32	6♑ 4 54	4R 39.0	24 38.0	1 34.5	24 40.0	9 21.3	14 11.4	22 21.1	6 38.0	12 32.7
29 W	10 31 2	6 12 50	12♑ 2 17	18 9 13	4 38.1	26 11.0	2 45.9	25 6.4	9 31.6	14 14.4	22 18.8	6 36.6	12 32.9
30 Th	10 34 59	7 10 50	24 8 10	0♒ 5 38	4 34.9	27 42.6	3 57.4	25 33.2	9 41.7	14 17.4	22 16.5	6 35.3	12 33.1
31 F	10 38 55	8 8 50	6♒ 2 1	11 57 42	4 29.3	29 13.0	5 9.0	26 0.5	9 51.8	14 20.3	22 14.2	6 34.0	12 33.3

*Giving the positions of planets daily at noon, in LONGITUDE Greenwich Mean Time

Noon Ephemeris: GMT* September 2001

Day	Sid.Time	☉	0 hr ☽	Noon ☽	True ☊	☿	♀	♂	♃	♄	♅	♆	♇
1 Sa	10 42 52	9♍ 6 52	17♒53 0	23♒48 13	4♋21.0	0♎42.0	6♌20.7	26♐28.1	10♋ 1.7	14♊23.0	22♒11.9	6♒32.6	12♐33.6
2 Su	10 46 48	10 4 56	29 43 37	5♓39 25	4R 10.5	2 9.7	7 32.4	26 56.2	10 11.6	14 25.7	22R 9.7	6R 31.3	12 33.9
3 M	10 50 45	11 3 1	11♓35 49	17 33 1	3 58.5	3 36.0	8 44.3	27 24.6	10 21.3	14 28.2	22 7.5	6 30.1	12 34.3
4 Tu	10 54 41	12 1 8	23 31 10	29 30 26	3 45.9	5 0.9	9 56.2	27 53.5	10 30.9	14 30.7	22 5.2	6 28.8	12 34.6
5 W	10 58 38	12 59 17	5♈31 0	11♈33 4	3 33.8	6 24.5	11 8.2	28 22.7	10 40.4	14 33.0	22 3.0	6 27.6	12 35.0
6 Th	11 2 34	13 57 27	17 36 49	23 42 29	3 23.3	7 46.7	12 20.2	28 52.3	10 49.8	14 35.3	22 0.9	6 26.3	12 35.5
7 F	11 6 31	14 55 40	29 50 20	6♉ 0 40	3 15.1	9 7.4	13 32.4	29 22.2	10 59.1	14 37.5	21 58.7	6 25.2	12 35.9
8 Sa	11 10 28	15 53 54	12♉13 49	18 30 8	3 9.6	10 26.6	14 44.6	29 52.5	11 8.3	14 39.5	21 56.6	6 24.0	12 36.4
9 Su	11 14 24	16 52 11	24 50 2	1♊13 56	3 6.6	11 44.3	15 56.9	0♑23.2	11 17.3	14 41.5	21 54.5	6 22.8	12 37.0
10 M	11 18 21	17 50 29	7♊42 15	14 15 26	3D 5.6	13 0.4	17 9.3	0 54.2	11 26.3	14 43.3	21 52.4	6 21.7	12 37.5
11 Tu	11 22 17	18 48 50	20 53 54	27 38 3	3R 5.7	14 14.9	18 21.7	1 25.5	11 35.1	14 45.0	21 50.4	6 20.6	12 38.2
12 W	11 26 14	19 47 13	4♋28 12	11♋24 36	3 5.6	15 27.6	19 34.2	1 57.2	11 43.8	14 46.7	21 48.3	6 19.5	12 38.8
13 Th	11 30 10	20 45 38	18 27 23	25 36 32	3 4.1	16 38.6	20 46.8	2 29.2	11 52.3	14 48.2	21 46.3	6 18.5	12 39.5
14 F	11 34 7	21 44 5	2♌51 51	10♌12 57	3 0.2	17 47.6	21 59.5	3 1.5	12 0.8	14 49.6	21 44.3	6 17.4	12 40.2
15 Sa	11 38 3	22 42 35	17 39 15	25 9 56	2 53.7	18 54.7	23 12.2	3 34.1	12 9.1	14 50.9	21 42.4	6 16.4	12 40.9
16 Su	11 42 0	23 41 6	2♍43 59	10♍20 13	2 44.6	19 59.6	24 25.0	4 7.0	12 17.3	14 52.1	21 40.5	6 15.5	12 41.7
17 M	11 45 57	24 39 39	17 57 20	25 33 55	2 33.9	21 2.3	25 37.9	4 40.3	12 25.3	14 53.2	21 38.6	6 14.5	12 42.5
18 Tu	11 49 53	25 38 14	3♎ 8 36	10♎40 1	2 22.7	22 2.6	26 50.8	5 13.8	12 33.2	14 54.2	21 36.7	6 13.6	12 43.3
19 W	11 53 50	26 36 50	18 6 59	25 28 25	2 12.4	23 0.4	28 3.8	5 47.6	12 41.0	14 55.1	21 34.9	6 12.7	12 44.1
20 Th	11 57 46	27 35 29	2♏43 31	9♏51 40	2 4.0	23 55.4	29 16.8	6 21.7	12 48.6	14 55.9	21 33.1	6 11.8	12 45.0
21 F	12 1 43	28 34 9	16 52 28	23 45 46	1 58.2	24 47.4	0♍29.9	6 56.1	12 56.1	14 56.5	21 31.3	6 10.9	12 46.0
22 Sa	12 5 39	29 32 52	0♐31 37	7♐10 14	1 55.0	25 36.2	1 43.1	7 30.7	13 3.5	14 57.1	21 29.6	6 10.1	12 46.9
23 Su	12 9 36	0♎31 35	13 41 57	20 7 15	1 53.8	26 21.5	2 56.3	8 5.6	13 10.7	14 57.5	21 27.9	6 9.3	12 47.9
24 M	12 13 32	1 30 21	26 26 41	2♑40 52	1 53.6	27 3.2	4 9.6	8 40.8	13 17.7	14 57.8	21 26.2	6 8.6	12 48.9
25 Tu	12 17 29	2 29 8	8♑50 26	14 56 3	1 53.3	27 40.8	5 22.9	9 16.2	13 24.6	14 58.1	21 24.6	6 7.8	12 50.0
26 W	12 21 26	3 27 57	20 58 23	26 58 4	1 51.8	28 14.0	6 36.3	9 51.8	13 31.4	14 58.2	21 23.0	6 7.1	12 51.0
27 Th	12 25 22	4 26 48	2♒55 43	8♒51 56	1 48.2	28 42.4	7 49.8	10 27.7	13 38.0	14R 58.2	21 21.4	6 6.5	12 52.2
28 F	12 29 19	5 25 40	14 47 15	20 42 10	1 41.8	29 5.7	9 3.3	11 3.8	13 44.5	14 58.1	21 19.9	6 5.8	12 53.3
29 Sa	12 33 15	6 24 34	26 37 8	2♓32 33	1 32.5	29 23.5	10 16.9	11 40.1	13 50.8	14 57.8	21 18.5	6 5.2	12 54.5
30 Su	12 37 12	7 23 30	8♓28 45	14 26 2	1 20.8	29 35.4	11 30.5	12 16.7	13 56.9	14 57.5	21 17.0	6 4.6	12 55.6

Longitude October 2001

Day	Sid.Time	☉	0 hr ☽	Noon ☽	True ☊	☿	♀	♂	♃	♄	♅	♆	♇
1 M	12 41 8	8♎22 28	20♓24 39	26♓24 48	1♋ 7.4	29♎40.8	12♍44.1	12♑53.4	14♋ 2.9	14♊57.1	21♒15.6	6♒ 4.1	12♐56.9
2 Tu	12 45 5	9 21 28	2♈26 38	8♈30 18	0R 53.3	29R 39.5	13 57.8	13 30.4	14 8.7	14R 56.5	21R 14.3	6R 3.6	12 58.1
3 W	12 49 1	10 20 30	14 35 54	20 43 31	0 39.8	29 30.9	15 11.6	14 7.6	14 14.4	14 55.9	21 12.9	6 3.1	12 59.4
4 Th	12 52 58	11 19 34	26 53 15	3♉ 5 10	0 27.9	29 14.9	16 25.4	14 44.9	14 19.9	14 55.1	21 11.7	6 2.6	13 0.7
5 F	12 56 54	12 18 40	9♉19 22	15 35 59	0 18.5	28 51.0	17 39.3	15 22.5	14 25.3	14 54.2	21 10.4	6 2.2	13 2.1
6 Sa	13 0 51	13 17 48	21 55 9	28 17 3	0 12.1	28 19.2	18 53.3	16 0.2	14 30.4	14 53.2	21 9.2	6 1.8	13 3.4
7 Su	13 4 48	14 16 59	4♊41 52	11♊ 9 50	0 8.5	27 39.5	20 7.2	16 38.2	14 35.4	14 52.2	21 8.1	6 1.4	13 4.8
8 M	13 8 44	15 16 12	17 41 15	24 16 23	0D 7.2	26 52.1	21 21.3	17 16.3	14 40.3	14 51.0	21 7.0	6 1.1	13 6.2
9 Tu	13 12 41	16 15 27	0♋55 30	7♋38 56	0 7.1	25 57.6	22 35.4	17 54.6	14 45.0	14 49.7	21 5.9	6 0.8	13 7.7
10 W	13 16 37	17 14 45	14 26 56	21 19 44	0R 7.2	24 56.7	23 49.5	18 33.1	14 49.5	14 48.2	21 4.9	6 0.5	13 9.2
11 Th	13 20 34	18 14 5	28 17 28	5♌20 14	0 6.1	23 50.5	25 3.7	19 11.7	14 53.8	14 46.7	21 3.9	6 0.3	13 10.7
12 F	13 24 30	19 13 27	12♌27 57	19 40 27	0 3.0	22 40.5	26 17.9	19 50.5	14 57.9	14 45.1	21 3.0	6 0.1	13 12.2
13 Sa	13 28 27	20 12 52	26 57 22	4♍18 11	29♊57.2	21 28.3	27 32.2	20 29.5	15 1.9	14 43.4	21 2.1	5 59.9	13 13.7
14 Su	13 32 23	21 12 19	11♍42 13	19 8 36	29 49.0	20 16.0	28 46.5	21 8.6	15 5.7	14 41.5	21 1.3	5 59.8	13 15.3
15 M	13 36 20	22 11 48	26 36 20	4♎ 4 21	29 39.2	19 5.5	0♎ 0.9	21 47.9	15 9.3	14 39.6	21 0.5	5 59.7	13 16.9
16 Tu	13 40 17	23 11 19	11♎31 28	18 56 31	29 28.7	17 59.0	1 15.3	22 27.4	15 12.7	14 37.6	20 59.8	5 59.6	13 18.6
17 W	13 44 13	24 10 52	26 18 24	3♏36 5	29 18.9	16 58.3	2 29.7	23 7.0	15 15.9	14 35.4	20 59.1	5 59.6	13 20.2
18 Th	13 48 10	25 10 27	10♏48 42	17 55 30	29 10.9	16 5.4	3 44.2	23 46.8	15 18.9	14 33.2	20 58.4	5D 59.5	13 21.9
19 F	13 52 6	26 10 4	24 55 57	1♐49 45	29 5.3	15 21.5	4 58.7	24 26.7	15 21.8	14 30.8	20 57.8	5 59.6	13 23.6
20 Sa	13 56 3	27 9 43	8♐36 42	15 16 51	29 2.3	14 47.8	6 13.2	25 6.8	15 24.5	14 28.4	20 57.3	5 59.6	13 25.3
21 Su	13 59 59	28 9 24	21 50 23	28 17 35	29D 1.3	14 25.1	7 27.8	25 47.0	15 26.9	14 25.8	20 56.8	5 59.7	13 27.1
22 M	14 3 56	29 9 7	4♑38 53	10♑54 47	29 1.8	14 13.6	8 42.4	26 27.3	15 29.2	14 23.2	20 56.4	5 59.9	13 28.8
23 Tu	14 7 52	0♏ 8 51	17 5 53	23 12 46	29 2.6	14D 13.4	9 57.1	27 7.8	15 31.3	14 20.5	20 56.0	6 0.1	13 30.6
24 W	14 11 49	1 8 37	29 16 7	5♒16 34	29R 2.7	14 24.2	11 11.8	27 48.4	15 33.2	14 17.7	20 55.6	6 0.3	13 32.4
25 Th	14 15 46	2 8 25	11♒14 47	17 11 25	29 1.2	14 45.5	12 26.5	28 29.1	15 34.9	14 14.7	20 55.3	6 0.5	13 34.3
26 F	14 19 42	3 8 14	23 7 6	29 2 25	28 57.7	15 16.6	13 41.2	29 9.9	15 36.4	14 11.7	20 55.1	6 0.8	13 36.1
27 Sa	14 23 39	4 8 5	4♓57 56	10♓54 10	28 51.8	15 56.8	14 56.0	29 50.9	15 37.8	14 8.6	20 54.9	6 1.1	13 38.0
28 Su	14 27 35	5 7 58	16 51 35	22 50 36	28 43.9	16 45.1	16 10.8	0♒31.9	15 38.9	14 5.5	20 54.7	6 1.4	13 39.9
29 M	14 31 32	6 7 52	28 51 35	4♈54 49	28 34.5	17 40.8	17 25.6	1 13.1	15 39.8	14 2.2	20 54.6	6 1.8	13 41.8
30 Tu	14 35 28	7 7 48	11♈ 0 35	17 9 2	28 24.5	18 43.0	18 40.4	1 54.4	15 40.5	13 58.8	20D 54.6	6 2.2	13 43.7
31 W	14 39 25	8 7 46	23 20 20	29 34 33	28 14.8	19 50.9	19 55.3	2 35.7	15 41.0	13 55.4	20 54.6	6 2.6	13 45.7

*Giving the positions of planets daily at noon, in LONGITUDE Greenwich Mean Time

NOON EPHEMERIS: GMT* — NOVEMBER 2001

Day	Sid.Time	☉	0 hr ☽	Noon ☽	True ☊	☿	♀	♂	♃	♄	♅	♆	♇
1 Th	14 43 21	9♏ 7 46	5♉51 45	12♉11 56	28♊ 6.4	21♎ 3.7	21♎10.2	3♒17.2	15♋41.4	13♊51.9	20♒54.6	6♒ 3.1	13♐47.7
2 F	14 47 18	10 7 48	18 35 6	25 1 11	27R59.9	22 20.8	22 25.2	3 58.8	15R41.5	13R48.3	20 54.7	6 3.6	13 49.7
3 Sa	14 51 15	11 7 52	1♊30 10	8♊ 2 0	27 55.7	23 41.5	23 40.1	4 40.4	15 41.4	13 44.6	20 54.9	6 4.1	13 51.7
4 Su	14 55 11	12 7 57	14 36 39	21 14 6	27 53.8	25 5.2	24 55.1	5 22.2	15 41.2	13 40.9	20 55.1	6 4.7	13 53.7
5 M	14 59 8	13 8 5	27 54 21	4♋37 24	27D53.8	26 31.5	26 10.1	6 4.0	15 40.7	13 37.0	20 55.4	6 5.3	13 55.7
6 Tu	15 3 4	14 8 15	11♋23 18	18 12 4	27 54.9	27 59.9	27 25.2	6 45.9	15 40.0	13 33.2	20 55.7	6 5.9	13 57.8
7 W	15 7 1	15 8 27	25 3 45	1♌58 24	27 56.2	29 30.0	28 40.3	7 28.0	15 39.1	13 29.2	20 56.0	6 6.6	13 59.9
8 Th	15 10 57	16 8 41	8♌56 0	15 56 32	27R56.8	1♏ 1.6	29 55.4	8 10.0	15 38.1	13 25.2	20 56.4	6 7.3	14 2.0
9 F	15 14 54	17 8 57	22 59 55	0♍ 6 0	27 56.1	2 34.3	1♏10.5	8 52.2	15 36.8	13 21.1	20 56.9	6 8.1	14 4.1
10 Sa	15 18 50	18 9 15	7♍14 34	14 25 16	27 53.5	4 7.9	2 25.6	9 34.5	15 35.3	13 16.9	20 57.4	6 8.8	14 6.2
11 Su	15 22 47	19 9 35	21 37 42	28 51 22	27 49.3	5 42.3	3 40.8	10 16.8	15 33.6	13 12.7	20 58.0	6 9.6	14 8.3
12 M	15 26 44	20 9 57	6♎ 5 38	13♎19 51	27 43.8	7 17.1	4 56.0	10 59.2	15 31.8	13 8.4	20 58.6	6 10.5	14 10.4
13 Tu	15 30 40	21 10 20	20 33 17	27 45 10	27 37.8	8 52.4	6 11.2	11 41.7	15 29.7	13 4.0	20 59.3	6 11.3	14 12.6
14 W	15 34 37	22 10 46	4♏54 45	12♏ 1 17	27 32.2	10 27.9	7 26.4	12 24.3	15 27.4	12 59.6	20 60.0	6 12.2	14 14.8
15 Th	15 38 33	23 11 13	19 4 8	26 2 41	27 27.6	12 3.7	8 41.6	13 6.9	15 24.9	12 55.2	21 0.7	6 13.2	14 16.9
16 F	15 42 30	24 11 42	2♐56 26	9♐45 2	27 24.6	13 39.5	9 56.9	13 49.6	15 22.3	12 50.7	21 1.6	6 14.1	14 19.1
17 Sa	15 46 26	25 12 13	16 28 14	23 5 54	27D23.3	15 15.4	11 12.2	14 32.4	15 19.4	12 46.1	21 2.4	6 15.1	14 21.3
18 Su	15 50 23	26 12 45	29 38 2	6♑ 4 45	27 23.5	16 51.3	12 27.4	15 15.3	15 16.3	12 41.6	21 3.4	6 16.2	14 23.6
19 M	15 54 19	27 13 18	12♑26 16	18 42 54	27 24.8	18 27.1	13 42.7	15 58.2	15 13.1	12 36.9	21 4.3	6 17.2	14 25.8
20 Tu	15 58 16	28 13 53	24 55 3	1♒ 3 10	27 26.6	20 2.8	14 58.0	16 41.2	15 9.7	12 32.3	21 5.4	6 18.3	14 28.0
21 W	16 2 13	29 14 29	7♒ 7 47	13 9 27	27 28.3	21 38.5	16 13.4	17 24.2	15 6.0	12 27.6	21 6.4	6 19.4	14 30.3
22 Th	16 6 9	0♐15 5	19 8 44	25 6 17	27R29.3	23 14.0	17 28.7	18 7.3	15 2.2	12 22.8	21 7.6	6 20.6	14 32.5
23 F	16 10 6	1 15 44	1♓ 2 41	6♓58 35	27 29.3	24 49.4	18 44.0	18 50.4	14 58.2	12 18.0	21 8.7	6 21.8	14 34.8
24 Sa	16 14 2	2 16 23	12 54 35	18 51 16	27 28.0	26 24.6	19 59.4	19 33.6	14 54.0	12 13.2	21 9.9	6 23.0	14 37.0
25 Su	16 17 59	3 17 3	24 49 12	0♈48 58	27 25.6	27 59.7	21 14.7	20 16.8	14 49.7	12 8.4	21 11.2	6 24.2	14 39.3
26 M	16 21 55	4 17 44	6♈51 2	12 55 51	27 22.4	29 34.7	22 30.1	21 0.0	14 45.1	12 3.6	21 12.5	6 25.5	14 41.6
27 Tu	16 25 52	5 18 27	19 3 51	25 15 21	27 18.8	1♐ 9.5	23 45.5	21 43.4	14 40.4	11 58.7	21 13.9	6 26.8	14 43.9
28 W	16 29 48	6 19 11	1♉30 39	7♉49 57	27 15.2	2 44.2	25 0.9	22 26.7	14 35.5	11 53.8	21 15.3	6 28.1	14 46.1
29 Th	16 33 45	7 19 56	14 13 24	20 41 3	27 12.1	4 18.8	26 16.2	23 10.1	14 30.5	11 48.9	21 16.8	6 29.5	14 48.4
30 F	16 37 42	8 20 42	27 12 55	3♊48 56	27 9.9	5 53.3	27 31.7	23 53.5	14 25.3	11 44.0	21 18.3	6 30.8	14 50.7

LONGITUDE — DECEMBER 2001

Day	Sid.Time	☉	0 hr ☽	Noon ☽	True ☊	☿	♀	♂	♃	♄	♅	♆	♇
1 Sa	16 41 38	9♐21 29	10♊28 57	17♊12 46	27♊ 8.7	7♐27.7	28♏47.1	24♒37.0	14♋19.9	11♊39.1	21♒19.8	6♒32.3	14♐53.0
2 Su	16 45 35	10 22 18	24 0 10	0♋50 50	27D 8.5	9 2.1	0♐ 2.5	25 20.5	14R14.4	11R34.2	21 21.4	6 33.7	14 55.3
3 M	16 49 31	11 23 7	7♋44 30	14 40 49	27 9.1	10 36.4	1 17.9	26 4.0	14 8.7	11 29.3	21 23.1	6 35.2	14 57.6
4 Tu	16 53 28	12 23 58	21 39 26	28 40 2	27 10.1	12 10.6	2 33.4	26 47.5	14 2.8	11 24.3	21 24.8	6 36.7	14 59.9
5 W	16 57 24	13 24 51	5♌42 16	12♌45 49	27 11.3	13 44.8	3 48.8	27 31.1	13 56.8	11 19.4	21 26.5	6 38.2	15 2.3
6 Th	17 1 21	14 25 44	19 50 22	26 55 37	27 12.3	15 19.0	5 4.3	28 14.7	13 50.7	11 14.5	21 28.3	6 39.7	15 4.6
7 F	17 5 17	15 26 39	4♍ 1 18	11♍ 7 7	27R12.8	16 53.0	6 19.7	28 58.3	13 44.4	11 9.6	21 30.1	6 41.3	15 6.9
8 Sa	17 9 14	16 27 35	18 12 49	25 18 6	27 12.7	18 27.5	7 35.2	29 42.0	13 38.0	11 4.7	21 32.0	6 42.9	15 9.2
9 Su	17 13 11	17 28 33	2♎22 44	9♎26 26	27 12.1	20 1.7	8 50.7	0♓25.7	13 31.4	10 59.8	21 33.9	6 44.5	15 11.5
10 M	17 17 7	18 29 32	16 28 53	23 29 49	27 11.1	21 36.0	10 6.2	1 9.4	13 24.7	10 54.9	21 35.8	6 46.1	15 13.8
11 Tu	17 21 4	19 30 31	0♏28 55	7♏25 53	27 10.1	23 10.4	11 21.7	1 53.1	13 17.9	10 50.1	21 37.8	6 47.8	15 16.1
12 W	17 25 0	20 31 32	14 20 24	21 12 10	27 9.2	24 44.8	12 37.2	2 36.9	13 11.2	10 45.2	21 39.9	6 49.5	15 18.4
13 Th	17 28 57	21 32 34	28 0 53	4♐46 18	27 8.6	26 19.3	13 52.7	3 20.7	13 4.0	10 40.4	21 42.0	6 51.2	15 20.7
14 F	17 32 53	22 33 37	11♐28 10	18 6 18	27 8.3	27 54.0	15 8.2	4 4.5	12 56.8	10 35.7	21 44.1	6 53.0	15 23.0
15 Sa	17 36 50	23 34 41	24 40 31	1♑10 44	27D 8.2	29 28.7	16 23.7	4 48.3	12 49.6	10 30.9	21 46.3	6 54.7	15 25.3
16 Su	17 40 46	24 35 45	7♑36 54	13 59 2	27 8.4	1♑ 3.5	17 39.2	5 32.2	12 42.2	10 26.2	21 48.5	6 56.5	15 27.6
17 M	17 44 43	25 36 50	20 17 13	26 31 35	27 8.5	2 38.4	18 54.7	6 16.0	12 34.8	10 21.5	21 50.7	6 58.3	15 29.9
18 Tu	17 48 40	26 37 55	2♒42 22	8♒49 49	27 8.7	4 13.5	20 10.3	6 59.9	12 27.2	10 16.9	21 53.0	7 0.2	15 32.2
19 W	17 52 36	27 39 1	14 54 15	20 56 4	27R 8.7	5 48.6	21 25.8	7 43.8	12 19.6	10 12.3	21 55.4	7 2.0	15 34.5
20 Th	17 56 33	28 40 7	26 55 41	2♓53 35	27 8.6	7 23.9	22 41.3	8 27.7	12 11.9	10 7.7	21 57.7	7 3.9	15 36.7
21 F	18 0 29	29 41 13	8♓50 15	14 46 15	27 8.4	8 59.2	23 56.8	9 11.6	12 4.2	10 3.2	22 0.1	7 5.8	15 39.0
22 Sa	18 4 26	0♑42 20	20 42 7	26 38 28	27D 8.2	10 34.6	25 12.3	9 55.6	11 56.3	9 58.8	22 2.6	7 7.7	15 41.2
23 Su	18 8 22	1 43 26	2♈35 52	8♈34 55	27 8.3	12 10.0	26 27.8	10 39.5	11 48.5	9 54.4	22 5.0	7 9.6	15 43.5
24 M	18 12 19	2 44 33	14 36 14	20 40 21	27 8.6	13 45.4	27 43.3	11 23.4	11 40.5	9 50.0	22 7.6	7 11.5	15 45.7
25 Tu	18 16 15	3 45 40	26 47 52	2♉59 16	27 9.1	15 20.8	28 58.9	12 7.3	11 32.5	9 45.7	22 10.1	7 13.5	15 47.9
26 W	18 20 12	4 46 47	9♉15 2	15 35 36	27 9.9	16 56.1	0♑14.4	12 51.3	11 24.5	9 41.5	22 12.7	7 15.5	15 50.1
27 Th	18 24 9	5 47 54	22 1 18	28 32 24	27 10.7	18 31.3	1 29.9	13 35.2	11 16.5	9 37.4	22 15.3	7 17.5	15 52.4
28 F	18 28 5	6 49 2	5♊ 9 5	11♊51 23	27 11.4	20 6.2	2 45.4	14 19.1	11 8.4	9 33.3	22 18.0	7 19.5	15 54.5
29 Sa	18 32 2	7 50 9	18 39 17	25 32 37	27R11.7	21 40.8	4 0.9	15 3.1	11 0.3	9 29.2	22 20.6	7 21.5	15 56.[illegible]
30 Su	18 35 58	8 51 17	2♋31 4	9♋34 14	27 11.5	23 14.9	5 16.4	15 47.0	10 52.2	9 25.3	22 23.4	7 23.6	15 5[illegible]
31 M	18 39 55	9 52 25	16 41 37	23 52 34	27 10.6	24 48.5	6 31.9	16 30.9	10 44.1	9 21.4	22 26.1	7 25.6	16 [illegible]

*Giving the positions of planets daily at noon, in LONGITUDE Greenwich Mean Time

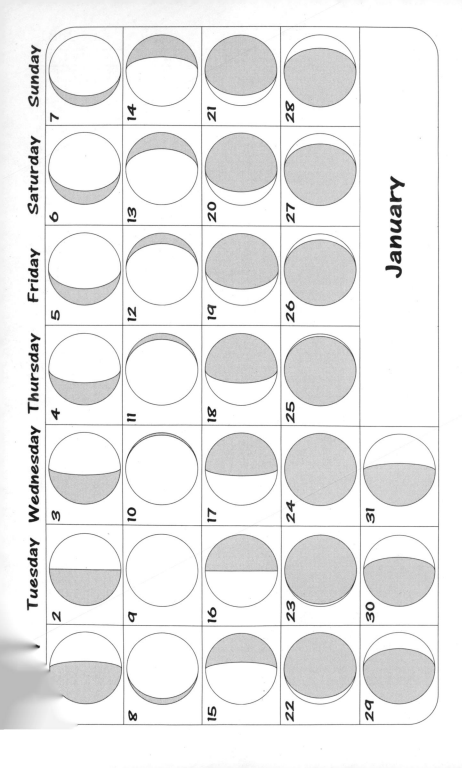

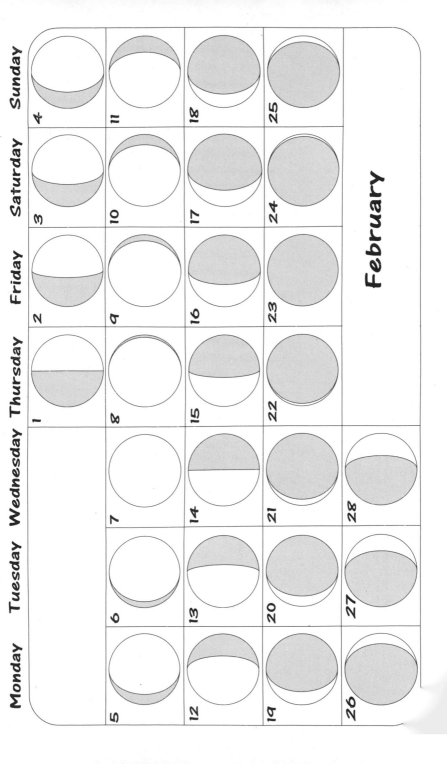

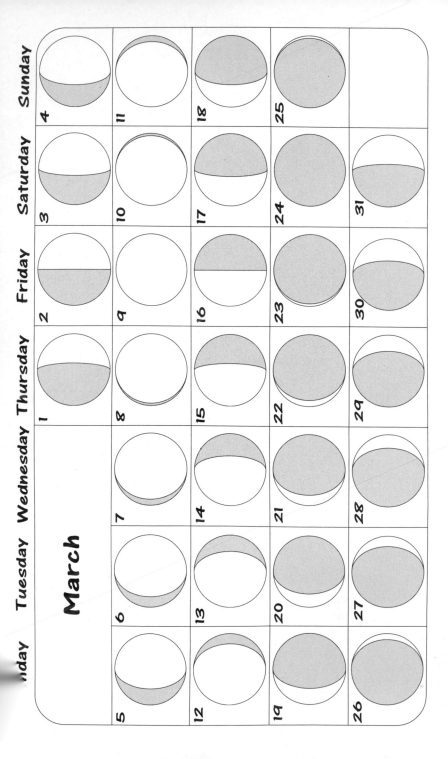

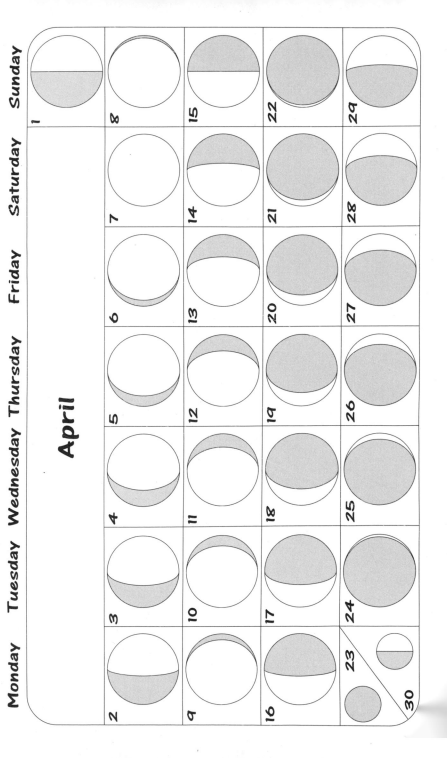

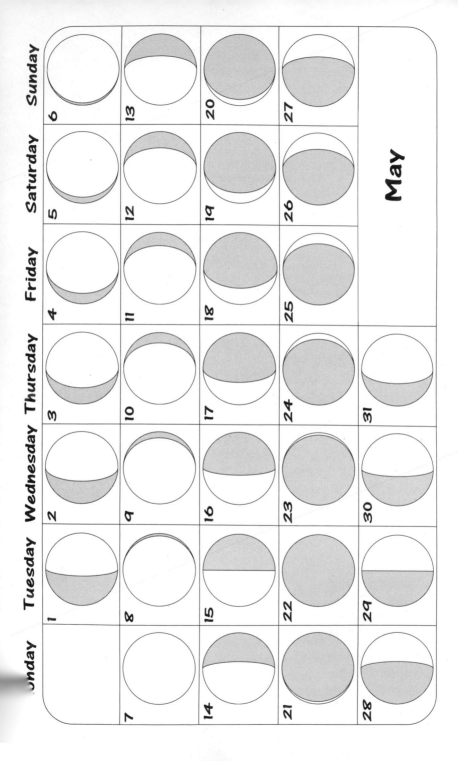

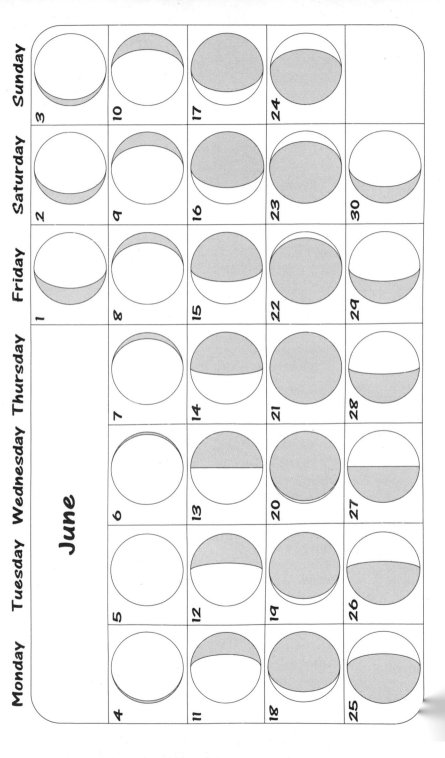

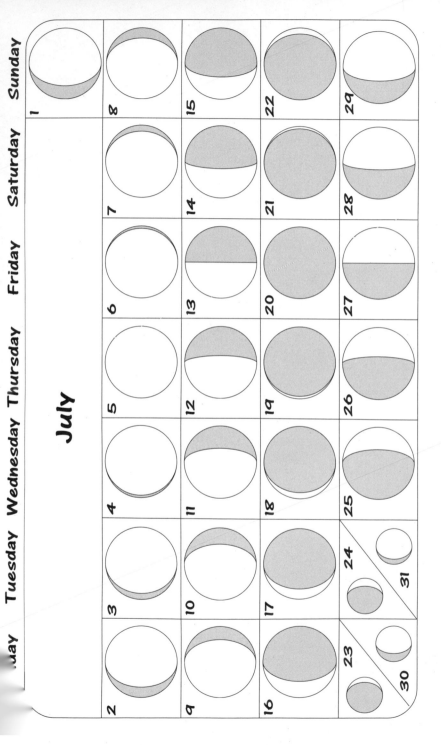

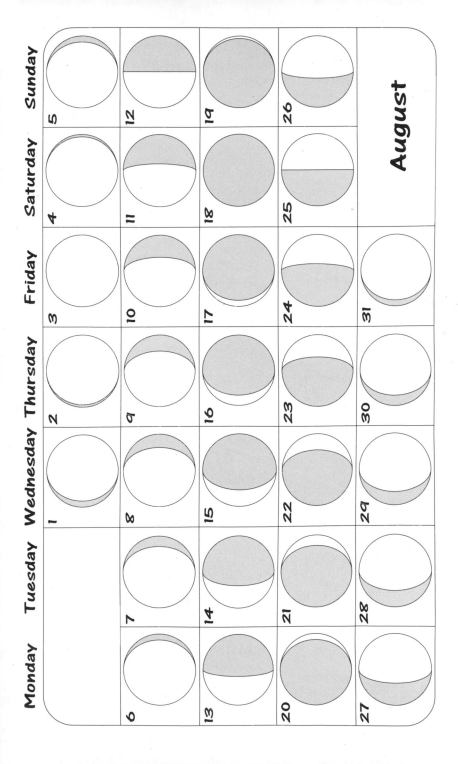

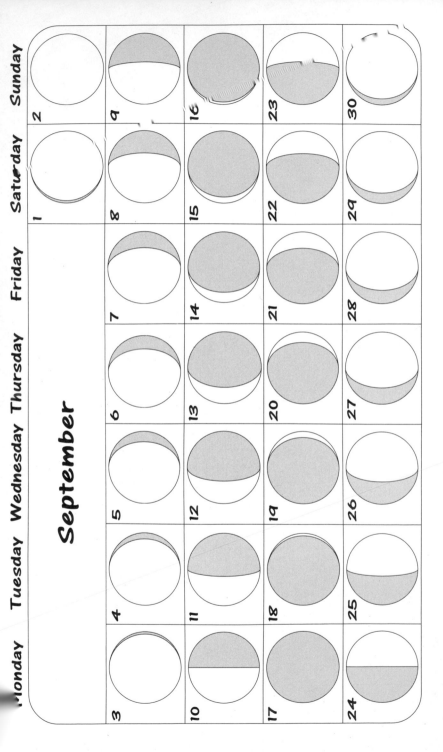

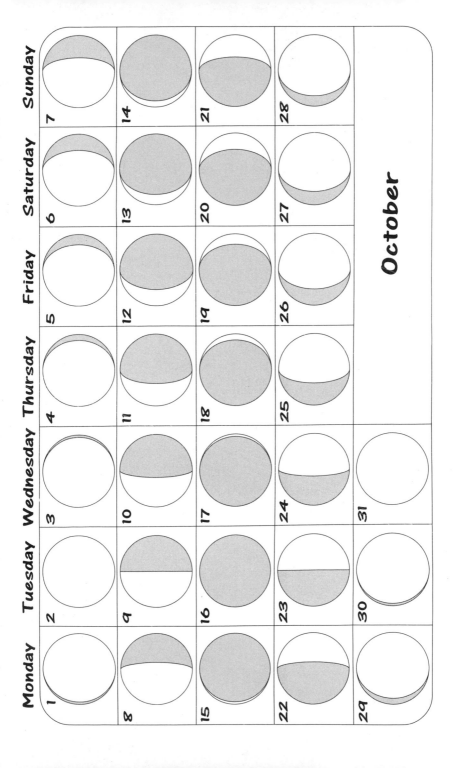

November

Monday	Tuesday	Wednesday	Thursday	Friday	Saturday	Sunday
			1	2	3	4
5	6	7	8	9	10	11
12	13	14	15	16	17	18
19	20	21	22	23	24	25
26	27	28	29	30		

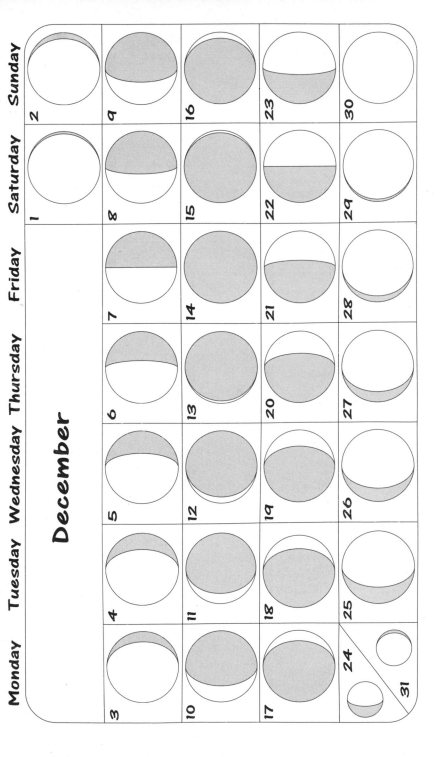

WORLD TIME ZONES

ID LW	NT BT	CA HT	YST	PST	MST	CST	EST	AST	BST	AT	WAT	GMT	CET	EET	BT	USSR Z3	USSR Z4	USSR Z5	SST	CCT	JST	GST	USSR Z10	ID LE
-12	-11	-10	-9	-8	-7	-6	-5	-4	-3	-2	-1	0	+1	+2	+3	+4	+5	+6	+7	+8	+9	+10	+11	+12
-4	-3	-2	-1	0	+1	+2	+3	+4	+5	+6	+7	+8	+9	+10	+11	+12	+13	+14	+15	+16	+17	+18	+19	+20

STANDARD TIME ZONES FROM WEST TO EAST CALCULATED FROM PST AS ZERO POINT:

IDLW:	International Date Line West	-4
NT/BT:	Nome Time/Bering Time	-3
CA/HT:	Central Alaska & Hawaiian Time	-2
YST:	Yukon Standard Time	-1
PST:	Pacific Standard Time	0
MST:	Mountain Standard Time	+1
CST:	Central Standard Time	+2
EST:	Eastern Standard Time	+3
AST:	Atlantic Standard Time	+4
NFT:	Newfoundland Time	+4 1/2
BST:	Brazil Standard Time	+5
AT:	Azores Time	+6
WAT:	West African Time	+7
GMT:	Greenwich Mean Time	+8
WET:	Western European Time (England)	+8
CET:	Central European Time	+9
EET:	Eastern European Time	+10
BT:	Bagdhad Time	+11
IT:	Iran Time	+11 1/2
USSR	Zone 3	+12
USSR	Zone 4	+13
IST:	Indian Standard Time	+13 1/2
USSR	Zone 5	+14
NST:	North Sumatra Time	+14 1/2
SST:	South Sumatra Time & USSR Zone 6	+15
JT:	Java Time	+15 1/2
CCT:	China Coast Time	+16
MT:	Moluccas Time	+16 1/2
JST:	Japanese Standard Time	+17
SAST:	South Australian Standard Time	+17 1/2
GST:	Guam Standard Time	+18
USSR	Zone 10	+19
IDLE:	International Date Line East	+20

HOW TO CALCULATE TIME ZONE CORRECTIONS IN YOUR AREA:

ADD if you are east of PST (Pacific Standard Time); SUBTRACT if you are west of PST on this map (see right-hand column of chart above).

All times in this calendar are calculated from the West Coast of North America where it is made. Pacific Standard Time (PST Zone 8) is zero point for this calendar except during Daylight Savings Time (April 1–October 28, 2001 during which times are given for PDT Zone 7). If your time zone does not use Daylight Savings Time, add one hour to the standard correction during this time. At the bottom of each page EST/EDT (Eastern Standard or Daylight Time) and GMT (Greenwich Mean Time) times are also given. For all other time zones, calculate your time zone correction(s) from this map and write it on the inside cover for easy reference.

SIGNS AND SYMBOLS AT A GLANCE

PLANETS

Personal Planets are closest to Earth.

⊙ **Sun:** self radiating outward, character, ego
☽ **Moon:** inward sense of self, emotions, psyche
☿ **Mercury:** communication, travel, thought
♀ **Venus:** relationship, love, sense of beauty, empathy
♂ **Mars:** will to act, initiative, ambition

Asteroids are between Mars and Jupiter and reflect the awakening of feminine-defined energy centers in human consciousness. See "Asteroids" (p.199).

Social Planets are between personal and outer planets.

♃ **Jupiter:** expansion, opportunities, leadership
♄ **Saturn:** limits, structure, discipline

Note: the seven days of the week are named after the above seven heavenly bodies.

⚷ **Chiron:** is a small planetary body between Saturn and Uranus representing the wounded healer.

Transpersonal Planets are the outer planets.

♅ **Uranus:** cosmic consciousness, revolutionary change
♆ **Neptune:** spiritual awakening, cosmic love, all one
♇ **Pluto:** death and rebirth, deep, total change

ZODIAC SIGNS

♈	Aries
♉	Taurus
♊	Gemini
♋	Cancer
♌	Leo
♍	Virgo
♎	Libra
♏	Scorpio
♐	Sagittarius
♑	Capricorn
♒	Aquarius
♓	Pisces

ASPECTS

Aspects show the angle between planets; this informs how the planets influence each other and us. **We'Moon** lists only significant aspects:

♂ CONJUNCTION (planets are 0–5° apart)
   linked together, energy of aspected planets is mutually enhancing
✶ SEXTILE (planets are 60° apart)
   cooperative, energies of this aspect blend well
□ SQUARE (planets are 90° apart)
   challenging, energies of this aspect are different from each other
△ TRINE (planets are 120° apart)
   harmonizing, energies of this aspect are in the same element
☍ OPPOSITION (planets are 180° apart)
   polarizing or complementing, energies are diametrically opposite
⚻ QUINCUNX (planets are 150° apart)
   variable, energies of this aspect combine contrary elements

OTHER SYMBOLS

☽ v/c: Moon is void of course from last lunar aspect till it enters new sign.
ApG–Apogee: Point in the orbit of a planet that's farthest from Earth.
PrG–Perigee: Point in the orbit of a planet that's nearest to Earth.
D or R–Direct or Retrograde: Describes when a planet moves forward (D) through the zodiac or appears to move backward (R).

DEF

GHI

JKL

MNO

PQR